Thanksgiving

THANKSGIVING

An American Holiday, An American History

Diana Karter Appelbaum

Facts On File Publications
New York, New York ● Bicester, England

Thanksgiving: An American Holiday, An American History

Copyright © 1984 by Diana Karter Appelbaum
First paperback edition 1985
All rights reserved. No part of this book may
be reproduced or utilized in any form or by any
means, electronic or mechanical, including
photocopying, recording or by any information
storage and retrieval systems, without permission
in writing from the Publisher.

Library of Congress Cataloging in Publication Data
Appelbaum, Diana Karter.
    Thanksgiving: an American holiday, an American history.

    Includes index.
    1. Thanksgiving Day. 2. Thanksgiving Day—Literary
collections. I. Title.
GT4975.A66   1985   394.2′683   83-20615
ISBN 0-8160-1291-1

Printed in the United States of America
10 9 8 7 6 5 4 3 2 1

Composition by Unitron Graphics

Contents

For Paul
Interlocutor and Friend

Acknowledgment

This book would not have been possible without the help of librarians at dozens of city and state historical societies. For their willingness to answer my queries and forward relevant material, I am most grateful.

An Invitation

Come home with me to Thanksgiving. Come into the kitchen of an old-fashioned New England farmhouse to savor the aroma of baking pies wafting from a brick oven and mingling with the joy of family reunion. Come to Thanksgiving Day in a Union Army camp, where bearded soldiers play football after their meal of turkey and trimmings sent by the folks back home. Come to Thanksgiving on the western frontier, where pioneer women, determined to celebrate the old holiday in their new homes, serve Thanksgiving buffalo steaks on prized china dishes.

Thanksgiving has been celebrated in all of these places and more since it began in Puritan New England long ago. How and where Thanksgiving began are the subjects that open this book. But the story of Thanksgiving does not end in colonial New England. The book describes the process by which Thanksgiving grew from a regional holiday into a national one, an evolution that was a triumph of Yankee salesmanship.

Thanksgiving Day itself is the central theme of every chapter: how it was celebrated, what it meant to the people who celebrated it, and what role Thanksgiving played in the public affairs of the day. Far from being exclusively a quiet, family holiday, Thanksgiving became a focus of controversy as it was pressed into service by patriots fighting for independence, appropriated for partisan purposes by contentious politicians, and made to serve as the occasion of abolitionist oratory.

The celebration of Thanksgiving, while aways infused with tradition, has changed substantially from generation to generation. A century ago, football replaced the turkey shoot as Thanksgiving Day's most characteristic sporting activity, but the turkey shoot was itself an innovation on a holiday once wholly devoted to grateful prayer. Pious in youth, Thanksgiving has been, by turns, a patriotic, partisan, nostalgic, jingoistic, gay, sporting, and domestic holiday. Thanksgiving changes, but it endures.

From the founding of New England to the present day, Thanksgiving has been a beloved part of American life. I invite you to explore Thanksgiving with me, to discover what Thanksgiving meant to our forebears and ponder what it means to us today.

That Elusive First Thanksgiving

1

On Thanksgiving Day a hush of contentment settles across the land as millions of American families pause to thank the Lord for the blessings we enjoy. Setting apart the last Thursday in November as a day of thanks is part of the fixed rhythm of our national life; the newest immigrants readily gather for a family meal on this day, and the oldest inhabitant searches in vain for remembrance of a year when Thanksgiving failed to be celebrated as autumn gives way to winter.

Every American knows how Thanksgiving is observed: the family gathers from near and far, offers grateful prayers and sits down to a feast of turkey, cranberry sauce and pumpkin pie. Even little children can relate the story of the first Thanksgiving at Plymouth Colony—how a small band of Pilgrims, in 1620, braved the perilous North Atlantic crossing in quest of religious freedom, how they landed in November and faced winter with meager supplies of food that dwindled rapidly. Half of that Pilgrim band died before spring. When summer weather proved benign and the

THE LANDING OF THE PILGRIM FATHERS

The breaking waves dashed high
  on a stern and rock-bound coast,
And the woods, against a stormy sky
  Their giant branches toss'd;

And the heavy night hung dark
  The hills and waters o'er,
When a band of exiles moor'd their bark
  On the wild New England shore.

Not as the conqueror comes,
  They, the true-hearted, came,
Not with the roll of the stirring drums,
  And the trumpet that sings of fame;

Not as the flying come,
  In silence and in fear,—
They shook the depths of the desert's gloom
  With their hymns of lofty cheer.

Amidst the storm they sang,
  And the stars heard and the sea!
And the sounding aisles of the dim woods rang
  To the anthem of the free!

The ocean-eagle soar'd
   From his nest by the white wave's foam,
And the rocking pines of the forest roar'd—
   This was their welcome home!

There were men with hoary hair
   Amidst that pilgrim-band—
Why had they come to wither there
   Away from their childhood's land?

There was woman's fearless eye,
   Lit by her deep love's truth;
There was manhood's brow, serenely high,
   And the fiery heart of youth.

What sought they thus afar?
   Bright jewels of the mine?
The wealth of seas, the spoils of war?—
   They sought a faith's pure shrine!

Ay, call it holy ground,
   The soil where first they trod.
They have left unstained what there they found—
   Freedom to worship God.

—Mrs. Felicia Dorothea Hemans

THE FIRST THANKSGIVING

Children do you know the story
    Of the first Thanksgiving Day,
Founded by our Pilgrim fathers
    In that time so far away?

They had given for religion
    Wealth and comfort—yes, and more—
Left their homes and friends and kindred,
    For a bleak and barren shore.

On New England's rugged headlands,
    Now where peaceful Plymouth lies;
There they built their rough log cabins,
    'Neath the cold forbidding skies.

And too often e'en the bravest
    Felt his blood run cold with dread,
Lest the wild and savage red man
    Burn the roof over his head.

Want and sickness, death and sorrow,
    Met their eyes on every hand;
And before the spring had reached them
    They had buried half their band.

But their noble, brave endurance
    Was not exercised in vain;
Summer brought them brighter prospects,
    Ripening seed and waving grain.

And the patient Pilgrim mothers,
    As the harvest time drew near,
Looked with happy thankful faces,
    At the full corn in the ear.

So the governor, William Bradford,
    In the gladness of his heart,
To praise God for all his mercies,
    Set a special day apart.

That was in the autumn, children,
    Sixteen hundred twenty-one;
Scarce a year from when they landed,
    And the colony begun.

And now, when in late November,
    Our Thanksgiving feast is spread,
'Tis the same time-honored custom
    Of those Pilgrims long since dead.

We shall never know the terrors,
    That they braved years, years ago;
But for all their struggles gave us,
    We our gratitude can show.

And the children of New England,
    If they feast or praise or pray,
Should bless God for those brave Pilgrims,
    And their first Thanksgiving Day.

                        —*Youth's Companion*

*Here is the myth of the first
Thanksgiving depicted by
America's great illustrator Newell
Convers Wyeth. A patriarch holds
an open bible while a Pilgrim
matron carries a roast turkey to a
table of diners, seated as guests
might be for Thanksgiving dinner
three centuries later.*

*Here, in Wyeth's vision, are some
of the ninety warriors who
accompanied Massasoit to the feast
being served by a Pilgrim woman.*

autumn harvest plentiful, the Pilgrim colony, appropriately grateful, established a day of thanksgiving and invited the local Indians to share their bounty, an event that has come to be commemorated every November.

This tale is immortalized in two poems that generations of American schoolchildren have memorized and recited at Thanksgiving assemblies.

Alas for the glories of uplifting myth and heroic legend, history does not flow in so smooth a channel. Certain as it is that the Plymouth colonists held a gay and grateful feast in the early autumn of 1621, it is unclear that the celebration can be labeled a "thanksgiving." America's Thanksgiving Day, as we know it, did not originate in one place and year.

The Plymouth Thanksgiving

Landing at Plymouth in December 1620, the Pilgrims faced winter without an adequate food supply, sheltered from the elements only by such dwellings as they could build quickly. Unseen, dreaded Indians lurked in the woods, their intentions unknown. Faith and prayer sustained the pious settlers—their first act upon setting foot on dry land was to kneel and pray. Records of the settlement are punctuated by notations of recurrent occasions when "solemne thanks and praise" were offered.

Only 55 of the 102 immigrants lived through that first winter, but when spring came, all 55 committed themselves to life in the New World and resolutely watched the *Mayflower* sail back to England without passengers. Tisquantum, an Indian of the Wampanoag tribe who had once been carried off by fishermen to England, where he learned to speak the settlers' tongue, befriended the colonists. They called him Squanto, and under his direction the colonists learned how to plant New World crops of corn and squash, where to catch fish and how to hunt. Squanto also served as negotiator and interpreter, helping to conclude a treaty that kept the peace for 50 years between the Pilgrims and the Wampanoag sachem, Massasoit.

The first autumn, an ample harvest insured that the colony

A target shoot designed to demonstrate the power of English muskets was a major feature of the three-day-long harvest celebration held in Plymouth in the fall of 1621.

would have food for the winter months. Governor Bradford, with one eye on the divine Providence, proclaimed a day of thanksgiving to God, and with the other eye on the local political situation, extended an invitation to neighboring Indians to share in the harvest feast. In order to guarantee that the feast served to cement a peaceful relationship, the three-day long meal was punctuated by displays of the power of English muskets for the benefit of suitably impressed Indian guests.

This "first Thanksgiving" was a feast called to suit the needs of the hour, which were to celebrate the harvest, thank the Lord for His goodness, and regale and impress the Indians. We have Edward Winslow's testimony that the feast was a success:

> Our harvest being gotten in, our Governour sent foure men fowling, so that we might after a more special manner rejoyce together, after we had gathered the fruit of our labours; they foure in one day killed as much fowle, as with a little helpe beside, served the Company almost a weeke, at which time amongst other Recreations we excercised our Armes, many of the Indians coming amongst us, and amongst the rest their greatest King Massasoyt, with some ninetie men, whom for three days we entertained and feasted, and they went out and killed five Deere which they brought to the Plantacion and bestowed on our Governour, and upon the Captaine, and others.

Preparing a feast for 90 Indians and 50 settlers must have taxed the strength of the four Englishwomen and two teenage girls on hand to do the cooking (13 Pilgrim women had been buried during the terrible first winter). They worked with the resources at hand, and, although they successfully fed the hungry men, the feast bore little resemblance to the modern Thanksgiving dinner. Partridges, ducks, geese and turkeys could be shot along the shores of Cape Cod Bay in the fall, and it may be that those who went a-fowling brought back some of each to be roasted or stewed. Although there is no proof that turkey was eaten at Plymouth that day, it is certain that there was venison and equally certain that some items were missing. There was no apple cider, no milk, butter or cheese (no cows had been aboard the *Mayflower*), and no bread—stores of flour from the ship had long since been exhausted and years would pass before significant quantities of wheat were successfully cultivated in New England.

What they did have were pumpkins and corn; these grew abundantly, and colonists ate them until they were cordially tired of both. With no flour and no molasses, there was no pumpkin pie, but there was plain, boiled pumpkin to eat. Corn was more versatile. It was boiled as "hasty pudding," kneaded into ersatz bread and fried in cakes. Cranberries may have been boiled for a sauce to accompany the meat. Perhaps there was even a little wild honey to sweeten the sour, red berries. Nine little girls and 15 boys were in the company, and they, or some of the hunters, may have gathered other wild fruits or nuts. Oysters, clams and fish rounded out the abundant, but far from epicurean, feast that the celebrators would have been more likely to call a "harvest home" than a "thanksgiving" celebration.

Thanksgivings were holy days of solemn prayer in the Puritan lexicon, days akin to sabbaths and fast days on which "Recreations" and "exercising of Armes" would not have been countenanced. Had the governor proclaimed a day of thanksgiving to Almighty God, Edward Winslow, one of the Pilgrim Fathers, would have written about the religious services the settlers held. Thus this feast was more harvest celebration than prayerful day of thanksgiving.

One successful harvest did not signal an end to the trials of Plymouth Colony: the following year brought a poor harvest and boatloads of new immigrants to be fed. After a long and hungry winter, the settlers planted corn in the spring of 1623 hoping for a good crop, only to have a drought begin in May that continued through June into July. An entire July day was devoted to prayer and fasting. Toward evening, clouds appeared, and by morning a gentle rain revived the corn and raised the spirits of the weary colony. The settlers were in a grateful mood when Miles Standish brought news of the sighting of the ship *Anne*, bearing Separatist brethren who had been left in Leiden, in the Netherlands, when the first colonists embarked on the *Mayflower*. Governor William Bradford proclaimed a day of thanksgiving, and grateful prayers were offered.

Some New Englanders cite this day, June 30, 1623, as the first Thanksgiving, since its prayerful spirit was in keeping with the Puritan version of a thanksgiving day. But in neither this case nor in the celebration of the bountiful harvest in 1621 did the colonists intend to establish an annual holiday.

The Massachusetts Bay Colony Thanksgiving

The Puritans who arrived at Charlestown in 1630 to establish Boston and the Massachusetts Bay Colony also held a day of prayer that many have called the "first Thanksgiving." A much larger and wealthier group than the Separatists down the coast at Plymouth, the Puritans of Massachusetts Bay constituted a well-funded and well-organized colony. Fifteen ships landed at the colony during the first six months and, by 1634, 10,000 settlers had arrived. Many skilled artisans, university graduates, ministers and representatives of the landed gentry were among these settlers, who saw themselves as new Israelites, a people chosen by God and led across the sea to found a shining "city upon a hill." Despite their wealth and ambition, however, they, like the Plymouth colonists, were refugees.

Both groups had common origins. Since Henry VIII split off the Church of England from the Catholic church in 1534, the Puritans had been struggling to purge the Church of England of its Catholic features. Saints' days, the Mass and icons were abhorrent to them. Ecclesiastical hierarchy was similarly repugnant. The Puritans believed that the only legitimate structure for the church was based on the individual congregation of converted souls, led by an elected minister.

The Separatists who founded Plymouth had grown frustrated with the pace of church reform in England. In 1606, they established a small congregation in the English village of Scrooby, having ceased to expect that the Church of England could purify itself sufficiently to meet their Protestant ideals. By divorcing themselves from the official church, these Separatists were exposed to official persecution and, in 1609, they left England to seek religious freedom in Holland. Ten years later they moved again, to found the colony at Plymouth. Meanwhile, the main body of Puritan Protestants continued to work for reform at home, until the ascension of the absolutist King Charles I to the throne in 1625 precipitated the persecution of the Puritans and drove many across the Atlantic to found Massachusetts Bay Colony.

The Massachusetts Bay colonists arrived in summertime, too late to clear fields and raise grain for the winter; and by autumn, supplies were running low. Governor John Winthrop sent Captain Pierce back to England in the ship *Lyon* to obtain food. Tradition holds that during the winter months the settlers were reduced to robbing the nests of squirrels for acorns and digging for mussels and clams on the mud flats at low tide. The expected time for the *Lyon*'s return came and went. Off Newfoundland, on its way to England, the *Lyon* had met a disabled vessel, the *Ambrose*, and had towed it home to Bristol, delaying its own mission. But the colonists, who could not imagine the reason for the delay, assumed that the ship had been lost and were in a state of despair. In February 1631, the situation was so bleak that Governor Winthrop declared a day of fasting and prayer for the 22nd of the month. Declaring a fast day when there is no food to eat may seem superfluous, but to convert grim necessity into an act of piety was the Puritan way.

On the morning of the scheduled fast day, the *Lyon* appeared in Boston Harbor, bringing supplies to the starving colonists and causing the governor to change the proclaimed day of fasting into one of prayer and thanksgiving.

The Massachusetts Bay celebration was a unique event commemorating a particular, providential delivery, but it did not establish an annual custom. Still, the craving for a founding myth demands satisfaction, and if Plymouth and Boston did not host the "first Thanksgiving," Maine and Virginia and, improbably enough, Texas and Florida stand ready to claim the honor.

THE FIRST THANKSGIVING
BOSTON, 1631

The curse of Cain was on the earth;
　The leaden heavens frowned;
The winter closed with cruel dearth
　And gripped the fruitless ground.

Behind us rose the sombre wood,
　Before us stretched the foam—
A thousand leagues of briny flood
　That sundered us from home.

The meagre mussel was our meat;
　We robbed the squirrels' hoard;
Our barren glebe beneath our feet,
　We cried upon the Lord.

"Arouse your souls against despair,"
　The godly Winthrop said,
"And choose a day of fast and prayer,
　For, surely, He who led

Our wanderings across the wave
　Shall hear us when we plead.
And stretch a mighty arm to save
　His people in their need."

Behold! When all is black and drear
　And want assails the land,
How God delighteth to appear
　To work with wond'rous hand!

For, even as we made to deal
　To one that hungered sore,
The utmost handful of our meal,
　A shout arose from shore.

An hundred watching eyes descried
　Through winter's misty pall,
The good ship Lion brest the tide
　With provender for all.

Then joined the voice of first and least
　A hymn of thanks to raise,
Our day of fasting changed to feast
　And prayer gave way to praise

So once in every year we throng
　Upon a day apart,
To praise the Lord with feast and song
　In thankfulness of heart.

—by Arthur Guiterman

A Spanish-American Thanksgiving

Along highway 217, just outside Canyon, Texas, is a roadside historical marker that reads:

Feast of First
Thanksgiving—1541

Proclaimed by Padre
Fray Juan De Padilla for Coronado
and His Troops in Palo Duro Canyon
79 Year Before the Pilgrims

Marker Placed by
Texas Society
Daughters of the American Colonists
1959

In 1540, Francisco Vásquez de Coronado, a daring young Spaniard, left his home in Mexico City to march north at the head of 1,500 men searching for gold and the legendary city of Quivira. He found, instead, Indians, buffalo, the Grand Canyon, and what are now Arizona, New Mexico, Texas, Oklahoma and Kansas. In May 1541, Coronado and his men were camped for 14 days along the Palo Duro Canyon in the Texas Panhandle, which offered abundant food, fresh water and pasture for their horses. On May 23, they held a service of thanksgiving. Then, after marching through Kansas and Oklahoma for several more months, Coronado gave up the idea of finding riches in the Southwest and returned to Mexico City. Claiming this as the first Thanksgiving is a fine example of Texas braggadocio.

Florida's First Thanksgiving

Half a century before the Pilgrims landed at Plymouth, a

small colony of French Huguenots established a settlement near present-day Jacksonville, Florida. On June 30, 1564, their leader, René de Laudonnière, recorded that "We sang a psalm of Thanksgiving unto God, beseeching Him that it would please Him to continue His accustomed goodness towards us." Unfortunately, the fledgling colony was wiped out in 1565 by a Spanish raiding party under the leadership of Pedro Menéndez de Avilés. The site of Florida's "first Thanksgiving" is marked by the Fort Caroline Memorial, a replica of the original fort on the St. Johns River.

Thanksgiving in Maine

Maine's claim to the first Thanksgiving derives from an early attempt at settlement under the charter of the Plymouth Company, led by George Popham in 1607. The Popham colonists arrived at the mouth of the Kennebec River in Maine on August 9, 1607, and held a service of thanksgiving in gratitude for a safe voyage and landing. Such spontaneous thanksgiving services for deliverance from danger were common in that pious age. However, since the attempt at colonization was abandoned within the year, the only tradition the Popham service spawned was that of Maine historians laying claim to still another "first Thanksgiving."

Thanksgiving in Virginia: Jamestown and Berkeley Hundred

Irrefutably first among permanent English settlements on the North American mainland was Jamestown, in Virginia. The early years were spent in struggle against disease, Indian attacks and hunger: at Jamestown, in the fall of 1609, 490 settlers were reduced to 60 by a winter of famine known as the "starving time." When Lord De la Warr sailed up the James River in the spring of 1610 carrying supplies from England, the beleaguered

Twentieth century Virginians reenact the landing of Captain John Woodleaf and settlers at the new Virginia colony of Berkeley Hundred.

settlement greeted him with a service of thanksgiving that some modern Virginians have labeled the "first Thanksgiving." Such a label is pure hyperbole. Far from establishing a national holiday for a nation not yet dreamed of, Jamestown colonists held a simple prayer service in gratitude for their providential rescue from starvation.

Proud Virginia historians, misconstruing the intention of an early colonist to have an annual day of Thanksgiving "perpetualy keept holy" as the origin of our national holiday, are even more likely to point to a service held at Berkeley Hundred on December 4, 1619, as the "first Thanksgiving." Captain John Woodleaf, leader of the small colony of Berkeley Hundred, wrote these "Instructions" in the colony charter:

> Wee ordaine that the day of our ships arrival at the place assigned for plantacon in the land of Virginia shall be yearly and perpetualy keept holy as a day of thanksgiving to Almighty god.

The anniversary may have been "keept holy" according to Captain Woodleaf's instructions in 1620 and 1621, but in March 1622, the fledgling colony was obliterated by an Indian attack. Although the Virginia General Assembly proclaimed thanksgiving observances for the remaining settlements in gratitude for their having survived the "bloudie massaker," this early proclamation in recognition of a singular event did not become a yearly celebration, and the memory of it soon faded.

However satisfying it would be to point to a particular day and say, "This was the first Thanksgiving," it would not be accurate. Thanksgiving was not a New England Athena, springing full grown and completely armed with roast turkey and cranberry sauce from the head of a Pilgrim Father. Thanksgiving gradually grew up in the unique culture of Puritan New England, an origin both more complex and more interesting than the legend of Pilgrim and Indian feasting at Plymouth in 1621.

A
Holiday
Is Born _____ 2

Although Maine, Massachusetts, Virginia, Texas and Florida
claim to have hosted the "first Thanksgiving," it was in the towns
of the Connecticut River valley and the farming villages of Plymouth Colony that the holiday as we know it evolved. Neither
created intentionally nor copied from a paradigmatic "first
Thanksgiving," the new celebration was a synthesis of four distinct and ancient traditions, elements of which united in the
unique cultural milieu of Puritan New England to give birth to
Thanksgiving. The newborn Thanksgiving holiday had a Puritan
"mother" from Connecticut, a Pilgrim "father" from Plymouth
and, for "grandparents," four traditions from the Old World.

Harvest Home

New Englanders came from Old England, where the Harvest

Home—one of the "grandparents" of Thanksgiving—was celebrated. The Harvest Home was a holiday on which the villagers
joined together to bring the last loads of grain from the fields and
share a merry feast when the work was done. English villages
followed local harvest customs; some dressed a maiden in white
to ride atop a loaded cart as "Queen of the Harvest." Others fashioned a figure from the grain itself to be robed in a white gown
and set in the center of a circle of rejoicing farmers. There was
sufficient taint of idol worship and evidence of licentious behavior in the old English Harvest Home for Puritans to reject the
custom summarily. They recoiled from these remnants of the
pagan customs that predated Christianity in England, but memories of the harvest feast lingered all the same.

The Puritans' shunning of the ancient Harvest Home left a
void in the New England year that might not have been problem-
atic had a similar attitude not been extended to other holidays.
But the Puritans had disapproved so many causes for celebration
that a holiday vacuum existed in the young colonies.

All saints' days had been swept off the calendar, along with
Christmas and Easter, on the grounds that these mixed "popish"
ritual with pagan custom. Sunday, the occasion in Europe for
afternoon ball games, cockfights, plays, gambling, fishing trips
and dances, became the Puritan Sabbath, a day passed in prayer,
church attendance and devotional reading. Every secular pleasure was forbidden by law and custom. Remaining to New Englanders were three holidays—Muster Day, Election Day and the
day of the Harvard Commencement. (Yale was not founded until
1701, whereas Harvard was founded in 1636.)

On Muster Day the colonial militias drilled. Citizen soldiers
shouldered muskets and marched up and down the village common, while an audience of small children spent their pennies on
lemonade and peppermint candy. After a few turns around the
common, the rustic troops adjourned to the village tavern for a
comradely round of ale and hard apple cider.

On Election Day, the men again gathered at the common,
only this time they left their muskets home, and hopeful candidates supplied the cider.

Harvard's early commencements were public revels. Kegs of
beer and tables of food were set out in Harvard Yard for guests

THE HOCK-CART, OR HARVEST-HOME

Come, sons of Summer, by whose toile
We are the lords of wine and oile,
By whose tough labors and rough hands,
We rip up first, then reap our lands,
Crown'd with the eares of corne, now come,
And to the pipe sing harvest-home;
Come forth, my lord, and see the cart,
Dressed up with all the country art.
The horses, mares, and frisking fillies,
Clad all in linen white as lillies.
The harvest swaines and wenches bound
For joy, to see the hock-cart crown'd.
Some blesse the cart; some kisse the sheaves;
Some prank them up with oaken leaves:
Some crosse the fill-horse; some with great
Devotion stroak the home-borne wheat;
While other rusticks, lesse attent
To prayers than to merryment,
Run after with their breeches rent.

—Robert Herrick
in Hesperides, 1648

WE PLOW THE FIELDS AND SCATTER

We plow the fields and scatter
The good seed on the land,
But it is fed and wa-tered
By God's al-might-y hand.
He sends the snow in winter,
The warmth to swell the grain,
The breezes and the sunshine,
And soft, refreshing rain.

All good gifts around us
Are sent from heaven above;
Then thank the Lord, O thank the Lord
For all his love. Amen.

He only is the maker
Of all things near and far;
He paints the way-side flower,
He lights the evening star.
The winds and waves obey him,
By him the birds are fed;
Much more, to us his children,
He gives our daily bread.

All good gifts around us
Are sent from heaven above;
Then thank the Lord, O thank the Lord
For all his love. Amen.

We thank thee, then, O Father,
For all things bright and good:
The seedtime and the har-vest,
Our life, our health, our food.
Accept the gifts we offer,
For all thy love imparts,
And, what thou most desirest,
Our humble, thankful hearts.

All good gifts around us
Are sent from heaven above;
Then thank the Lord, O thank the Lord
For all his love. Amen.

—Matthias Claudias

COME, YE THANKFUL PEOPLE, COME

Come, ye thankful people, come,
Raise the song of harvest home;
All is safely gathered in,
Ere the winter storms begin;
God, our Maker, doth provide
For our wants to be supplied;
Come to God's own temple, come,
Raise the song of harvest home.

All the world is God's own field,
Fruit unto his praise to yield;
Wheat and tares together sown,
Unto joy or sorrow grown;
First the blade, and then the ear,
Then the full corn shall appear;
Lord of harvest, grant that we
Wholesome grain and pure may be.

For the Lord our God shall come,
And shall take his harvest home;
From his field shall in that day
All offenses purge away,
Give his angels charge at last
In the fire the tares to cast,
But the fruitful ears to store
In his garner evermore.

Even so, Lord, quickly come
To thy final harvest home;
Gather thou thy people in,
Free from sorrow, free from sin;
There forever purified,
In thy presence to abide;
Come, with all thine angels, come,
Raise the glorious harvest home. Amen.

—*Henry Alford*

who came from the furthest reaches of the colony to hear the
speakers and drink ale, often to the point of intoxication, along
with the young Puritan ministers newly minted by the college.
Few of the revelers had any personal relationship with the graduates but, since Harvard was supported by the public treasury
and there were so few celebrations to enjoy, all felt entitled to
attend.

Christmas

Like the Harvest Home, Christmas—another of the old-
world "grandparents" of Thanksgiving—was remembered but
not celebrated by the Puritans. The practice of designating the
day of Jesus' birth, and especially of making merry on that day,
were viewed as one of the grave errors of the churches of both
Rome and England and as a departure from the purity of the early
church. Celebration of Christmas was so disparaged in the seventeenth-century Bay Colony that the General Court forbade labor-
ers taking off from work on that day under penalty of a five-
shilling fine. Not until the nineteenth century did New England
relent in this attitude and the Congregational churches began to
observe Christmas—but Massachusetts was two centuries old
before that happened. In the early years, everything associated
with Christmas was rejected out of hand; even the lowly mince
pie, eaten in every English household at Christmas, was banished
from the Puritan kitchen as being unholy food at any time of
year.

The spirit of Christmas, however, was sorely missed, and
during the 1600s, when Thanksgiving was becoming a popular
festival, small pieces of the English Christmas crept into the celebration of the Yankee Thanksgiving. Those quintessential
English Christmas dishes, plum pudding and mince pie, became
as indispensable a part of the Thanksgiving menu as turkey and
pumpkin pie itself.

Civil Proclamations

Thanksgiving Day, our unique American holiday, ought not to be confused with still a third "grandparent," the special days of thanksgiving proclaimed by civil authorities in Europe and throughout the American colonies. When some stroke of extraordinary good fortune befell a nation, the civil authorities often declared a day of thanksgiving and prayer, marked by special services in every church. The end of an epidemic, rainfall after a drought and victory in war were common reasons for such celebrations, and declarations of this sort were familiar to the first settlers on these shores. Coronado, Popham and the settlers at Jamestown, Plymouth and Boston acted in this tradition when they held their "first Thanksgivings."

Settlers in both New Amsterdam and Plymouth were familiar with the Dutch custom of celebrating October 3 as a day of thanksgiving commemorating the independence of Holland from Spain. English settlers recalled that the Anglican church marked November 5, the anniversary of the discovery of the Gunpowder Plot, as a day on which thanks were given that the scheme to blow up Parliament had failed. Puritan New England undoubtedly drew upon the tradition of civic thanksgivings in creating the new holiday.

Religious Proclamations

Fourth "grandparent" to the American Thanksgiving Day was the tradition of individual Puritan congregations declaring days of thanksgiving and prayer. The Puritans rejected all ecclesiastical hierarchy in favor of the sovereignty of the congregation. Authority equivalent to that belonging to Catholic or Anglican bishops was vested in Puritan congregations, which had sole power to ordain clergymen, admit or excommunicate members and declare days of fasting and of thanksgiving. Like the proclamations of civil authorities, congregational thanksgiving days were declared for special causes.

Synthesis of the Traditions

The Thanksgiving holiday born in Puritan New England in
the 1630s and 1640s was shaped by four traditions—the Harvest
Home, Christmas, proclamations of civic thanksgiving and congregational days of thanksgiving and prayer. But it also had distinct characteristics of its own that enable us to identify this holiday as the beginning of our contemporary Thanksgiving Day.

Days of thanksgiving in colonial New England were occasions of prayer and of feasting and family reunion, proclaimed
annually by civil authorities for general causes. Individual Plymouth Colony congregations held days of thanksgiving for the
harvest with some frequency in the 1630s and 1640s, but not
every year. The day of thanksgiving at Scituate in 1636, for example, began

> In ye Meetinghouse, beginning some halfe an hour before nine
> and continued untill after twelve aclocke, ye day being very
> cold, beginning with a short prayer, then a psalme song, then
> more large in prayer [a longer prayer than the first], after that an
> other Psalme, and then the Word taught [the sermon by Rever-
> end John Lothrop], after that prayer—and then a psalme—then
> making merry to the creatures [attending to creature comforts,
> in this case a holiday meal], the poorer sort being invited of the
> richer.

Here was Thanksgiving Day in embryo, a day of prayer followed
by "making merry" at family dinners.

Other features of the holiday developed in Connecticut. The
Connecticut River valley towns of Wethersfield, Windsor and
Hartford were settled in 1635 and 1636 by families from Massachusetts Bay who shared with their sister colony a thoroughgoing
dedication to Puritanism. The church in each town followed the
established, Puritan custom of holding days of public thanks or of
prayer and fasting as the occasion warranted, but the leaders of
the colony departed from tradition by proclaiming a day of public
thanksgiving each autumn in gratitude for general well-being and
for the harvest just gathered. Although records from the early
years are incomplete, a proclamation of thanksgiving for Septem-

Five Puritan girls sing at Thanksgiving Services in an old New England meetinghouse where men and women sit segregated by sex and by age. The kneeling angel is the anachronistic embellishment of the Victorian artist.

The Thanksgiving feasts of yore were laboriously prepared over open hearth fires. This guide at Plimouth Plantation in Plymouth, Massachusetts re-creates the cooking methods of the seventeenth century colonists.

ber 18, 1639, survives, as do proclamations for 1644 and for every year from 1649 onward.

This was the crucial innovation. The entire Western world shares the custom of special thanksgivings for special causes and, as we have seen, individual Plymouth colony congregations sometimes held harvest thanksgivings followed by a festive meal. When Connecticut made Thanksgiving Day an annual festival for general causes, however, a new holiday was born. Thanksgiving in Connecticut was held every autumn, not for special reasons, but in gratitude for the ordinary blessings of the "year past" and for the "fruits of the earth." It was held whether the harvest was abundant or meager and regardless of events that had befallen the colony since the previous Thanksgiving Day.

If the year had gone well, specific causes for gratitude were enumerated in the proclamation—good weather, ample harvests or the blessings of civil and religious liberty. If the year had brought misfortune, such few blessings as there were nonetheless were enumerated, and the colony dutifully turned out to give thanks. Only once, from 1649 to the present, has a disaster so overwhelmed the people of Connecticut that they omitted their Thanksgiving celebration.

In June 1675, Metacomet, sachem of the Wampanoag Indians, known to history as King Philip, ended the peaceful coexistence with the Plymouth Colony begun by his father, Massasoit, in 1621 by attacking the Plymouth town of Swansea. Total warfare ensued between the colonists and the Indian tribes of Narragansett, Wampanoag, and Nipmuck. Indian warriors raided isolated farms and villages, brutally murdering every inhabitant. New England soldiers, Christian Indians among them, attacked Indian villages, sometimes burning alive their entire populations. Twenty years passed before all of the devastated colonial villages were resettled, and organized tribal life in southern New England was at an end forever, so great was the destruction.

Surrounded by devastation and living in dread of attack, the citizens of Connecticut found no cause to give thanks in 1675. By the autumn of 1676, however, the tide had turned. Philip was dead, his warriors had been sold as slaves in the West Indies and along the Barbary Coast of Africa and New

England's peaceful future had been secured. The General Court of Connecticut urged the people of the colony to thank their Lord for "appeareing so gloriously for their help in subdueing of our enemies . . ." and for other causes including "the comfortable and plentifull harvest . . ." by keeping "a day of Publique Thankesgiving. . . ."

Never again would a governor of Connecticut omit to declare Thanksgiving Day. Born of a devout Puritan impulse to thank the Lord for His goodness once each year, nurtured along the banks of the Connecticut River by farmers who followed pious devotions with a wholesome celebration of crops harvested and families reunited, Thanksgiving Day was poised to become a holiday beloved by a nation.

Thanksgiving Comes of Age in New England _____ 3

While the idea of an annual Thanksgiving Day took root in Connecticut, Massachusetts Bay was still rejecting an annual celebration in favor of days of thanks set only when there was something special for which to be thankful. In the words of Reverend John Cotton, "We sometimes upon extraordinary occasions . . . do set apart a day of humiliation or upon special mercies we set apart a day of Thanksgiving." Indeed, Massachusetts colonists were not shy about setting such days apart; individual congregations and the colony as a whole observed dozens of them during the seventeenth century, but each was a unique day of gratitude for specific occurrences, not an annual event.

As the years passed, some Massachusetts Bay residents began to feel that annual days of thanks, such as were held in Connecticut and by the churches in Plymouth, were a good idea.

A debate was joined. Many prominent citizens believed that, in the words of Judge Samuel Sewall, "t'was not fit upon mere Generals [that is, upon merely general, and not specific, causes] to Command a Thanksgiving." Judge Sewall, who had trained for the ministry at Harvard, was a member of the Governor's Council and for 26 years a member and then chief justice of the Superior Court. A theologically conservative Puritan, Sewall is remembered as one of the judges in the Salem witchcraft trials who condemned 19 people to death, a role he later repented.

Sewall's position against an annual thanksgiving was shared by many ministers who feared that such yearly celebrations when no particularly noteworthy beneficences had been received, would make the people overly confident of the Lord's generosity and insufficiently humble and chary of Providential wrath. Theologically, the argument was a strong one, but the people wanted Thanksgiving. The congregation at Salem, for example, noting that in 1668 "the General Court" has not appointed "any public days of Thanksgiving or Fasting and prayer," declared December 23 as a fast and January 14 as a thanksgiving "with respect unto the mercies of the year past."

Colonial authorities were torn between the two positions, and a debate in the Governor's Council in 1690 highlights their dilemma. According to Judge Sewall's diary, "Mr. Torrey is for a Fast or at least a Fast first. Mr. Willard is for a Thanksgiving first. Mr. Torrey fears lest a Thanksgiving should tend to harden the people in their carnal confidence." Torrey carried his point and a public fast day was held, but the proponents of Thanksgiving could not be put off. Samuel Willard, rector of Old South Church in Boston, was an erudite and conservative theologian whose ability to put aside theology in favor of sound policy won for him the acting presidency of Harvard. He sensibly opposed burning people accused of witchcraft and, in the case of Thanksgiving, defied theological considerations to accommodate the popular desire for a Thanksgiving holiday. With his support, a thanksgiving was celebrated that winter, albeit in February.

An autumn Thanksgiving took root slowly in Massachusetts Bay, being held most years after 1660 and coexisting with frequent, periodic or specially declared fasts and thanksgivings. But, by the end of the century, its roots were so deep that no later governor dared to omit proclaiming the day.

Plymouth

Colonists at Plymouth seem not to have had strong objections to the idea of proclaiming thanksgivings for general causes, but they did feel strongly that power to declare such days was vested in the churches, not in civil authorities. During the colony's first four decades, numerous days of thanks were held by individual congregations, sometimes by several congregations simultaneously and for general causes, but none was proclaimed by the colonial government.

In some years devout but hard-pressed congregations were at a loss to know whether to hold a fast day and repent the causes of their trials or to hold a thanksgiving for the meager blessings they could still count. The year 1690 was a year of poor harvests and intermittent Indian warfare for the people of Plymouth. A day of prayer was clearly in order. The congregations of English settlers, despondent over their troubles, held a day of fasting; while the congregations of Christianized Indians "appointed a day of Thanksgiving to God for his mercy in supplying their extream and pinching Necessities under their late want of Corn. . . ."

As time passed, the congregations guarded their prerogative of proclaiming days of thanksgiving less jealously, and it may have seemed convenient for all the towns to do together what each already did individually. In 1668, the Plymouth General Court "propose[d] unto the several congregations of this government, that on the 25th day of November next, which will be ye fourth day of the week, to be kept as a sollemne day of thanksgiving," the cause of which was to take "notice of the goodness of God to us in the continuance of our civill and religious liberties, the generall health that wee have enjoyed, and that it hath pleased God in some comfortable measure to blesse us in the fruits of the earth."

Thanksgivings were so familiar a part of congregational life that, in effect, the General Court was regularizing an ongoing custom. It is noteworthy that whereas the Puritan leaders in Connecticut and Massachusetts Bay "ordered" or "proclaimed" Thanksgiving Day, Separatist leaders in Plymouth, more mindful of the principle of congregational independence from government authority, "proposed," "desired," or "recommended" the observance in proclamations sent to each congregation.

In all three colonies, the practice was for the authorities to make a copy of the proclamation for each congregation. In the words of Plymouth Colony records: "A coppy of this was sent speedyly to the severall congregations of this government," and the holiday was formally proclaimed by the action of individual ministers reading the order from the pulpit.

Plymouth held its last independent Thanksgiving in 1692 to celebrate union with Massachusetts Bay and thereafter observed the days proclaimed by the General Court at Boston.

Maine, New Hampshire and New Haven

Maine was a sparsely settled district of Massachusetts Bay for most of the 1600s and followed that colony's laws. New Hampshire was founded by migrants from Connecticut, who settled the river valley to the west, and from Massachusetts, who settled the eastern hills and seacoast. Each group followed the customs of its home colony for a time, but as New Hampshire matured, the governor proclaimed Thanksgiving Day, doing so for the first time in 1695, and by the first decade of the eighteenth century, annual proclamations were issued.

The small colony of New Haven, which extended along the shore of Connecticut and included the eastern reaches of Long Island, held at least occasional days of thanksgiving before it was absorbed by Connecticut in 1665.

Rhode Island

As for Rhode Island, it is well to recall that the colony was settled by men and women too independent-minded and outspoken to get along with the religious establishments of Connecticut, Massachusetts Bay or Plymouth. Folks in neighboring colonies called the place Rogues' Island. The tiny colony, founded in 1636, was a kaleidoscope of religious opinion, with adherents of an apparently infinite number of sects among its citizens. In Massachusetts, Thanksgiving cut across religious lines, being observed by Anglican and Puritan alike. No one, however, could tell Rhode Islanders how to worship or even when. Stubborn Rhode Island was the last New England colony to begin to observe Thanksgiving. Rhode Islanders went to church on a few thanksgivings ordered by Governor Andros during the Dominion of New England and, during the French and Indian Wars, held a few fast days and a public thanksgiving on November 22, 1759, after the capture of Quebec by British and colonial troops. Additional thanksgivings were occasionally set apart by individual congregations, but a statewide, annual Thanksgiving Day only became customary in Rhode Island after nationwide days were proclaimed by the Continental Congress during the Revolutionary War.

Thanksgiving Becomes Popular

Every New England colony continued to proclaim occasional days of thanksgiving or of fasting and prayer in recognition of extraordinary events long after Thanksgiving had become an annual autumn holiday. The capture of Louisburg, at the mouth of the Gulf of St. Lawrence, by colonial troops on July 3, 1745, during the French and Indian Wars, for example, was the occasion of public thanksgivings throughout the colonies. And on August 24, 1749, the people of Massachusetts celebrated a day of thanksgiving for rain that had alleviated a severe drought. Special fast days were declared for such extraordinary events as the earthquake that terrified Massachusetts residents on October 30, 1727, sending them to their churches to fast and repent the sins that had brought this terror into their midst.

In all of the colonies, public behavior on thanksgiving days

and fast days was regulated by "blue laws." A statute in effect in
Massachusetts Bay, Connecticut and New Haven colonies in the
seventeenth century decreed that "Every person shall . . . attend . . . the publick ministry of the Word . . . he shall forfeit
for his absence from every such publick meeting five shillings."
In the small communities of early New England, the easy and
eager enforcement of such ordinances made absences from meetings rare occurrences. Colonial New England in the 1600s was a
hotbed of devout, Puritan conformity. Everyone went to meeting
on thanksgiving days, and no one thought of doing anything livelier afterward than eating dinner at home with the family.

The rising generation was another story altogether. Massachusetts, in 1692, New Hampshire, in 1700, and Connecticut, in
1750, enacted laws admonishing the young folk not to "Use any
Game, Sport, Play, or Recreation on . . . Thanksgiving . . . on pain that every Person so Offending shall for every
offence Forfeit the Sum of Ten Shillings." It was little use. The
holy day was becoming a holiday, and the legislation had little
power to alter the forces of social change.

As suggested by these statutes, early New England days of
thanksgiving, both those proclaimed in recognition of special
beneficences and the annual autumn Thanksgiving days, were at
the outset primarily days of prayer. Morning services, including
prayers, hymns and a sermon, occupied about four hours. The
congregation then went home to dinner and returned to church
for another two hours or so of evening prayers and a final install-
ment of the morning's sermon. This pattern of two services punctuated by a dinner was modeled on the schedule of the New England Sabbath day. Though very pious, it was probably not very
much fun.

Thanksgiving dinner grew in importance in the late seventeenth century, adding homecoming relatives, extra pies and plat-
ters of roast meat. Congregations made room for this more elaborate dinner by eliminating the afternoon service on Thanksgiving Day, first in country districts where the walk to meeting was
long and cold, then in the 1720s in Boston itself. Soon the feast
was as important as the morning prayer service.

Colchester, Connecticut, waiting in the fall of 1705 for a
shipment of molasses delayed by an early snowstorm, finally

The piety of this family, with heads bowed as grandfather asks the blessing, reflects the spirit of the Puritan Thanksgiving. The coat of arms and portrait on the wall, however, are the fanciful embellishments of the Victorian artist.

decided that Thanksgiving could not be held without molasses for pumpkin pies. The residents of the town met and voted to put off Thanksgiving for one week. On November 9, seven days after the rest of the state, Colchester had its Thanksgiving—pies and all.

A generation that deemed pies an indispensable part of Thanksgiving Day also enjoyed recreations of the sort forbidden on the Sabbath. First, visiting or walking to a neighbor's house, activities avoided by the devout on the Lord's Day, became acceptable, and then, gradually, parlor games, dances, ice skating, and ball games became part of Thanksgiving Day.

At first, no particular day of the week was reserved for Thanksgiving, but some days were thought more appropriate than others. Puritans observed the Sabbath as a Biblical ordinance and did not intrude their thanksgivings upon it. Since Saturday was occupied with preparations for the Sabbath, and Monday was the day just after, these were not convenient choices. Friday was ruled out because it was the fast day of the Catholic church, and any day of prayer held on a Friday would have had "Romish" overtones. However, Thursday was lecture day in Boston: ministers offered afternoon sermons for those with the leisure time to attend weekday religious meetings. Perhaps for this reason Thursday early became the favorite day for fasts and thanksgivings, and although other days were occasionally chosen, Thursday became the traditional choice.

The Custom Prevails

Congregations with purely local reasons for giving thanks retained the prerogative of setting aside days of thanksgiving and exercised it with some frequency into the early years of the eighteenth century. But when an entire colony shared cause for gratitude, the ministers would recognize God's graciousness with a decision to hold a thanksgiving, and the governor and the council would proclaim the day. This system worked very well while civil and religious authorities were in close accord, but there arrived the awful day when Charles II was restored to the throne of England and revoked the self-governing charter of Massachusetts Bay. Several fast days were held as New Englanders hoped that divine intervention would save their precious charters. The good Lord did take Charles II from this life, but only to replace him with James II, who sent a royal governor to rule New England. Massachusetts, waiting in the fall of 1685 for the arrival of the dreaded governor, nearly missed Thanksgiving.

The General Court was paralyzed by fear that some phrase in the proclamation would bring the wrath of England down on the colony. "The difficulty of Printing an Order [for Thanksgiving] is," according to Judge Sewall, "lest by putting in or leaving out, we offend England." At least five sessions of the General Court essayed to write a proclamation that would leave out what would displease England, without putting in that which would offend their constituents, who were bitterly resentful of English tyranny. The politicians failed. Then the ministers met and proclaimed Thanksgiving for December 3, 1685.

Sir Edmund Andros, royal governor of the Dominion of New England, arrived in Boston on December 20, 1686, and it is not recorded that he and the people under his rule agreed on any single issue from that day until he was driven form his post three years later. Governor Andros was traveling in Connecticut in the fall of 1687 when the ministers of Massachusetts agreed to name November 17 a day of thanksgiving. He returned to Boston on November 16 and promptly annulled their proclamation, declaring proclamations of thanksgiving to be the prerogative of the governor and appointing December 1 as Thanksgiving Day for all of New England.

The people of Massachusetts, Connecticut, New Hampshire and Plymouth sullenly observed the governor's date, but stubborn Rhode Islanders refused to let a governor tell them when to worship. Many of them worked in the fields on that day or omitted to attend divine services, both illegal acts in defiance of Governor Andros' edict that the people set the day apart for prayer. Samuel Stapleton of Newport, arrested and brought before the court on charges of having opened his shop on the governor's thanksgiving, gave a good, Quaker answer, "that he was above the observation of days and times."

The ministers were still simmering over Andros's high-handed autumn thanksgiving when he declared a special thanksgiving for Sunday, April 18, in gratitude for the queen's pregnancy. Not only were Sabbath day thanksgivings contrary to all New England tradition but New Englanders cordially disliked their Catholic King James II and would have been pleased had his wife, Mary of Modena, borne no children at all. Most New England congregations were spared the unpleasant duty of offering thankful prayers for the expected Catholic heir because the Thanksgiving proclamations failed to arrive. Whether this failure was the ruse of a Protestant messenger, a contagious case of ministerial dissemblance or an actual error, history does not reveal.

The government took note of the undelivered proclamations and when the council designated the anniversary of the beheading of Charles I as a "day of fasting and humilitation," the proclamations were served on the reluctant congregations by sheriffs. New Englanders, who had prayed for the success of Parliament and had sheltered the regicides who beheaded Charles, were now being forced to pray for a king whom they hated. It was an insult not to be borne, and many congregations defiantly let the day pass unobserved. Early in April, news reached Boston of Protestant William and Mary's invasion of England, which became known as the Glorious Revolution. The people rose and threw the hated Andros into jail, restored their provincial assemblies to power and declared days of thanksgiving for the ascension of William and Mary.

When the eighteenth century dawned, governors of Connecticut, Massachusetts (incorporating Plymouth) and New Hampshire were in the annual habit of proclaiming an autumn thanksgiving, which was observed as a day of both prayer and feasting. No colony west or south of New England celebrated a New England–style thanksgiving, although every colony did, on occasion, observe the separate and ancient custom of appointing special days of thanks. New England pastors and governors were also ready to declare special days of fasting or thanksgiving as the occasion warranted, but the annual autumn Thanksgiving Day had become something more. It was a holiday that could no more be stopped by a governor's whim than be created by one. It was a holiday created by the people of New England.

Revolutionary
Holiday _____ 4

When a rift began to open between the emerging American nation and its English mother country, Thanksgiving was enlisted for service in the patriot cause by politicians writing proclamations of thanksgiving and by preachers endorsing revolutionary ideas in their sermons. Most British-born and -educated Anglican ministers were Loyalists who left their American parishes and returned to England during the war; but Presbyterian, Congregational and other Protestant clergymen mounted their pulpits to sound the trumpets of independence in their Thanksgiving sermons.

The Beginnings of Rebellion

The prelude to rebellion began in 1764, when Parliament attempted to defray the cost of defending the American colonies

during the French and Indian Wars by passing, first, the Acts of
Trade and Navigation, which imposed duties on a number of
colonial imports, and then, on March 22, 1765, the infamous
Stamp Act. This tax, assessed by means of a revenue stamp
affixed to papers of all kinds—including newspapers, legal docu-
ments and even playing cards—was the first instance of parlia-
mentary imposition on the colonies of a levy other than customs
duties. The colonies rang with protest: patriots refused to buy
imported goods or to use the revenue stamps, and mobs
destroyed the homes and offices of stamp distributors in several
cities. Days of fasting and prayer were held to encourage people
to repent whatever sins might have brought on this visitation of
imperial revenue-grabbing.

When the time for Thanksgiving 1765 came around, Governor Thomas Fitch of Connecticut issued a proclamation suggesting that thanks be offered only "for the Continuation of those
Privileges civil and religious which we still enjoy." Connecticut
and its democratically elected governor were unanimous in
opposing the Stamp Act. Governor and citizen alike worshiped in
Congregational meetinghouses that Thanksgiving Day—Yankee
congregations listening with equal approval to their governor's
assertive proclamation and the ministers' concurring sermons.

Massachusetts, on the other hand, was ruled by a royal governor, Sir Francis Bernard, whose proclamation suggested that
thanks be offered for "the continuance of the Happiness and
Liberty, which have been secured to us by His Majesty's illustrious House." The royal governor may have given thanks for his
personal "happiness and liberty," but the citizens of Massachusetts went to meeting on Thanksgiving Day to pray for repeal of
the Stamp Act.

Repeal, when it came in March 1766, was greeted with
rejoicing throughout the colonies and by a round of public
thanksgivings in New England. Governor Benning Wentworth of
New Hampshire had set a public fast for May 21, but when news
of the repeal reached Portsmouth on that very day, the mourners
rejoiced. In Massachusetts, churches held individual days of
thanksgiving. Reverend Jonathan Mayhew, grumbling over "the
improbability of our being called together for this end by proclamation" by Governor Bernard, offered a Thanksgiving sermon

on the text: "Our soul is escaped as a bird from the snare of the fowlers, the snare is broken and we are escaped," which he dedicated to William Pitt, engineer of the Stamp Act repeal in Parliament.

The colonies were still celebrating when Governor William Pitkin issued the annual Thanksgiving proclamation for Connecticut: "God hath in a singular manner appeared for us in the course of his merciful Providence, in the late gloomy Day of Prayer, Anxiety, and Distress, averting impending Evils, and saved to us our important civil Rights and Liberties,—a Favour of Heaven never to be forgotten!"

Thomas Hutchinson became governor of Massachusetts Bay in 1771, a year of unprecedented prosperity throughout the colonies, when it seemed possible that the Stamp Act might indeed be forgotten and the Trade and Navigation acts endured without further protest by affluent Americans. Perhaps the revolutionary fervor might die down. Virginia, according to Thomas Jefferson, "seemed to fall into a state of insensibility to our situation," and even that firebrand John Adams resolved in his diary to "become more retired and cautious; I shall certainly mind my own farm and my own business."

Samuel Adams also perceived the danger in the situation. "It is to be feared that the people will be so accustomed to bondage as to forget that they were ever free," he wrote, and cast about for some way to stir the people up. At this juncture, Governor Hutchinson issued his Thanksgiving proclamation, suggesting, among other reasons, that the people offer thanks for the "continuation of our civil and religious privileges." It was just what Sam Adams had been waiting for.

At a time when so many traditional privileges had been suspended, Adams charged, the governor's proclamation was "contrived to try the feelings of the people," and a campaign was mounted to dissuade ministers from reading the proclamation from the pulpit. "A more artful method of exciting the general attention of the people, which would otherwise have ceased, for want of subject, could not have been projected," complained Hutchinson in retrospect during his long exile in England, brought about by an enduring inability to perceive that the agitation for independence was unlikely to cease.

Not merely "artful," the ploy was also successful. This letter from an angry Bostonian bears witness to the outrage that Adams and his fellow instigators succeeded in stirring up over the incident:

> We were therein called upon to give thanks for the continuance of our civil and religious privileges and for the increase in our trade and commerce. Such a palpable affront to a people who are daily complaining of the abridgement of their liberties and the burthens upon their Commerce, gave universal disgust, and the proclamation was treated with greater contempt than anything of the kind had ever before been in this part of the world. Out of twenty Congregations in this Town [Boston] it was read in but one, and even there by far the greater part of the people signified their contempt by leaving the church the minute the Parson began to read it.

Actually, the proclamation was read in two churches: Old South, where a young assistant minister watched his congregation leave the meetinghouse as he read, and in Governor Hutchinson's own church, the New Brick, where Reverend Ebenezer Pemberton, the governor's personal friend, was a man of moderation who hoped for an accommodation with Britain.

The attitude of the clergy was more nearly typified by the selection of the following sermon text from the Book of Nehemiah by Reverend Samuel Cooke of the First Congregational Church in Arlington, Massachusetts:

> Behold, we are servants this day, and for the land that thou gavest our father, to eat the fruits thereof and the good thereof, behold! we are servants in it; and it yieldeth much increase unto the kings whom thou hast set over us because of our sins: also they have dominion over our bodies, and over our cattle, at their pleasure, and we are in great distress.

By 1774, affairs had reached such a pass that the Associated Pastors of Boston resolved not to read any proclamations that a royal governor might issue.

On June 1, the Boston Port Bill was to go into effect, closing Boston Harbor to shipping until compensation was paid for tea thrown overboard at the "Tea Party" in December 1773. Enacted by Parliament along with the Port Bill were the Government and Administration of Justice acts, designed to punish rebellious

Massachusetts, and the odious Quartering Act, empowering royal governors to commandeer space in private homes for soldiers' quarters. Together, they were known as the Intolerable Acts by Americans, who had no intention of tolerating royal coercion. Citizens of Massachusetts responded by setting up Committees of Correspondence to govern themselves, leaving General Thomas Gage, who succeeded Hutchinson as governor of Massachusetts Bay, actually master only of Boston itself, which he ruled with the support of five regiments of British regulars.

Other colonies rallied to Boston's aid, sending food and money to the beleaguered city. In Virginia, the House of Burgesses passed a resolution that Thomas Jefferson helped to draft denouncing the occupation of Boston as a "hostile invasion" and declaring June 1 a "day of fasting, humiliation and prayer." Enraged by this proclamation of a fast for such a cause, Governor John Dunmore promptly dissolved the Virginia legislature. Before going home, the Burgesses met at Raleigh Tavern in Williamsburg to resolve that "an attack made on one of our sister colonies, to compel submission to arbitrary taxes, is an attack made on all British America." The road to independence had been taken.

New England mourned, fasted and prayed when the Port Bill went into effect, but when autumn came, Thanksgiving was kept as usual. Governor Jonathan Trumbull of Connecticut issued a bold proclamation for Thanksgiving Day 1774: "Preserve our Liberties and Peace; restore and preserve them to all the rest of the British colonies in America. . . . Unite our Councils, and guide us into the most wise and happy measures for the preservation of all our just Rights."

This daring prayer for the preservation of rights contrasts dramatically with traditional phrasing, which in earlier years had meekly thanked the monarch for the "continuation of our privileges." The leap from expressing gratitude for privileges to considering "measures" for the "preservation of rights" was an important step toward rebellion, but it was as far as Trumbull was prepared to advance in 1774. His proclamation continued with a plea that "GOD would enable and dispose the King . . . to be the Father of, and favorable to all the British

Colonies in America, and to hear us when we call," and closed
with the ancient epithet "God Save the King."

Open Rebellion

Massachusetts, by contrast, was finished with proclamations
pleading for the favor of His Britannic Majesty and was ready to
issue a new kind of document. Meeting at Cambridge on October
22, 1774, the rebel colonial assembly declared Thursday, December 15, a day of Thanksgiving "by order of the Provincial Congress, John Hancock, President." No British governor signed the
proclamation, no royal coat of arms appeared at the top of the
page and, for the first time on an American Thanksgiving proclamation, the motto "God Save the King" was missing. Bay State
ministers rose to the occasion with revolutionary sermons. "The
way to escape an attack is to be in readiness to receive it," said the
Reverend William Gordon of Roxbury, Massachusetts, "The
colonies should pursue the means of safety as vigorously as ever,
that they may not be surprised." Rebellious colonists continued
to store arms at Concord.

Even as the first shots of the Revolution rang out on Lexing-
ton Green on April 19, 1775, the people of Connecticut were
gathered in their churches, fasting and praying for a peaceful resolution to the conflict. Fast days were kept throughout the colonies
as the war began, but the conflict quickly moved beyond hope of
peaceful resolution.

November 23, 1775, was observed as Thanksgiving Day by
the Continental Army besieging Boston, as well as by the people
of Massachusetts. Five months later, in March 1776, General
William Howe and his army were driven from Boston by cannon
placed under George Washington's orders on Dorchester
Heights. Massachusetts had real cause for jubilation. "He hath so
far supported us in our Exertions against the arbitrary Claims and
military violence of Britain . . ." rang the exultant words of the
Massachusetts Thanksgiving proclamation for Thursday, December 12, 1776, and "Hath given us a compleat Victory over a
whole Army of our Enemies."

Victory: A Reason for Thanksgiving

The Continental Congress had found reasons enough to declare days of fasting and prayer; 1777 would bring the first opportunity to declare a national day of thanksgiving. Major General John Burgoyne, marching south from Canada in June 1777 with 6,000 men and orders to secure the Hudson Valley for England, was soundly defeated by the dashing tactics of General Benedict Arnold and his Continentals. Burgoyne surrendered on October 17 at Saratoga, leaving England shocked and America jubilant that a British army could be beaten so quickly and completely by unseasoned colonial troops. In Philadelphia, Congress declared December 18 a "day of solemn Thanksgiving and praise" for this "signal success."

Thanksgiving Day 1777, the first such celebration ever proclaimed by a national authority for all 13 states, was more the continuation of an old custom than an extension of the New England Thanksgiving holiday. It was a special thanksgiving, kept for special causes. The victory at Saratoga was a stunning success for the army of the infant republic, and a special day of thanks was in order. Delegates to the Continental Congress viewed the appointment as just such a special thanksgiving, voting to appoint a committee to "set apart a day for Thanksgiving, for the signal success lately obtained over the enemies of these United States."

The custom of special thanksgivings was familiar throughout the colonies. Proclamations for such days had been issued, for various causes, in every colony from their inception. In the autumn of 1759, colonies from New Hampshire to Georgia had celebrated the fall of French Canada to British and colonial troops with days of thanksgiving. The New England colonies kept two thanksgivings each in 1759, one for the fall of Quebec and one in the annual tradition. Thanksgiving Day, December 18, 1777, was likewise treated as a special thanksgiving by New Englanders who celebrated their annual holiday first—Connecticut and Massachusetts on November 20 and New Hampshire and Vermont on December 4—and then joined the other colonies in a holiday of special thanksgiving that ministers made the occasion for patriotic sermons.

While the Thanksgiving Day declared by the Continental Congress was in the tradition of special days of thanks, the proclamation, written by a committee chaired by Samuel Adams of Massachusetts, contained overtones of New England's annual holiday. First, Thursday was designated for Thanksgiving by Massachusetts-born Adams, accustomed from birth to celebrating Thanksgiving on a Thursday. Second, the proclamation went beyond citing the "signal success" at Saratoga; it offered thanks for "innumerable bounties," asked divine assistance in "the prosecution of a just and necessary war, for the defense and establishment of our liberties," requested blessings upon the government and the commanders of the army and navy, and begged prosperity for trade, manufactures, husbandry, education and religion. In short, when Adams set his hand to write a proclamation for a special thanksgiving, out came a document very like a traditional proclamation for New England's annual holiday.

News of the victory at Saratoga reached General Washington on October 18, 1777, and he ordered a celebration of thanksgiving for that very afternoon, complete with sermons and discharges of artillery. The practice of victorious generals ordering days of thanks for their troops is an ancient one, paralleling the custom of civil days of special thanksgiving. On such days a chaplain led prayer services, special rations were issued and the orders of the day allowed a holiday for as many soldiers as possible.

George Washington first witnessed such a thanksgiving while serving with the British army. In the fall of 1758, General John Forbes marched across Pennsylvania at the head of three brigades of British and colonial troops, took Fort Duquesne from the French and renamed it Pittsborough for the British statesman William Pitt. The new British fortress was known as Fort Pitt and grew into modern Pittsburgh. Sensibly grateful for the easy victory (the outnumbered French had abandoned the fortified point at the headwaters of the Ohio before the British arrived), Forbes ordered a day of thanks for November 26. The Reverend Charles Beatty, a Presbyterian chaplain, delivered a sermon of thanksgiving to the assembled troops, among whom was a young colonel from Virginia who 19 years later would declare a similar thanksgiving for the Continental Army under his command.

Within a few weeks of Washington's proclamation of 1777, the army was encamped at Valley Forge for a winter of deprivation. On December 18, the day set aside by the Continental Congress for thanksgiving, General Washington ordered that "the chaplains perform divine service and earnestly exhort[ed] all officers and soldiers . . . to attend with reverence the solemnities of the day"; no mention was made of feasting or extra rations because the commissary had none to give. A homesick officer, Lieutenant Colonel Henry Dearborn of New Hampshire, wrote in his diary

> This is Thanksgiving Day, but God knows we have very little to keep it with, this being the third day we have been without flour or bread and are living on a high uncultivated hill, in huts and tents, lying on the cold ground. Upon the whole I think all we have to be thankful for is that we are alive and not in the grave with many of our friends.

Spring brought relief from the cold, and on May 6 a messenger arrived at the ragged encampment bearing news of the treaty of alliance with France. Washington immediately "set apart a day for gratefully acknowledging the divine Goodness and celebrating the important Event which we owe to his divine Interposition." General Lafayette, other French officers, Mrs. Washington and many other ladies were present for the celebration, which began as the soldiers assembled to hear their chaplains read the notice of the alliance, offer grateful prayers and deliver appropriate sermons. The celebration also included a discharge of 13 guns punctuated by a cheer, "Long live the King of France!" A second discharge was followed by the shout, "Long live the European Powers!" and to a third discharge the troops responded, "The American States!"

As commander of the army, Washington had enlisted religion in his efforts to create a disciplined fighting force from a ragtag band of untrained volunteers. He persuaded Congress to appoint and pay a chaplain for each brigade and ordered every soldier "not engaged in actual duty" to report for services every Sunday. Each Thanksgiving proclamation issued by the Congress was received respectfully by the army. Washington directed the chaplains to "perform divine service" and ordered the troops to attend. A regular church-goer, he expected worship services to "improve the morals" and "increase the happiness of the soldiery" and to reduce "profane cursing, swearing, and drunkenness" among the enlisted men. This was probably hoping for too much. Nevertheless, regular worship on Sunday and thanksgivings became as commonplace in the Continental Army as it was in towns and villages throughout the colonies.

Congress concurred with Washington's decision to hold a special thanksgiving in honor of the French alliance, declaring Thursday, December 30, 1778, a day of thanksgiving to Almighty God for "disposing the heart of a powerful monarch to enter into an alliance with us, and aid our cause."

While the proclamation of 1777 can best be considered to have been a special thanksgiving for the victory at Saratoga, this proclamation of 1778, the second by the Continental Congress, was for a thanksgiving completely in the New England style. A special thanksgiving for the French alliance would have been set in May or June. Instead, Congress designated a Thursday in autumn to give thanks for the alliance, for sundry victories, for the continuing union of the states, and to pray that schools, trade, husbandry, manufactures and piety might flourish.

Congressional tardiness—the proclamation was not issued until November 17—caused New England to celebrate twice: Connecticut and Massachusetts had already set aside November 26 and New Hampshire December 10 before the congressional thanksgiving was declared.

Revolutionary thanksgiving days, gladly celebrated by ministers of most denominations, posed a special dilemma for clergymen of Loyalist or moderate political sentiment. Opening the church for services on a thanksgiving day declared by the Continental Congress was tantamount to a declaration of support for the rebellion. Not opening the church, however, entailed the risk of having one's home and property confiscated and of being run out of town as a Tory. The Reverend Mr. Bass, Anglican rector of Newberry Port, Massachusetts, faced this quandary.

When many Anglican clergymen returned to England, Bass elected to remain in America and weather the war by making such conciliatory gestures as omitting collects for the king from the order of prayer. Like other Anglican ministers, Reverend Bass received his salary as a missionary for the Society for the Propagation of the Gospel, in London. The society got wind of his behavior and fired him in January 1779 for three offenses: having read the Declaration of Independence in his church, having preached a charity sermon for funds to clothe "rebel soldiers" and having kept "all fasts and thanksgivings appointed by Congress."

The first two charges Bass, in a frantic and unsuccessful attempt to regain the society's good graces and his British salary, denied; but on the charge of having opened his church for Thanksgiving the reverend justified himself in this way: "This I have done at the repeated request of my parishioners, who represented to me the danger the Church, if shut up on such days, would be in of being demolished. . . ."

An annual Thanksgiving proclamation by the Continental Congress was fast becoming a tradition. On December 9, 1779, and December 7, 1780, the United States joined in celebrating Thanksgiving Day by congressional proclamation. Special thanks were given for the rescue of "the army from imminent dangers at the moment when treason was ripened for execution" in the 1780 proclamation, written only a month after the capture of Major John André foiled Benedict Arnold's plan to deliver West Point to the British. But this was only one of many causes for gratitude listed in the proclamation. These were thanksgiving days set to give thanks for the ordinary blessings of health and good harvests, as well as for continuing success in the war for independence.

A letter from a Boston schoolgirl to her "Dear Cousin Betsey" describes one family's Thanksgiving in Boston in 1779. It was a family holiday much like Thanksgiving in the twentieth century, but with wartime food shortages to cope with and the Puritans' serious approach to the proper form of worship:

> When Thanksgiving Day was approaching our dear Grandmother Smith . . . did her best to persuade us that it would be better to make it a Day of Fasting and Prayer in view of the Wickedness of our Friends and the Vileness of our Enemies. I am sure you can hear Grandmother say that and shake her cap border. . . . But my dear Father brought her to a more proper frame of Mind. . . .

. . . All the baking of pies and cakes was done at our house and we had the big oven heated and filled twice each day for three days before it was all done, and everything was Good, though we did have to do without some things that ought to be used. Neither Love nor Money could buy Raisins, but our good red cherries dried without the pits, did almost as well. . . .

The tables were set in the Dining Hall and even that big room had no space to spare when we were all seated. . . . There were our two Grandmothers side by side . . . and happy they were to look around upon so many of their descendants. . . . Then there were six of the Livingstone family next door. They had never seen a Thanksgiving Dinner before, having been used to keep Christmas Day instead, as is the wont in New York and Province. . . .

Of course we could have no Roast Beef. None of us have tasted any beef this three years back as it all must go to the Army, and too little they get, poor fellows. But, Mayquittymaw's Hunters were able to get us a fine red Deer, so that we had a good haunch of Venisson on each Table. These were balanced by huge Chines of Roast Pork at the other ends of the Tables. Then there was on one a big Roast Turkey and on the other a Goose and two big Pigeon Pasties [pies]. Then there was an abundance of good vegetables of all the old Sorts and one which I do not believe you have yet seen. Uncle Simeon had imported the Seede from England just before the War began and only this year was there enough for Table use. It is called Sellery and you eat it without cooking.

For six years the war continued, often with little apparent prospect that the Continental forces could bring it to a successful conclusion. The war years saw more fast days than thanksgivings proclaimed. Amid destruction, death and dim hope for the future, fasting and prayer surely must have often seemed more appropriate to the needs of the hour. Still, the colonies fought on until in 1781 the nation had something substantial for which to be thankful.

A Thanksgiving for Peace

On October 19, 1781, the British army surrendered at Yorktown. Brigadier Charles O'Hara, deputed by Earl Cornwallis for the task, handed his sword to American General Benjamin Lincoln, as British and American military bands played the melancholy tune "The World Turned Upside Down." Americans and Europeans who witnessed the defeat of a mighty empire by a band of upstart colonies thought, indeed, that it had.

Congress met in a mood of jubilation. On October 24, two days after Philadelphia received news of the victory, its members adjourned at two o'clock and marched in procession to attend a special service of thanksgiving at the nearby Dutch Lutheran Church. Two days later the committee that had been appointed in September to write the annual Thanksgiving proclamation returned a document to Congress authorizing a Thanksgiving Day for December 13, 1781. This Thanksgiving, like the others declared by Congress, was observed by closing places of business, just as on Sunday. God-fearing citizens attended church, while the less godly took advantage of their day off to crowd the taverns and get soundly drunk, arousing the disapprobation of churchgoers who believed that the day was set apart for grateful, sober prayer.

Thanksgiving Day, November 28, 1782, was celebrated by 13 states grateful for peace, but still without a treaty officially .ending the war. In April 1783, news of the conclusion of the Treaty of Paris reached America. North Carolina Governor Alexander Martin proclaimed the Fourth of July as a Day of Solemn Thanksgiving for his state, recommending that the people offer thanks to "Almighty God . . . For conducting them gloriously and triumphantly through a just and necessary War, and . . . the restoration of Peace, after humbling . . . our enemies and compelling them to acknowledge the Sovereignty and Independence of the American Empire."

The Continental Congress set December 11, 1783, and October 19, 1784, as Thanksgiving days in gratitude for peace. Thanksgiving 1784 was the seventh in a series of thanksgivings proclaimed by the Continental Congress in the New England tradition of setting aside one Thursday every autumn as a day of grateful prayer. Representatives from other parts of the country, however, were beginning to resist this attempt to impose a "New England holiday" on the other states. After the Congress of 1784 adjourned, no nationwide thanksgivings were proclaimed until Washington assumed the presidency under the new constitution.

Political Feast in a Young Republic ___ 5

On September 25, 1789, the first Congress of the United States was in session in New York City. The 13 colonies had defied the expectations of Europe by peacefully and voluntarily uniting under a new constitution; leaders of the rebellion were now leaders of a young republic. It was a remarkable achievement, for successful rebellions occur with some frequency in history, but a revolution that results in liberty, judicious self-government and prosperity is a rare event. These United States had cause for self-congratulation.

Pros and Cons of Thanksgiving

Elias Boudinot, member from New Jersey, rose from his seat to propose that the House and Senate jointly request of President Washington a proclamation for a day of thanksgiving for "the

*The first Thanksgiving
proclamation by a President of the
United States was issued by George
Washington in 1789 in gratitude for
the enactment of the Constitution.*

many signal favors of Almighty God, especially by affording them an opportunity peace ably to establish a constitution of government for their safety and happiness." Some congressmen dissented; after all, the newly enacted constitution was still a controversial document in the young republic. Thomas Tucker of South Carolina objected that a proclamation would be premature:

> Why should the President direct the people to do what perhaps they have no mind to do? They may not be inclined to return thanks for a Constitution until they have experienced that it promotes their safety and happiness. . . . If a day of Thanksgiving must take place, let it be done by the authority of the several States. They know best what reason their constituents have to be pleased with the establishment of the Constitution.

Tucker's comments came at a time when North Carolina and Rhode Island had not yet ratified the Constitution, and in every colony defeated opponents of Federalism sulked—pro- and anti-Constitution forces giving birth to the beginnings of a two-party system.

On the question of a thanksgiving day for the Constitution, the Federalists won, but not without a final sally from Tucker. Thanksgiving, he maintained, "is a religious matter, and as such it is proscribed to us."

Tucker's arguments did not persuade his colleagues, but did reflect a serious and widely shared concern for the separation of church and state. There would be no established church in the new republic, nor anything that smacked of one. In his proclamation for Thanksgiving Day 1795, President Washington carefully addressed "All religious Societies and Denominations and . . . all persons, whomsoever, within the United States" and omitted any reference to Christianity.

On Thanksgiving Day, 1789, Washington himself worshiped at a church of his own Episcopal denomination, St. Paul's Chapel in New York City. In an act of Thanksgiving charity, the president had sent £7 10s 4d (English currency was still in general use) to supply "provisions and beer" to debtors confined in the New York City jail. Around the nation, citizens worshiped according to the dictates of conscience: New England farmers gathered in

Congregational meetinghouses; residents of Salem, North Carolina, celebrated a Moravian love feast with traditional German
hymns, and at New York's Shearith Israel Synagogue, Rabbi Gershom Sexias, one of the clergymen who had officiated at Washington's inaugural, followed the Hebrew prayer service with an
English Thanksgiving sermon.

Prayers of thanks for the new Constitution were the order of
the day throughout the nation as anti-Federalists waited for a
turn of the wheel of political fortune that would bring them to
power. In Massachusetts, they had to wait only until Sam Adams
became governor in 1793. Although the national government
issued proclamations of thanksgiving only for special occasions,
New England governors continued to proclaim Thanksgiving
every year. Sam Adams's first Thanksgiving proclamation, for
November 20, 1794, struck a blow at Federalism by omitting the
conventional phrase asking a blessing upon the president and
officers of the federal government.

The clergy of the Bay State, Federalists to a man, preached
ringing denunciations of Governor Adams and his Democratic-
Republican (anti-Federalist) policies. "This omission is strange
and singular," said Reverend David Osgood of Medford,
"beyond anything of the kind that I recollect to have seen since
the first union of the states in the memorable year 1775." And
Reverend Osgood knew where to place blame for the offending
omission; it lay with the "baneful influence of . . . Democratic
societies."

Two parties now competed for power in the republic, both
drawing support from every segment of society and section of the
country. Jeffersonian Democratic-Republicans (anti-Federalists)
included Virginia aristocrats, frontier farmers and others who rallied to the ideal of a pure democracy. They were opposed to a
strong federal government, fearing that centralized power could
lead to tyranny, and were similarly suspicious of churches with
centralized hierarchies. These sentiments led Democratic-Republicans to view with approval the French Revolution, with its
enthusiasm for liberty and its anticlerical stance.

Federalist voters included northern merchants, church
members, and others who were pleased that stability and social
order would be secured by a strong central government. Federal-

ists, who had written provisions into the Constitution for a bica-
meral legislature and election of senators by state legislatures,
feared that too direct a democratic process would lead to mob
rule. They believed that churches, apart from their spiritual func-
tion, were important bulwarks of social order. Although all
Americans reacted favorably to the initial news of the revolution
in France, the Federalists were soon horrified by the anarchy and
atheism that prevailed there.

When Washington and his Federalist cabinet acted to keep
America neutral in the war being waged by revolutionary France
against Prussia, Austria and Great Britain, Democratic-Republicans formed Jacobin clubs and attempted to raise troops to come
to the aid of France. The issue was not so much who would hold
power in Europe, as whether America should model itself on par-
liamentary England or revolutionary France.

During the political struggle, a number of western Pennsylvania farmers were busy converting their surplus corn into whiskey. Kegs of whiskey shipped over the steep Appalachian roads
could earn cash in city markets where bulky corn could not prof-
itably be sent. Whiskey was their only cash crop, and these western farmers felt unjustly burdened by the new federal excise tax
on distilled spirits. The men of Washington, Pennsylvania,
resolved to fight anyone who tried to make them pay the tax, and
Governor Thomas Mifflin steadfastly refused to enforce so unpopular a law. President Washington seized on this "Whiskey
Rebellion" as a test of federal authority, called out 15,000 militia
from four states to march over the Alleghenies and watched the
rebellion dissolve.

Pleased by this exploit and delighted by diplomatic success
in keeping American neutral in the European war, Washington
issued a Thanksgiving proclamation for February 19, 1795, that
angered Democratic-Republicans on three counts and offended
Episcopalians on one. "The present condition of the United
States," he wrote, "affords much . . . satisfaction . . . " referring to "Our exemption hitherto from foreign wars," which many
Democratic-Republicans were itching to enter; "the suppression
of the late insurrection," over a tax that many continued to
oppose; and "for the possession of constitutions of government
which unite and by their union establish liberty with order," an

order that many still saw as antithetical to true liberty.

Throughout the nation, however, Thanksgiving sermons of Federalist clergymen rang with praise for Washington and his policies. "The sermons," in the words of Jedidiah Morse of Charlestown, Massachusetts, "spoke the language of Federalism." The press was staunchly anti-Federalist, however, and editorials on the issue of a thanksgiving condemned the president in the language of Jeffersonianism.

As though he did not have trouble enough from his opponents, Washington incurred the displeasure of the Episcopal church by appointing as thanksgiving the day following Ash Wednesday. Writing that it was "disagreeable . . . to be called from the season of humiliation and repentance, to a day of rejoicing and thanksgiving," Bishop Samuel Seabury refused to read the president's proclamation at St. James Church in New London, Connecticut. Episcopal churches were, however, generally supportive of a thanksgiving day when it came in its proper season.

One effect of the Revolution was to sever the American Episcopal church from the Church of England. The General Convention of the new Episcopal church, meeting in 1789 to formulate a liturgy, included a "Form of Prayer and Thanksgiving for the fruits of the earth" in the new prayer book. In states where the governor proclaimed Thanksgiving Day, this gave the Episcopalians a liturgy suitable to the occasion; parishes in other states had the option of celebrating Thanksgiving Day using the new liturgy.

Washington proclaimed two special days of thanksgiving during his presidency, but did not move to make the holiday an annual one for the nation. In the wake of the series of eight annual proclamations by the Continental Congress, however, the holiday expanded beyond its prewar base in Connecticut, Massachusetts and New Hampshire. Both Rhode Island, which has not celebrated an annual thanksgiving before Independence, and Vermont, which has not existed before the war, now observed Thanksgiving Day each year. The third state to make an attempt to establish Thanksgiving Day in the eighteenth century was New York.

John Jay, in his first year as governor of New York, declared

Thursday, November 26, 1795, as Thanksgiving Day. Despite forebodings of the political controversy that a Thanksgiving proclamation could provoke, Jay issued a proclamation recommending that thanks be given for, in addition to sundry noncontroversial causes, "preserving us from being involved in wars, . . . which at this moment afflict and distress many nations," and for "the valuable life and usefulness of the President of the United States." Democratic-Republicans, still itching to support France and chaffing under Washington's Federalist administration, denounced this proclamation as vehemently as any single act of Jay's regime, accusing him of overreaching his authority to curry political favor with Federalist clergyman. Jay, chastened by the outcry, did not venture further Thanksgiving proclamations.

By 1798, revolutionary France had sent its armies on the rampage in Europe and French privateers attacked American merchant ships on the high seas. American Democratic-Republicans were so enamored of the French Revolution that they actually armed privateers in Charleston Harbor to prey on American shipping under French letters of marque. President John Adams and his Federalist cabinet struggled desperately to avoid war with France under a policy of armed neutrality. On May 9, 1798, and again on April 25, 1799, Adams sought divine assistance, proclaiming days of fasting and prayer for this nation placed "in a hazardous and afflictive situation, by the unfriendly disposition, conduct and demands of a foreign power, evinced by repeated refusals to receive our messengers of reconciliation and peace, by depredations on our commerce and the infliction of injuries on very many of our fellow citizens."

The Political-Religious Imbroglio

On both of these fast days, and on Thanksgiving Day, November 1798, in New England, the Federalist clergy took to their pulpits to decry the atheism of revolutionary France, implying that this antireligious spirit had spread to American Democratic-Republicans. Reverend Jedidiah Morse of Charlestown,

Massachusetts, used his Thanksgiving sermon to inform the congregation that the devil himself had taken up residence in Paris. Democratic-Republican partisan Abraham Bishop asked, "How much, think you, has religion benefited by sermons, intended to show that Satan and Cain are Jacobins?"; and the Boston *Independent Chronicle,* a Democratic-Republican newspaper, opined that, "Our clergy would serve the cause of religion at this day of deism more effectually by vindicating the truths of the gospel than the measures of government."

The point was well taken, but it was out of step with the times. It had become customary for Thanksgiving proclamations, whether issued by Federalist or Democratic-Republican governors, to have political overtones, and for ministers to preach highly partisan sermons on the day of thanks, sermons that were often reprinted as political tracts. Even the prayers were sometimes political. A story is told of one Federalist cleric who found the election of Thomas Jefferson so distasteful that he prayed, "O Lord, endow the President with a goodly portion of Thy grace, for Thou, O Lord, knowest he needs it."

At the close of the American Revolution, the vast majority of New Englanders attended Congregational churches. Congregational clergymen had long been leaders in the secular, as well as the sacred, affairs of New England. They had led in founding the colony, ran its educational institutions and had been involved in or intimately associated with the leaders of the colonial government from its inception. These men now felt duty bound to instruct their flocks in the righteousness of Federalist policies.

This stance put the clergymen out of step with their congregations, especially in the frontier districts of northern and western New England, where voters favored Jeffersonian policies. The dissonance led increasingly to desertion of Congregational meetinghouses for membership in Methodist and Baptist churches and to the disestablishment of Congregationalism as the official church.

Most Democratic-Republicans, like most Federalists, were faithful Christians, but anticlericalism, deism and even atheism found voices among the more radical and Francophile party members, bringing down the opprobrium of Federalist clerics like Reverend Joseph Lymen of Hatfield, Massachusetts, who preached a Thanksgiving sermon in 1804 condemning the French Revolution "whose whole object was the destruction of all religion, morals, social order and civil government. . . . " Reverend Lymen warned that "The seeds of corrupt doctrine were diligently sewn in our own country . . . " by Jacobins and Democrats, until, "We have lived to see the day, the ignominious, the gloomy day, when that God and Saviour whom our fathers so affectionately loved and humbly adored, *when that God who came from heaven to earth, was conceived of the Holy Ghost, and born of the Virgin Mary,* has been publicly blasphemed in our country as the *bastard son* of an artful, lewd and polluted country girl."

Reverend Lymen was referring to the "heaven daring blasphemer," Thomas Paine and his antibiblical work *The Age of Reason,* but the depth of his outrage stemmed from association of Thomas Paine and French revolutionary ideals with the Democratic-Republican party of deist President Thomas Jefferson.

With such a man in power, many ministers believed, Christianity itself, not merely the republic, was in danger. "The emissaries of Satan," maintained Reverend Lymen, "and the heralds of infidelity are uncommonly busy. . . . But has not Christ also aroused his ministers to testify for him against the prevailing wickedness. . . ." The shock of the European Enlightenment was brought home to Reverend Lymen and his colleagues in the persons of elected government officials who openly denied the doctrines of the Virgin Birth, the Trinity and even the divinity of Jesus. It is no wonder that they felt called upon to "testify" against these "emissaries of Satan," and to enter the political arena in defense of the faith.

Political sniping between Federalist clergymen and Democratic-Republican officials became a pitched battle with the election of Elbridge Gerry to the governor's mansion of Massachusetts in 1811. Gerry is ruefully remembered by political scientists as the godfather of the gerrymander, a political tool that acquired its name when Gerry drew an election district that would return three Jeffersonian state senators, by squirming across county lines in a shape resembling a salamander. The new governor fired a salvo in his Thanksgiving proclamation, accusing the Federalist-dominated Massachusetts clergy of being controlled by "passion, prejudice and worldly delusion."

Many ministers refused to read the proclamation. Reverend Abiel Holmes tried to read it from his pulpit in Cambridge, but was interrupted by an "indecent shuffling of . . . feet," as Harvard students, Federalists like their well-to-do fathers, registered their disapproval of the governor's politics. Reverend Holmes demanded and received an apology from the students who explained that they meant no disrespect for the minister but disliked their Jeffersonian governor. Battered by the cross fire between Federalists and Democratic-Republicans, Thanksgiving acquired a political aura that hindered efforts to make it a national holiday.

Presidents and Thanksgiving

Among the early presidents, only Washington, Adams and Madison declared national days of prayer. At the request of Congress, President Madison set aside August 20, 1812, September 9, 1813, and January 12, 1815, as days of fasting and prayer during the War of 1812. These fast days were, predictably enough, the occasion of sermons angrily denouncing or warmly supporting the war effort, depending on the politics of the preacher.

News traveled slowly in those days, so although the Treaty of Ghent, which ended the war, was signed on December 24, 1814, Americans went to church to pray for peace on January 12, unaware that a treaty had been signed. Down in New Orleans, on January 8, British and American troops, likewise unaware that the war had ended, fought, and the Americans won the Battle of New Orleans. When news of the treaty finally reached American shores, Madison proclaimed a day of thanksgiving for April 13, 1815. Americans gave thanks that the unpopular war had ended, some praising God that it had turned out so well, and others that it had turned out no worse.

James Madison, a Founding Father committed to ensuring the separation of church and state, studied the arguments closely before deciding that national days of thanksgiving did not overstep this boundary. He concluded that the propriety of Thanksgiving proclamations hinged on two key elements, first, that the president might recommend but must not order any citizen to participate in public worship, and, second, that the invitation be issued on a basis of equality to all religious groups and denominations, leaving citizens free to worship according to the dictates of individual conscience.

Thomas Jefferson disagreed, considering himself barred from proclaiming days of thanksgiving because "Civil powers alone have been given to the President of the United States, and no authority to direct the religious exercises of his constituents." Accordingly, Jefferson proclaimed no public days of prayer during his administration.

New England born John Quincy Adams refused a request made by a Presbyterian minister, Reverend Lawrie, to proclaim Thanksgiving Day for the District of Columbia on the last Thursday in November, 1825. President Adams wrote in his diary that he had no objections to issuing such a proclamation, but preferred to follow the advice of his Cabinet in the matter. Every Cabinet member present at the meeting viewed the proposed Thanksgiving proclamation as politically unwise. Since Thanksgiving would be a novelty in the District, Adams would open himself to charges of exercising Presidential authority arbitrarily and of "introducing New England manners."

Other early presidents agreed with Jefferson that the Constitution did not grant to the president power to issue Thanksgiving proclamations, decided to avoid provoking the political invective that previous proclamations had aroused or preferred to leave this prerogative for state governors to exercise and refrained from proclaiming days of thanksgiving.

The constitutional argument against such proclamations was raised again during the Jackson administration when an epidemic of asiatic cholera led many citizens and clergymen to urge the president to proclaim a day of fasting and prayer. Jackson refused to do so, on the grounds that such proclamations fell outside "the limits prescribed by the Constitution for the President. . . ." After a lengthy debate on the constitutional issue, the Senate voted 30 to 13 and the House 86 to 70 to appoint a national fast day by congressional action alone—but then adjourned without doing so.

Two more national fast days were proclaimed by early nineteenth-century presidents: one by President John Tyler for May 14, 1841, in mourning after the death in office of President William Henry Harrison; the other by President Zachary Taylor for August 3, 1849, during another cholera epidemic. Following his fast day proclamation, and because the epidemic abated with the coming of cooler weather, many citizens wrote to request that Taylor issue a Thanksgiving proclamation. President Taylor explained his reason for declining to do so in a letter to Reverend Nicholas Murray, moderator of the General Assembly of Presbyterian Churches, a group then urging a national Thanksgiving Day. Without alluding to the constitutional issue, Taylor simply pointed out that Thanksgiving proclamations had become a customary gubernatorial prerogative and that many governors had already issued their annual proclamations.

New Englanders ignored the on-again, off-again nature of the Thanksgiving proclamations issued by the Continental Congress and the federal government. Thanksgiving was an eagerly anticipated and joyfully celebrated part of New England life, unaffected by the vagaries of national government. One Thursday each autumn, New England bowed its head to offer thanks for all that the Lord in His bounty had bestowed, and rose up to celebrate all that for which thanks had been given.

It Never Rained on Thanksgiving 6

Even in the most picturesque New England villages, there must have been years when it rained on Thanksgiving, years when the sky was overcast and the November world looked grey, and years when it was too warm for the skating pond to freeze but too cold to play out-of-doors. It stands to reason that such meteorological misfortune must have befallen old-time New England, for it certainly occurs on Thanksgiving Day in our own generation. There is, however, no evidence that the weather on Thanksgiving Day in old New England was ever less than perfect. Each year the sun shone brightly, the air was crisp and clear, the sky blue and the pond—frozen.

The Church Service

Whether Thanksgiving dawned cold and clear or muffled by

falling snow, everyone went to church. Absence was unthinkable on this, the premier feast day of the New England calendar from the seventeenth through the early nineteenth centuries, since the purpose of Thanksgiving Day was to render thanks unto the Lord. Moreover, everyone wanted to see and to be seen.

On Thanksgiving the churches filled with men who had left town as boys and who returned for the holiday, bringing tall boys of their own; old people on visits greeted friends and the children of friends they had not seen for months or years on end; village swains and belles eyed their cousins and the cousins of friends who widened their narrow social circle during this holiday week; and the inquisitive could note each new bonnet or gown adorning a village matron, carefully observing both style and fabric and privately calculating the cost.

These churchgoers were pious people and, once curiosity had been satisfied, they were content to watch the minister enter the church and to begin the first hymn.

Services opened with a reading of the governor's Thanksgiving proclamation, which had already been read on each of two Sabbaths preceding the feast day. The excitement generated by the proclamation in usually sedate New England meetinghouses can hardly be overestimated. Edward Everett Hale, who as pastor of Boston's South Congregational Church for many years read the governor's proclamation to his own congregation, here recalls a scene from his boyhood:

> The time is the middle of November, on a Sunday morning. A boy of four years old . . . has the fortunate privilige of sitting on the cross-seat of the pew, . . . (his mother) whispers to him that he had better listen now, for the minister is going to read the proclamation. The boy stands up on his seat and . . . watches with rapture Mr. Palfry unfolding the large paper sheet, which might have been a large newspaper, and sees the sheet cover even the pulpit Bible.
>
> Mr. Palfry . . . reads the Governor's proclamation with sense and feeling, so that even a child follows along, about the taking care of the poor, the happiness of home, but specially about the sucess of the fisheries. . . . But home, poor people, fisheries and all sink into their own insignificance when the minister ends—with grand words:

Given in the Council Chamber at Boston, in the year of our Lord, 1826, and of the Independence of the United States the fiftieth.

Levi Lincoln, Governor

This fine relationship between "Thanksgiving Day" and "Independence Day," of which the glories, six months ago, are a certain hazy dream, is not lost upon the child.

Another hymn was followed by the minister's long prayer on the theme of thanksgiving, which might last an hour or more. That prayer, interminable by modern standards, would not have seemed so to New Englanders of that era. Congregations judged the quality of a minister by his ability to petition the Almighty at length and in pleasing language. Moreover, these were people who knew that they had a good deal to be grateful for. After a third hymn, the congregation, which had remained standing for the whole lengthy prayer, sat down to hear a sermon that usually lasted about two hours. The end of the sermon signaled the congregation to rise for another hymn and prayer before returning home to dinner.

The Groaning Board

Thanksgiving dinner was a feast that had been in preparation for weeks and even months before the great day arrived; nearly everything on the holiday table was raised and prepared right on the farm where it was eaten. Turkey held the place of honor at Thanksgiving, but our New England forebears had appetites heartier by far than those of their modern-day descendants, and turkey was accompanied by a huge chicken pie made of the meat of three of four birds. Beside these were placed roasted ducks and geese, two or more, depending on the size of the company, and a joint of mutton, pork or beef—sometimes all three. Winter vegetables—squash, turnips, potatoes and cabbages—were boiled in quantity, and small mountains of mashed vegetables, piled onto huge chargers, stood beside the turkey and geese at the great feast.

Smaller dishes filled with the sauces that delight the New

Farm hands load a wagon with
vegetables, fowl, barrels of apples
and jugs of cider for the trip to
market while a farm boy drives a
flock of turkeys along the road.

England palate were tucked into the remaining space. Cranberry sauce was there, of course, but also apple butter, spiced crab apples, pickled pears and peaches, wild-grape catsup, currant jelly and gooseberry jam. As each fruit came into season it was painstaking chopped, spiced, boiled and stored in the farmhouse pantry. On an ordinary Sabbath, one or two of these delicacies might grace the table, but on Thanksgiving, the best of everything the farm could offer was spread on the table in generous quantity.

Preparing the Dinner

Meat, vegetables and sauces were all prepared in impressive array, but the truly distinguishing feature of the Thanksgiving feast, and the task that occupied housewives for days beforehand, was the variety of pies to be baked and served; for pies are the crowning glory of New England cuisine.

Thanksgiving really began on that morning, ten or more days before the feast itself, when mother began to chop mincemeat for the pies. Young members of the family were drafted to seed the raisins, shell the nuts, peel the apples and mince the beef. These ingredients were turned into a huge wooden bowl, and the womenfolk took turns chopping until each felt surely that her arm could lift the chopper no more. When the ingredients were minced exquisitely fine, mother basted them liberally with brandy and molasses, showered them with spices and turned the mixture into piecrusts. Ten days, she declared, was necessary for a mince pie to "ripen" to a peak of flavor.

Each pie was pricked with a design, perhaps a pattern of graceful ferns, the intertwined initials of a cousin and her beau who would have a Thanksgiving wedding, or even a replica of the *Mayflower*. All were drawn with the tines of a fork before the pies went into the oven. As the pies baked to a golden brown, a Thanksgiving aroma filled the house, and the youngsters vowed they would die of impatience before the great day arrived.

The array of golden pies in the pantry increased as mother directed each day's labor to ensure that there would be "pies enough." Youngsters peeled and sliced an endless succession of

Rolling pin in hand, the matriarch directs the small boy bearing a platter with the Thanksgiving plum pudding. Other family members busily carry firewood, pluck fowl, slice pumpkins, trim pie crusts and grind spices in an old fashioned mortar. A keg of cider is on tap under the table, and a trough with a chopping knife on the floor shows that someone has been chopping mince meat.

apples and quinces. Dried cherries had to be sorted, and each tiny cranberry sliced to remove the seeds, for wild cranberries grew smaller and seedier than our modern, cultivated berries do. An old trick learned from the Indians eased the task: "Quarts and quarts of berries from the farm's own wild bog were soaked overnight, then cut up; each tiny berry sliced in half. 'Play with your hands in the water,' said Great-grandmother. 'Don't splash, play gently. Now lift the berries.' The seeds did fall out." When the children's energies could no longer be contained by the kitchen, they were given pails and sent out to gather butternuts while the women rolled out more pies.

This orgy of baking gave one boy in each family a full-time job of splitting wood and carrying it inside to replenish the woodbox. Cord after cord of oak and hickory went to heat the brick ovens and the big cast-iron stoves that replaced them midway through the nineteenth century, and the boy who split all that wood unquestionably earned his dinner.

Pies were baked in careful order. First was mince, because it needed time to ripen, then fruit pies in their infinite variety, since these kept well. Preparation of pumpkin, custard and chicken pie was left until Wednesday for fear of spoilage.

Spoilage of food prepared so far in advance was not so big a problem as might be supposed; the houses actually provided a variety of excellent storage opportunities. A pantry opening off the well-heated kitchen approximated in wintertime the temperature of a modern refrigerator and was a safe repository for pies and pastry. Any northern chamber remote from a fireplace or chimney was unlikely to achieve a temperature above freezing during the winter months, and thrifty housewives were in the habit of preserving some foods by freezing. Extra Thanksgiving pies could be left in a frosty room and eaten as late as March or April. Overnight, when the fires burned down, it was not unusual for the temperature in every room in the house to drop below freezing, and so butter, eggs and whatever else that must be preserved without freezing were stored in the cellar, along with apples, cider and root vegetables, which could be kept fresh all winter at ground temperature.

Pies, turkey, mutton, poultry, vegetables and sauces—the work of many hands, and many days—were all set on the table at midday on Thanksgiving and the diners sat down to help themselves, with utter disregard for "the French doctrine of courses." The idea of arranging a meal so that soup, salad, fish and meat dishes follow in orderly succession did not gain currency in the United States until self-conscious Victorian brides began an anxious study of books of etiquette. In the early days of the republic, mother spread the table, father offered a blessing and everyone ate, filling and refilling plates at will. The only separate course at Thanksgiving dinner was dessert, a glorious plum pudding carried in on a platter just when the company was too full to eat another bite of turkey or pumpkin pie.

A plum pudding has nothing to do with plums and less to do with little boxes of powder that one purchases in a supermarket, boils with milk and spoons into bowls. Plum pudding resembles exceedingly rich cake, mixed of flour, suet, sugar and spices and studded with raisins and currants, which were quaintly referred to as plumbs or plums. What defines it as a pudding and not a cake is that the mixture is not baked, nor is leavening added. It is tied in a pudding bag and steamed to a rich moistness of texture that no cake can ever achieve.

Plum pudding capped the preparations as it did the feast. When the last pie was in the oven, the sauces stewed, the vegetables prepared and the poultry dressed for roasting, mother marshaled her store of spices, currants and flour and prepared to tie up the pudding.

The Gathering of the Family

Suddenly, preparations were interrupted by a sound in the dooryard. Knives and bowls were abandoned as the family rushed to greet the first of the relatives to arrive home.

There is an urge in the breast of every New Englander that drives him or her home to Thanksgiving as inexorably as the instinct that makes salmon fight the currents of the Penobscot River to spawn in the brook where they were born. Perhaps the first arrival is a son returning home from his first job in the city, perhaps a wagonload of cousins, aunts and uncles from a nearby

*Thanksgiving Day—Arrival at the
Old Home*

town, or a granddaughter from her first session of teaching school. No matter who arrives first, soon all will be sheltered together under the broad farmhouse roof.

In the 1700s and 1800s, American families were frequently separated by large distances as sons and daughters left home to till farmland in less settled regions or to seek opportunities in the growing cities. Thanksgiving was the annual ingathering, the time when everyone strove to be home for the holiday. Mothers sending their children into the world secured a promise that the youths would "be home to Thanksgiving," and a wistful, homesick day was the lot of those forced to spend the holiday far from home.

The farther New Englanders scattered, the stronger the tradition of returning home to Thanksgiving grew. Margaret Sangster remembered that "Always the great feature was the family gathering. Somebody came from Massachusetts, somebody came from Texas, somebody from California, or the North Pole, or South Africa, traveling fast by night and day, just to kiss an old mother or grasp an old father's hand at Thanksgiving."

In 1858, it was reliably estimated that upwards of 10,000 people left New York City alone to spend the holiday in New England. A few years earlier a debate swirled in Pennsylvania over the question of whether the governor ought to proclaim a thanksgiving day for his constituents. Philadelphia grocers threw their weight behind the proposal, arguing that the increasingly large number of Philadelphians who abandoned their city to travel to New England the fourth week in every November was exceedingly bad for business. How much influence the grocers had on the governor is difficult to estimate, but Pennsylvanians were soon enjoying Thanksgiving as a legal holiday right at home.

Families began to gather days before the festival itself. College students and apprentices often had an entire week of liberty to spend at home. Lucky city youngsters might be brought to the farm days before the holiday feast and have the privilege of assisting in preparations. The old houses filled until it seemed they must burst. "Bedrooms had been fixed up everywhere and snowy beds prepared in rubbish rooms and closets, while the warm, dry loft above the wood-house, with its row of 'bunks,' looked, Jake said, 'a good deal like a camp-meeting.' "

Remembering Others

Each new female arrival was drafted into the work of the kitchen, and the men stood ready to serve as errand boys. Perhaps some last-minute purchase had to be made in town; more likely, one of the farmer's sons would be sent to carry Thanksgiving baskets laden with poultry and pies for poor families in the neighborhood. Certainly, a basket of freshly killed fowl and winter vegetables would be dispatched with dutiful respects to the minister and his wife.

Sending a tribute of the choicest produce to the minister was a token of the esteem in which he was held. It was not considered a gift, but the rightful due of the most respected resident of a New England village. More prosaically, it was a significant part of his salary in an era when ministerial wages were calculated in cords of firewood, barrels of apples, sides of beef, skeins of wool and a little cash.

No custom is more central to Thanksgiving than feeding the poor. In New England, as in the other colonies, the poor were provided for year-round. In times of peace, poor relief was the largest expense of local government, and assistance to less fortunate neighbors was the rule at all times. But Thanksgiving was special. On Thanksgiving the poor were not merely provided for, they were provided with a meal as hearty as that enjoyed by the wealthiest citizen. To that end, whole turkeys, pies, meat and fruits were dispatched to the homes of needy families, and it was considered a privilege to seat at one's dining table lonely widows, stranded travelers, students unable to return home and anyone else unable to enjoy the feast with their own kin.

A Family Interlude

Strangers were gladly welcomed to the Thanksgiving feast, but the night before the holiday was reserved as a family time.

When the aunts had crimped the last piecrust and dressed the poultry for roasting in the morning, when the cousins had put away their skates and sleds, when all of the horses were stabled and the last uncle had arrived by stagecoach, the family gathered by the parlor fireplace. The events, great and small, of an entire year had to be shared with loved ones who lived so far away. The family had only these few days of Thanksgiving together before they would once more be separated.

Soon the talk gave way to storytelling, fresh tales of the exploits of youths just starting out in the world and stories of adventures now 40 years old, told by graybearded men who had told them every Thanksgiving since; stories dear and familiar to every listener save only the youngest, who listened with widening eyes to the tale of how grandpapa once shot a wolf, or was shipwrecked in the China sea or marched to fight the British under General Washington.

The great fireplace roared with its immense wood fire, lighting the room like day, and was still assisted in this by many home-made candles in quaint ancient candlesticks, the large snuffers from their tray being frequently needed to trim these lights. The family circle—shall I ever forget it? The silver-haired grand-father, with his fine old face and his commanding presence, on one side of the fire, while placidly knitting on the other side is his faithful and gentle wife. [Their sons] the Senator, the Reverend Doctor of Divinity, his brother, a merchant from the West, another, raiser of fine stock in Pennsylvania; wives, daughters, children on the floor inside the circle, and the flow of wit, learning, story and reminiscence going on without ceasing. . . .

Apples, all the rustic nuts of the season, lemonade in profusion, and generous homemade cider stood upon a side table. Barrels of the same were in the cellar. The grandfather, taking a glass in his fine old hands, lifted up his calm voice and said: "Children, friends, another year sees us united here. Perhaps the coming one will take some of us away. God's will be done. A health to every one." Then all tongues were loosened and the children's hour began. We would gather around grandfather's chair and beg to hear the "bear story." That was always fresh and new to us. And the venerable old man would tell the oft-

One relative plays a fiddle while others dance and toss the children into the air in a scene of family pleasure.

FROLIC WITH THE CHILDREN.

repeated story of a great bear that used to range the fields of corn. . . .

We roasted apples and chestnuts in the coals and hot ashes, we played all manner of sly tricks upon one another, until the stern mandate, "Go to bed, children," would arouse a chorus of indignant remonstrance, entreaties and shouts of dismay. The sentence would be suspended for one-half hour on promise of quiet being maintained, and the terms of the armistice openly violated by us all before half the time has passed.

When the State of Ohio was called New Connecticut, grandfather had made a long journey thereto on horseback, and had acquired lands there, and had encountered many adventures, the relation of which would excite our admiration and wonder. The great snake story—snakes in writhing masses, of immense size and ferocity—that story excited our wonder and fear, and grandfather was regarded as a hero, even to escape alive and to return and tell of it.

As the evening wore on, the youngsters grew sleepy and the elders would begin to talk, . . . the youngsters were forgotten until presently it was discovered that they were all asleep in careless, unstudied attitudes on the floor, while the playing firelight disclosed tumbled curls, robust little limbs, and flushed faces, making so pretty a picture that all hearts were too touched and pleased at the sight rudely to dispel it by awakening them.

I have many treasured recollections of boyhood's days, but none more pleasant than those of Thanksgiving day at grandfather's, forty years ago.

Early Thanksgiving Morning

Sleeping in on Thanksgiving Day was the special treat of farmers and farmwives, who could stay in bed on this day, perhaps even until the sky began to glow with the first light of dawn—an hour or two, that is, beyond the usual farmhouse rising time. Children, on the other hand, were out of bed early, bursting with the excitement of the day. Some of them stayed at home to play with visiting cousins or daringly raided the pantry for the abundance of nuts, cookies and apples stored there, but for many the best treat was a sunrise ice-skating party.

Boys spend a snowy Thanksgiving afternoon coasting downhill on sleds with wooden runners.

Warmly dressed, skates slung over their shoulders and lanterns in hand, they hurried out to meet the sons and daughters of neighboring houses. At the edge of the pond they stopped to strap on their skates, wooden ones with long steel runners curling up over the toe, held to the boots with leather straps. In an act of countrified chivalry that was a sure sign of budding romance, a swain might carry his lady's skates to the pond and there strap them on for her, gaining for himself the privilege of skating arm-in-arm around the pond.

By the time the sun was fairly over the treetops, the skating party dispersed and hurried home for breakfast. It was a hearty breakfast, cooked according to traditions that reigned firmly in each family—perhaps sausage or fried chicken, ham steaks or codfish balls, accompanied by fried potatoes, doughnuts or pancakes smothered in maple syrup. Food enough, in short, to keep a body warm through a three-hour service in an unheated meetinghouse and to stave off the hunger pangs until dinner was served.

Sitting Down Together

Dinner was, as it remains today, the high point of Thanksgiving Day. Families that ate in the kitchen every day of the year on this special day gathered in the parlor where two or more tables were somewhat unevenly joined to form a large table spread with a white cloth. Many times, even pushing together all of the tables that would fit in the largest room was inadequate, and the children were obliged to sit at a second table to one side or in an adjoining room.

On the table were laid whatever silver the family possessed, alongside brightly polished pewter. Mother's prized china was set before the chairs of grandparents and honored guests, pieced out by earthenware and tinware plates for use by the younger diners. Then the ladies began to carry in dinner.

The roasted turkey took precedence on this occasion, being placed at the head of the table; and well did it become its lordly station, sending forth the rich odor of its savory stuffing, and finely covered with the froth of the basting. At the foot of the board, a sirloin of beef, flanked on either side by a leg of pork and a loin of mutton, seemed placed as a bastion to defend innumerable bowls of gravy and plates of vegetables disposed in that quarter. A goose and a pair of ducklings occupied side stations on the table, the middle being graced, as it always is on such occasions, by that rich burgomeister of the provisions called a chicken pie. This pie, which is formed of the choicest parts of fowls, enriched and seasoned by a profusion of butter and pepper, and covered with an excellent puff paste, is, like the celebrated pumpkin pie, an indispensable part of a good and true Yankee Thanksgiving; the size of the pie usually denoting the gratitude of the party who prepares the feast. . . . Plates of pickles, preserves and butter, and all the necessaries for increasing the seasoning of the viands to the demands of each palate, filled the interstices on the table, leaving hardly sufficient room for the plates of the company, a wine glass and two tumblers for each, with a slice of wheat bread lying on one of the inverted tumblers.

This feast of intimidating proportions was laid in 1827 for a party of ten.

When the food was on the table and each diner was seated, all bowed their heads while father said grace. Grace on Thanksgiving was an opportunity to give thanks for the blessings of the day, a harvest gathered and a family united, but it was also an occasion to take stock of the blessings of the year just passed. Each sad occurrence was recounted, each blessing mentioned with gratitude.

Father thanked the Lord for Cousin Esther's safe delivery of a baby girl last December, for the excellent run of maple sugar in the spring and for Nehemiah's creditable performance in his new job. He was grateful for a summer of fine weather and for a bountiful harvest of nearly every crop. Father was saddened by Uncle Samuel's death and quietly recalled his virtues while a tear ran down Aunt Hetty's cheek. Then father asked a blessing individually for each member of the family, especially noting the improvements each child had achieved during the past year. Grace ended with a final plea that blessings of peace, prosperity and health be renewed for the coming year, and the family said, "Amen."

If some of the food cooled during the long grace, no one objected. After all, the first purpose of Thanksgiving Day was to thank the Lord for His blessings, and there was so much to be grateful for. New England was a good place to live. By working hard, most couples could make a rocky New England farm produce enough food to raise a family; if wealth was out of reach, they were grateful that hunger was equally a stranger. New England lived in peace for most of its history, and victory in the war of independence ensured that the people could continue to govern themselves answerable to no king but God.

The End of the Day

After dinner the house was quiet: "the elders were generally somnolent . . . stealing quiet naps in sequestered nooks"; the women, of course, first had to wash the mountain of dishes, while the menfolk might take out their pipes and sit smoking in the parlor. On a clear day some of the company was likely to go out for a walk; and, if there was snow, the children would be sure to show their cousins the best "side-hill" for coasting.

> Once, Thanksgiving coincided with Indian summer—that period of warm, peaceful sunny days after the first hard frosts, before the harsh winter. Even Great-grandmother, in cap and shawl, went for a little walk in the garden. We children rode the farm horses bareback. The men sat on the stone walls in the sun and inspected the barns and livestock. Farm life was best, they all agreed, especially the city men. It was a lot of work, but farm people ate better.

This is the classic picture of a New England clan gathered for the holiday afternoon—menfolk chattering while the women tidy up and the children burn up their dinners in whatever activities the weather will allow; an afternoon lull to be followed by the gala excitement of the Thanksgiving ball.

All of the young people in town, and most of the older folk, too, gathered on Thursday evening for a gala dance that was a social highlight of the New England year. Country lads and lasses who worked hard on the farms all year, their social lives often

As grandfather carves the turkey, a large family enjoys Thanksgiving dinner in the dining room of a comfortable home. A wishbone lies at one end of the children's table and a tall glass of celery stands at the center of the main table.

Grandfather and grandchild asleep in a chair at the dining table after the feast.

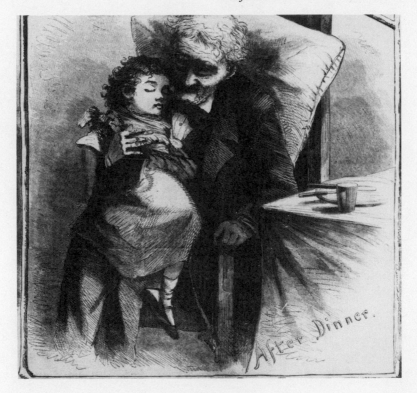

*Family members of every
generation enjoy dancing in the
parlor in this old fashioned
Thanksgiving scene.*

limited to seeing neighboring families at meeting on Sundays, looked forward to the gaiety of Thanksgiving week. The week was filled with sleigh rides, sledding and skating parties and visits to the homes of friends—all capped by the Thanksgiving dance.

The Puritan founders of New England did not approve of dancing, but with each new generation, Governor Winthrop, Reverend Cotton Mather and their contemporaries faded farther into history. Not every weekend, of course, but when a special holiday warranted celebration the young folk danced under the protective chaperonage of mothers and aunts, and even with such careful supervision the dances they indulged in were nothing so scandalous as a waltz or a polka. These were country dances, partners alternating in circles or whisking up and down an aisle of clapping dancers in a reel. It was fun, exciting and romantic. Every village youth went in hope of meeting the charming niece of some neighbor visiting for the holiday, and many a courtship began at the Thanksgiving dance. The evening, associated with such gaiety and ensured of a gathering of relatives, became a favorite one for weddings.

This family holiday in an old-fashioned New England homestead became and remains the archetypal Thanksgiving Day. It is this gathering of loving relatives, the pious pause to render thanks to our Creator, the feast of turkey, pumpkin and mince, the dances and sports, the clear blue sky and snow-covered hillsides that every American wishes to remember from childhood and hopes to re-create on the last Thursday in November. This rollicking, reverent holiday that we cherish is also the holiday that pioneers took with them to new homes in the West.

Old
Holiday
in a
New Home _____ 7

Our national government was established by 13 small sea-board states with tenuous dominion over vast expanses of wilderness west of the Alleghenies. Few as the citizens of the new nation were, many of them were driven westward by the desire to possess land of their own. Virginians led the way through the Cumberland Gap into Kentucky; Pennsylvanians built flatboats at Pittsburgh and floated down the Ohio River; and Carolinians pressed the frontier into Georgia and Tennessee.

Thanksgiving Goes West

New Englanders joined the westward movement in large numbers. By the close of the eighteenth century, the good farm-lands of southern New England, and even the rocky hillsides of New Hampshire and Vermont, were densely settled. Sons and daughters of New England farmers either had to find work in the cities or find new land elsewhere; tens of thousands chose to move west. Spilling over the borders of their homeland, scions of New England families settled central and western New York State, the northern counties of Pennsylvania and large sections of Ohio. New Englanders settled Michigan, Iowa and Wisconsin and comprised a major portion of the populations of Indiana and Illinois. About 800,000 New Englanders settled in these frontier regions between 1790 and 1820. By 1850, the number would reach a million and a half.

Along with household goods, plows and ox teams, these immigrants brought familiar social institutions to their new homes, including the belief that Thanksgiving Day ought to be celebrated every year as autumn turns into winter.

From the earliest colonial days, New Englanders had moved to the frontier in groups. Young people, in a New England town with insufficient farmland to keep the rising generation at home, would send representatives to scout and purchase a town site in a new district. They would move there together, often forming a new church before departing and taking a young minister along with them. When the first autumn came to the new settlement, the congregation would ordain a day of thanksgiving, often the same day proclaimed by the governor of their native state.

New York Embraces Thanksgiving

In the 1790s, Thanksgiving Day was regularly celebrated in this fashion by numerous New England immigrant congregations throughout upstate New York, and other New Yorkers celebrated the holiday along with them. Presbyterians observed Thanksgiving Day as proclaimed by the Synod of New York, and many Episcopal parishes held services of thanksgiving as provided for in their new Book of Common Prayer. The City Council of New York began, in 1799, to declare Thanksgiving Days.

Governor De Witt Clinton drew on this widespread tradition of church and local proclamations of Thanksgiving when, in 1817, he issued a seemingly unobjectionable proclamation for a statewide Thanksgiving. However, he aroused the stubborn opposition of the farmers of Southampton and Easthampton on Long Island. These descendants of Connecticut families observed Thanksgiving every year on a date set in their own unique way. Cattle belonging to farms in the Hamptons spent the summer in a large herd on 9,000 acres of common pasture at Montauk Point. They were driven home when the weather became cold, a date that varied from year to year, and Thanksgiving was set on Thursday of the following week. The farmers did not want to give up their traditional way of setting the date. Governor Clinton, however, prevailed, and New Yorkers have celebrated Thanksgiving in unison every autumn since.

Pennsylvania Is Reluctant

In 1817, the same year that Governor Clinton made Thanksgiving an official holiday in New York, Governor Simon Snyder of Pennsylvania declared that the third Thursday in November should be a day of general thanksgiving in his state. Governor William Findlay continued the practice the following year, setting Thursday, November 19, as Thanksgiving Day, but the holiday did not take root in Pennsylvania. Some "Pennsylvania Dutch" seem to have resented the idea as a usurpation of their own Harvest Home festival. Other Pennsylvanians simply ignored the holiday, and no further proclamations were issued for two decades.

Michigan Follows New England

Further west, victory in the War of 1812 opened Michigan Territory to American settlement, and it filled rapidly with pioneers, mostly of New England stock. In 1824, the Legislative Council of the territory formally requested that Governor Lewis Cass proclaim a day of thanksgiving. Governor Cass, a son of New Hampshire, appointed Thursday, November 25, 1824, as

Thanksgiving Day. The holiday was observed in the new territory that year and every year thereafter. This pattern—settlement of a territory by New Englanders, who then prevailed on the governor to issue a Thanksgiving proclamation—would repeat itself throughout the West.

Ohio Settlers Agitate for Thanksgiving

Settlers in Ohio's Western Reserve celebrated the holiday much as their neighbors did in Michigan—as a religious holiday with morning church services and dinner with family or neighbors in the afternoon. Sometimes, however, they were forced to act without the sanction of a gubernatorial proclamation. The northeastern corner of Ohio was settled after 1795 by communities of Connecticut immigrants who named the villages of Windham, Clinton, New Lyme, Hambden and others after their hometowns. The self-governing Congregational churches of these communities observed Connecticut's Thanksgiving Day on their own authority, but with expectations the governors of Ohio would soon begin to issue Thanksgiving proclamations as governors of New England had long done.

One Ohio governor did issue a proclamation in 1821, but the holiday was proclaimed only erratically by Buckeye governors for several years, despite the desires of Ohio Yankees. In 1838, a letter to the Cleveland *Herald and Gazette* asked, "Can you inform the people why Governor Vance has not appointed a day of thanksgiving in this state? If he knew how many Yankees there were in these parts, he would have signed a proclamation long ago. . . . We must have roast turkies, chicken and pumpkin pies and those delicacies so dear to the heart of the 'down east Yankee.' "

The governor failed to take up the suggestion, and November 1838 found the editor complaining that "The Governors of all 'down east' as well as New York and Michigan have set apart the 29th of the present month as a general Thanksgiving day. It is a good old Yankee custom. . . . Why does not Governor Vance

A Thanksgiving dinner among the descendants of the Puritans.

give us his Proclamation? We of the Reserve regard the customs of our fatherland [New England] with a reverence and affection that cannot brook their neglect."

When the governor remained unmoved, the Cleveland editor took it upon himself to proclaim on Thanksgiving eve: "Tomorrow is the festal anniversary hallowed by the custom of our New England forefathers. Let it be kept . . ."—and the Yankee denizens of the Western Reserve did just that.

The year 1839 brought a new governor of Ohio who was somewhat more appreciative of the importance of Thanksgiving. But though Governor Wilson Shannon had the grace to proclaim Thanksgiving Day, he clumsily chose a Saturday, impelling the *Herald* on Wednesday, November 27, to remind, "All Yankees . . . that tomorrow is Thanksgiving Day in Yankee-land," and prompting many Reserve Yankees to ignore the governor and celebrate on their traditional day. In 1840, Shannon came only a little closer to the mark, appointing a Tuesday in late December. After that, Ohio governors got the hang of things and issued an uninterrupted series of Thanksgiving proclamations for Thursdays in late November or early December.

Thanksgiving Takes Root in Wisconsin

Wisconsin was settled in the 1820s and 1830s by pioneers who came from New England and upstate New York via the new Erie Canal and the Great Lakes. Once the first demands of life in the wilderness had been met, the settlers moved to establish institutions they had enjoyed back home. A Christmas Day editorial in the Milwaukee *Sentinel* of 1838 asked, "Why can't we have a Thanksgiving out West here as we used to in good old New England? We do wish the governor would think of this thing." Others agreed with the homesick editor.

Meeting on March 4, 1839, the Council of the Territorial Legislature passed a resolution requesting Governor Henry

Lured by bait, turkeys walk through the opening under the log wall. Then they will try hopelessly to escape through the gaps between the logs until the trapper returns to wring their necks.

Dodge to proclaim a thanksgiving day for the people of Wisconsin. The resolution of the council passed the House of Representatives by a vote of 17 to 4, but not before the legislators had had some fun with it.

Responding to opposition from some of his colleagues, Representative Blackstone moved to amend the resolution by inserting the title "Resolution to encourage the growth of pumpkins." Now the four cynical representatives who opposed Thanksgiving voted "Aye," while the holiday's supporters opposed the facetious new title. Governor Dodge complied with the original resolution by making Thursday, October 24, 1839, the first Thanksgiving Day in Wisconsin.

The not insubstantial obstacles to celebrating Thanksgiving under frontier conditions were overcome by determined pioneers. Mrs. Mary Spielman Roller, an 18-year-old bride from Buffalo, New York, arrived in Milwaukee with her husband in 1835. They had a cow, four turkeys and little else. With some effort, a pen was built and a "fine brood of young turkeys was raised, and they became famous all over the settlement as they stood for a real, old fashioned Thanksgiving Dinner."

It required constant vigilance by the Rollers to guard their flock from Indians, who had "discovered that it was easier to catch them in the coop" than stalk them in the woods. Shortly before the long-anticipated Thanksgiving feast, the pen broke, turkeys scattered through the woods and the whole settlement turned out to chase Thanksgiving dinner. The last bird was recovered only after a fistfight between Mr. Roller and an Indian who apparently felt that a loose turkey in the woods was fair game.

Thanksgiving took root quickly in Wisconsin soil. On the holiday, businesses closed, the *Sentinel* suspended publication and the post office restricted local mail delivery. Taverns lured residents with no family to Thanksgiving banquets, and the Milwaukee House hosted a Thanksgiving ball for a "fine collection of beaus and belles." Markets overflowed with wild game, poultry and barrels of fresh Baltimore oysters. When German immigrants began to settle in Wisconsin, the Milwaukee Lager Beer Saloon advertised that it offered patrons a free Thanksgiving turkey lunch and "some kegs of *genuine* Lager."

Illinois Settlers Observe the Holiday

The early settlers in Illinois came down the Ohio River from Virginia by flatboat or up the wagon road from Kentucky, like young Abe Lincoln and his parents. When New Englanders began to move into the state in the 1830s, political friction sprang up between the predominantly Whig Yankees and the mostly Democratic southerners. Like transplanted New Englanders in other states, they missed their New England holiday. Thus they were pleased in the fall of 1838, when the Chicago *Democrat* announced that it was publishing Governor Joseph Duncan's proclamation of Thanksgiving Day for Thursday, November 26. Simeon Francis, editor of the *Sangamo Journal* in Springfield and a Connecticut Yankee by birth, praised the governor's proclamation in an editorial and asked if any of his readers had raised pumpkins and would someone kindly send the editor one for pie.

Yankee pioneers set about celebrating the old holiday in their new homes and were probably still eating leftover turkey when the December 1 issue of the *Sangamo Journal* reported that the proclamation had been a hoax. The perpetrator, the *Journal* declared, had been "that vehicle of loco focoism, the Chicago *Democrat*." (Loco-focos were members of a radical faction of the Democratic party.) This elaborate practical joke reflected political tensions between northern and southern settlers who were increasingly at odds over slavery.

In 1841, the Presbyterian State Synod of Illinois recommended that Thursday, November 25, be celebrated as Thanksgiving Day. Mayor Francis Sherman of Chicago concurred, proclaiming Thanksgiving for that day in his city. A document in the collection of the Chicago Historical Society shows the sincere desire for Thanksgiving proclamations of the citizens of early Chicago. The handwritten petition with 27 signatures reads:

> To the Honorable
> The Mayor and Aldermen of the City of Chicago
> The undersigned inhabitants of the City of Chicago would respectfully represent that ever since the incorporation of our city it has been the laudable custom to appoint by proclamation

A farm family killing, scalding, picking feathers, plumping and preparing turkeys for the market.

of the Mayor a day of Public Thanksgiving and Prayer to Almighty God for the mercies and blessings of a past year. In observance of so praiseworthy a custom the petitioners would respectfully ask that His Honor the Mayor may be directed to issue his proclamation appointing some fit day within a short time to be observed as such a day of Thanksgiving and your petitioners will ever pray so.
Chicago, November 16, 1842

If the custom had, in fact, been observed "since the incorporation of our city," Chicago had its first Thanksgiving in 1837. Of a certainty, the first official statewide Thanksgiving Day in Illinois fell on Thursday, December 29, 1842. The Synod of the Presbyterian Church formally urged Governor Thomas Carlin to issue such a proclamation, and he complied, recommending that the people of Illinois "meet in their respective houses of worship" on the appointed day.

All the churches scheduled services, but Simeon Francis, worried lest some Illinoisan might lack the knowledge and experience to celebrate the holiday properly. In an editorial he undertook to instruct his fellow citizens in the "immemorial usage" of Thanksgiving Day:

A large supply of the good things of life are required, such as turkies, chickens, geese, partridges, and such like. Families give out their invitations to the dinner a week ahead, so that all can go like clock-work. All the eatables, including a large lot of pumpkin pies, are prepared for the oven the night beforehand.

At 11 o'clock on Thanksgiving Day, all the supernumeraries of the family (leaving only those at home necessary to perform the duties of cooking) proceed to church where the service is of great length, rendered so by the singing of one or two extra hymns. This is done to impress the inner man with due solemnity of the importance of the Day—and also has the effect of sharpening the appetite of the outer man for the things that are about to be set before him.

The tables are soon filled and the important business of eating is performed with all due deliberation.

The remaining part of the week, (Thanksgiving should always be set on Thursday, as Governor Carlin has very properly done in this case), should be spent in visiting, social parties and such, and when Saturday night comes, in reckoning up

The young woman is preparing apples for Thanksgiving pies—we may only guess what sort of preparations the young man has in mind as they sit in the kitchen together.

matters it is usually found that, in neighborhoods, old grudges are healed, new courtships are under progress, and the people are generally better satisfied with their condition and happier by far than before the Thanksgiving holiday.

Westerners who came to the new territories from Virginia, Kentucky and other regions outside New England took such advice to heart. Although intermittent grumbling continued to come from a few citizens, like the Indianians who ridiculed Governor David Wallace's 1839 Thanksgiving proclamation as the "Governor's Sunday," most pioneers were soon celebrating the old holiday in their new homes.

Iowa Gives Thanks

In 1844, Governor John Chambers proclaimed the first Thanksgiving Day in Iowa Territory. Like other western governors, Chambers issued his Thanksgiving proclamation "at the request of many of my Fellow Citizens." He suggested that all Iowans worship and celebrate the day, but the Davenport *Gazette* had no doubt that "former residents of New England" would greet the proclamation with special joy. The Iowa City *Standard* assessed the new holiday in an editorial: "We believe this is the first Thanksgiving Proclamation ever issued in Iowa; we are glad to welcome the good old Pilgrim custom to our midst, and trust that when the day comes around with its plentiful cheer, none will omit to send up to the Almighty Giver a tribute of praise."

Many Iowans undoubtedly spent their first Thanksgiving Day in family gatherings and worship services and then the evening in decorous and pious assembly. The good folk of Iowa City, for example, attended an "appropriate celebration by the Sunday School scholars, under the management of their teachers," and in the evening "assembled at the Methodist Episcopal Church, to listen to a most delightful entertainment of vocal and instrumental music, and an admirable lecture on music as a science." But down in Burlington, folks with a taste for holiday entertainment of a livelier sort spent their first Thanksgiving morning "shooting

*The triumphant hunter brings
home a wild turkey.*

deer and prairie chickens on the Bottoms" and in the evening attended a ball at the City Hall.

Each territory in the old Northwest, like New York with its New England–bred upstate population, began to celebrate Thanksgiving as the natural result of settlement by New Englanders. In no territory did Yankees feel bound to await a gubernatorial proclamation before celebrating their holiday. Groups of homesick Yankees banded together to celebrate Thanksgiving wherever they found themselves when November came around. Invariably, they introduced the custom to neighbors who had not heard of it before. Some of the very earliest western Thanksgiving days were celebrated by missionaries who moved into Indian country well ahead of the settlers.

In 1845, Methodist missionaries at the Shawnee Mission Indian School in Mission, Kansas, invited some nearby Quaker missionaries over for Thanksgiving. Thanksgiving was a new holiday for the Quakers, who accepted the invitation and left this record of the event:

> Turkey was the main meat course at this celebration. Wild turkies were plentiful and the Methodists had cooked several. The Quakers were surprised; they had never heard of the turkey as a bird of Thanksgiving. But, following a special religious service, they pulled the roast from the wishbones with almost as much gusto as the Methodists.

Hawaii Melds the Old and the New

While a river of New England immigrants was settling the Midwest, a small but determined stream of Yankees left New England harbors sailing south, then west around Cape Horn, to bring the gospel to the Sandwich Islands, the modern state of Hawaii. Missionaries arrived in the islands, which Captain James Cook had named for the Earl of Sandwich in 1778.

Traders had introduced firearms, alcohol and western diseases to the once idyllic islands, resulting in a breakdown of

Hawaiian religion and culture and enabling Yankee missionaries rapidly to convert the Hawaiians to Christianity. The missionaries established schools, developed an Hawaiian alphabet and became trusted advisors of King Kamehameha III. Sandalwood trade with China and a brisk business resupplying Yankee whaling ships kept the islands in regular contact with New England.

Life in Hawaii was challenging and strange for Yankee missionaries, but group solidarity and a sense of purpose buoyed their spirits. "I do not think there are any people in New England who enjoy the pleasure of friendship more than we do. We are one from the same land, have the same interests, the same work, the same enemies, the same friends . . . " wrote a woman missionary in 1841. This band of Yankees, together in a far-off land, naturally decided to celebrate Thanksgiving in an attempt to re-create a bit of New England in their new home.

Thanksgiving Day was celebrated as early as Thursday, December 6, 1838, by the congregation at Honolulu. There was a church service, followed by dinner, the missionaries dining together and remarking that it "seemed like old times—thanksgiving in the United States." In 1841, the 25 adults and 32 children of the Honolulu mission station decided to eat Thanksgiving dinner together in a room specially decorated for the occasion. "Evergreens were brought from the mountains, and converted into wreaths and festoons to adorn the walls. Shells, lava, and minerals were arranged in one corner to form a grotto. If the tiny windows did not look really gothic, it was not the fault of the committee." (Gothic style architecture was then the height of fashion.)

Into this resplendent chamber the women brought dishes that they had prepared, vying "with each other in producing the old-fashioned dishes [New England style] of chicken and pumpkin pie. Oranges and bananas took the place of apples." After dinner, "The happiness of the elders was too calm, too deep to seek expression in a dance, but the children played 'blind man's bluff' and 'hunt the slipper.' . . . "

In 1849, the quiet Thanksgiving celebration of transplanted Yankees gave way to a national Thanksgiving proclaimed by King Kamehameha. The missionary newspaper, *The Friend*, registered its approval.

Among the many good imports into this Kingdom, we rejoice that on the last day of 1849 a National Thanksgiving made its appearance. His Majesty, Kamehameha, could not have made an appointment that would call up in the minds of Americans in his dominions, more pleasing and time hallowed associations. Thanksgiving is a season as fondly cherished and observed by the descendants of the Pilgrims, as Christmas is by the people of the "old countries."

Delighted as they were, the editors of *The Friend* chided the king on one point:

To be sure, Thanksgiving on the 31st of December, when that occurs on Monday, rather shocks our ideas of the festival, which we have always been accustomed to celebrate on Thursday and that Thursday ordinarily the last of November; but not supposing it possible for the King to err, we would merely express the wish that his ministers consult their almanac next year before making the appointment.

On his first Thanksgiving Day, King Kamehameha, the queen, the premier and other officials attended a Thanksgiving recital put on jointly by the Protestant schools in Hawaii. After a program, partly in English, partly in Hawaiian, of prayers, hymns and declamations by several schoolchildren, the "schools marched in procession, with banners unfurled and streamers flying to the Reverend Mr. Smith's church where a feast was prepared a la Hawaiian."

Surely two groups never made more determined efforts to learn the ways of the other's culture. Here were New England Yankees praying in Hawaiian and serving a luau for Thanksgiving dinner. Here were Hawaiians singing hymns and temperance songs in a Protestant church on Thanksgiving Day. As if to underline this earnest cultural accommodation, the Hawaiian guests at the Thanksgiving luau ate "poi with a spoon," while the Yankee missionaries "accomplish[ed] the same feat with their fingers."

The first Thanksgiving was such a success that King Kamehameha proclaimed more, although not every year. In 1856, he cleverly proclaimed Thursday, December 25, as Thanksgiving Day, thus enabling New Englanders to celebrate their traditional holiday on the same day when English and French traders and seamen celebrated theirs. In the words of the missionary newspaper, "The union of these festival days appears to have given general satisfaction. The Europeans and Americans, the Episcopalians and the Puritans, were satisfied to spend the day they listed."

Hawaii became increasingly tied to the United States, and when President Lincoln declared Thanksgiving Day for the nation, the holiday was observed "by the American citizens resident in Honolulu, and the numerous seafaring visitors belonging to the fleet of whale ships in port." But if the intention of Americans in Hawaii was to celebrate Thanksgiving along with Americans back home, the remoteness of the islands sometimes thwarted their desires. Reverend Jonathan Smith Green, missionary pastor of the Makawas Church on Maui, kept a diary of his activities. In 1865 he wrote:

> Thursday November 30th, wife got up a Thanksgiving dinner having become impatient waiting for President Johnson's proclamation and being so much of a Yankee that she could not live without a Thanksgiving dinner. So inviting Porter, Hattie, and daughter Mary and coming home we sat down about 5 1-2 o'clock pm to a tolerably comfortable dinner. Well, we had hardly swallowed the last mouthful, when in dropped the *Pacific* of November 2nd and on looking it over I found the President's proclamation for the real Thanksgiving day. As Porter and Hattie were on hand, we talked it over and concluded to observe the day officially, and Porter said come and dine with us.
>
> On the Sabbath I read from the pulpit the President's proclamation and gave notice of a public meeting . . . and on the said 7th day of December 1865 . . . we prayed, sang and preached.

Thanksgiving Day as proclaimed by American presidents was for many years observed by Americans in Hawaii, and by the missionaries and their congregations. When Hawaii was an independent republic, from 1894 to 1898, President Sanford Dole proclaimed Thanksgiving Day for his constituents; after Hawaii was annexed by the United States in 1898, Hawaiians naturally celebrated Thanksgiving Day with other Americans.

Yankees Celebrate in California

San Francisco witnessed its first Thanksgiving when a band of homesick New Englanders gathered to celebrate the old holiday in 1847. The City by the Bay was then a seaport of some 800 souls, 80 of whom, mostly eastern merchants and officers of Yankee ships in the harbor, gathered at the City Hotel. They dined on turkey and Oregon cranberries and appear to have drunk as much as they ate, washing down the turkey with sherry, champagne, port and a domestic wine, "Don Luis" from Los Angeles. Glasses were lifted in response to a series of toasts to objects of esteem, including "the fair daughters of New England," "the South American Republics (let them strive to imitate the virtue and patriotism of their Brothers and Sisters of North America),""Our country, our Flag" and even "the cranberries of Oregon." Revelry followed feasting as the diners adjourned to a grand ball in the hotel parlor, the opulence of which vividly contrasts with early Thanksgiving experiences of settlers on the western prairie.

By the 1840s, New Englanders had carried their holiday into the new territories settled by Yankees and to the outposts of American civilization. The task now before them was to persuade fellow citizens in the eastern and southern states to join in celebrating Thanksgiving Day.

Proclaiming Thanksgiving Throughout the Land _____ 8

New England's unique culture—featuring free schools for every child, a religious tradition in which ordinary folk wrestled with complex theological questions and two centuries of self-government—produced in the early nineteenth century a generation of young people uniquely well fitted to fill the demand for educated professionals in the growing urban centers of the republic.

Even as tens of thousands of New Englanders cleared farmland on the western frontier, thousands of their cousins became clerks in the banking houses of New York, shopkeepers in Louisiana, schoolteachers in Virginia, editors in Pennsylvania, lawyers in Ohio, physicians in Missouri and clergymen in Illinois. In every state of the Union, and overwhelmingly so in the new states of the West, New England disproportionately furnished the professional men and women. Congressman John C. Calhoun, South Carolina's great statesman and a Yale man, reflected this dominance when he remarked that he "had seen the time when the natives of Connecticut, together with the graduates of Yale College, in Congress, constituted within five votes of a majority of that body."

Transplanted Yankees Sow the Seeds of Thanksgiving

In the 1830s and 1840s, this cadre of Yankee editors, teachers, ministers and citizens began a campaign to make Thanksgiving a national holiday. There was no central leadership, no coordinated strategy, not even an awareness by each individual that others, elsewhere, were working toward the same end. There was only a simple desire of New Englanders living in other states to celebrate this holiday beloved of childhood in their new homes. When virtually the entire population of a territory was made up of New Englanders, as was the case in Michigan and Iowa, this was a relatively simple proposition. Increasingly, however, New Englanders were in a position to persuade governors of such states as Missouri, Maryland and Mississippi of the desirability of proclaiming Thanksgiving Day.

By the early 1840s, Thanksgiving had spread far beyond the borders of New England. Connecticut, Massachusetts, New Hampshire, Rhode Island, Vermont and Maine still celebrated the holiday born two centuries earlier along the banks of the Connecticut River, but governors of New York, Michigan, Illinois, Iowa, Wisconsin and Indiana also proclaimed an annual thanksgiving day, and in 1843 Pennsylvania and Missouri joined the growing list. Governor David Rittenhouse Porter proclaimed Thursday, December 21, 1843, Thanksgiving Day for Pennsylvania and, in contrast to the efforts of earlier governors to establish the holiday, his initiative took root.

Reverend Samuel Lowrie of Pittsburgh recalled as an elderly gentleman how he had spent that first Thanksgiving day as a seven-year-old boy:

> The part assigned to me was to baste the turkey, which was to be roasting in a reflector oven before the open grate fireplace,

while the church service was going on, so as to be ready to be offered to the company promptly when they came from church. . . . The canned oysters that came from Baltimore were properly cooked and served. . . . There were, of course, pumpkin pie and apple butter and, also sweet cider from Grandfather Thompson's cider mill and press.

The following year there was no Thanksgiving in Pennsylvania, but Thanksgiving Day was proclaimed by Governor Francis Shunk for November 27, 1845, and has been observed every year since.

Folks in Pittsburgh learned how to celebrate Thanksgiving the same way their governors learned how to write Thanksgiving proclamations. Though they had never written one before, Yankees showed them how. Pennsylvania governors issued proclamations in the style of governors of Connecticut and Massachusetts, and people celebrated by following the lead of their New England–born preachers, editors, teachers, writers and neighbors.

Louisiana observed Thanksgiving for the first time on Thursday, January 15, 1846. An exultant New England–born resident of Water Proof, Tensas Parish, Louisiana, wrote to relatives in Indiana:

You little thought when telling us of the good Thanksgiving dinner you expected to eat at Mrs. Douglass' that we too were going to enjoy the privilege of showing our thankfulness for mercies past by partaking of a sumptuous repast. But it is even so, thanks to His excellency Governor Mouton! He has seen the evil of his ways, and has at length repented and announced that *this year* and *ever after* the people of Louisiana must celebrate a day of Thanksgiving. The day set apart is the fifteenth of January 1846.

We are going to try to have a *real* Yankee dinner, pumpkin pies and everything to match.

The promise of Thanksgiving Day "this year and ever after" proved true; Louisiana celebrated Thanksgiving on a Thursday in November or December from November 26, 1846, on. Thanksgiving Day, December 9, 1847, was especially joyful, coming just six days after General Zachary Taylor led a triumphal parade of soldiers fresh from victory in the Mexican War through the streets of New Orleans.

Governor Thomas Reynolds proclaimed the first Thanksgiving Day in Missouri for December 3, 1843, specifying as did many governors, that he addressed his constituents "without any distinction of sect, denomination or creed." William J. Hammond, a newspaperman working for the *Missouri Republican*, described the day in a letter to his mother:

It was the first Thanksgiving Day ever observed in this State, and you may suppose the most was made of it. . . . There was all sorts of frolicking. . . .

In the morning the . . . Churches were thrown open for religious exercises, and all were crowded to overflowing. The afternoon . . . was observed by the gathering together of all the members of families . . . as I had no fireside to go to . . . nor no relation to talk with . . . the afternoon was spent by me walking around like a lost sheep waiting to be gathered into the fold. But the afternoon would not last always, and night came, and with it brought my time for fun. There were Methodist Sewing Societies, Presbyterian Tea Parties, and Balls in abundance and it was some time before I could make up my mind which to attend. I finally concluded to stick to first principles and go to a Methodist Sewing Society.

The one which I attended was held at Mrs. McKee's. . . . At an early hour quite a company was assembled. . . . All passed very pleasantly till about 8 o'clock, when Miss Mary took a particular spite against the Piano, and commenced hammering it, with vocal accompaniments, which frightened me considerably and I sloped. The evening not being far advanced, I . . . [gave] the Presbyterians a pop by going to their Tea Party; they had a splendid supper, good speeches were made by several gentlemen, and I regretted that I did not go there first as I never spent my time more agreeably.

Missouri's first Thanksgiving was a success, but Thanksgiving did not become an official annual holiday in Missouri until 1855. Between 1843 and 1855, some governors proclaimed the holiday, others omitted to do so. An editorial from the December 7, 1849, Liberty, Missouri, *Weekly Tribune* scolded: "We observe that many of the States have long since appointed certain days for thanksgiving, and yet the Governor of Missouri is mum on the subject." Governor Austin King was negligent only in 1849; the following year he proclaimed Thursday, December 12, as Thanksgiving Day.

Such erratic proclamations were common. Thanksgiving Day might come in September, October, November, December or even January, and in many states it was some years proclaimed, some years neglected, according to the whim of the governor. This irregularity of dates had a single, distinct advantage: it was often possible to partake of a turkey dinner with cousins in New York on Thanksgiving Day and still be able to ladle cranberry sauce onto sliced turkey with cousins in Vermont on Thanksgiving Day a week later. But the practical-minded, Mrs. Sarah Josepha Hale chief among them, found this variety untidy and confusing.

Mrs. Hale's Campaign

Sarah Josepha Hale was a remarkable woman. Born near Newport, New Hampshire, in 1788 to a revolutionary war veteran and his wife, Sarah Hale was left a poor widow with five children to support in an era when no profession open to women enabled them to earn an adequate living. Mrs. Hale determined to support her family with her pen and wrote *Northwood; or Life North and South* a novel that set out to demonstrate the superiority of democratic, virtuous, rural New England by contrasting it with decadent, slaveholding southern society. One entire chapter was devoted to a description of Thanksgiving Day in the hero's New Hampshire farm family and to the author's opinion that Thanksgiving Day "should be the same as the Fourth of July, a national holiday." To Mrs. Hale, more than to any other individual, goes the credit for making it so.

The success of *Northwood* led to a job as editor of the *Ladies' Magazine* in Boston, one of the earliest women's magazines and the first to be edited by a woman. In 1837, the *Ladies' Magazine* merged with the *Lady's Book* of Philadelphia, and Mrs. Hale became editor of the new *Lady's Book and Magazine,* published by L. A. Godey. In 1841, she moved her home and editorial offices to Philadelphia.

Godey's Lady's Book was, for the next two decades, the most widely distributed periodical of any kind in the United States. It was read in New York town houses, on southern plantations and in cabins on the western frontier. Not precisely comparable to any single periodical today, the *Lady's Book* under Mrs. Hale's direction exercised an influence of the magnitude of *Seventeen, Redbook, Good Housekeeping* and *Better Homes and Gardens* combined. When *Godey's* printed a new bonnet style, milliners from coast to coast fashioned copies for their customers. *Godey's* published plans for "model cottages," and carpenters from Baltimore to Portland built houses "like the picture in the *Lady's Book*." Hers was a powerful position, and Mrs. Hale chose to use it to make Thanksgiving a national holiday.

Sarah Hale began her campaign to make the last Thursday in November the national Thanksgiving Day in 1846. Whether she was inspired by the recent gubernatorial decision to make Thanksgiving a holiday in Pennsylvania, or whether she in some way influenced the governor to proclaim the holiday, is impossible to say. Old issues of the *Lady's Book* do show that she waged an unremitting campaign for a nationwide Thanksgiving holiday beginning that year.

Each year Mrs. Hale wrote a rhapsodic editorial on the desirability of a national Thanksgiving Day. November issues of the *Lady's Book* featured Thanksgiving poetry and stories of families reunited on Thanksgiving Day. Household advice columns carried directions on how to stuff a turkey and bake a mince pie. Mrs. Hale intended to tell her readers about Thanksgiving and teach them to celebrate it until the holiday became as familiar a household custom in Mississippi and Nebraska as it was in New Hampshire.

Thanksgiving Takes Root

In addition to her editorials, Mrs. Hale wrote letters. Each summer the governor of every state and territory received a letter from her urging them to proclaim the last Thursday in November as Thanksgiving Day. Her requests, and the similar efforts of others, fell on fertile soil. America, always a God-fearing nation, was experiencing a ground swell of religious fervor in the 1840s and 1850s. Protestant churches, leading institutions in the culture of the time, favored officially proclaimed days of thanksgiving.

The Presbyterian church played an especially important role in introducing Thanksgiving to new states. Presbyterian state synods commonly proclaimed days of thanksgiving for Presbyterians in states where the governors did not, and sometimes formally petitioned the governor to proclaim Thanksgiving Day. Presbyterian synods began to issue Thanksgiving proclamation after the Revolution, but Presbyterian enthusiasm for Thanksgiving was augmented by the odd circumstance that when New England Congresgationlists moved west, they usually became Presbyterians.

The old New England doctrine of congregational autonomy proved unequal to the task of establishing churches throughout the rapidly expanding frontier. Presbyterianism was doctrinally compatible with Congregationalism, and had the advantage of a strong, centralized hierarchy. Presbyterian churches with New England–bred congregations led the way in establishing Thanksgiving Day in new states, but churches of other denominations also endorsed the holiday, ministers, as a rule, being in favor of anything that brought people into church.

Thanksgiving had the additional advantage of being introduced to people who, while not accustomed to celebrate it, were at least familiar with it as a New England custom, much as Americans today recognize Mardi Gras as a customary holiday in New Orleans. Young Rutherford B. Hayes, sent East to a Connecticut prep school in 1838, wrote home to his family in Ohio:

> Thanksgiving was the 30th of November. I suppose you have heard of the richness of the dinner in this Yankee Country on that day; but it beat everything all hallow I ever saw. Our dessert alone, I should think, would cost fifty dollars . . . we had things [I] never dreamed of there being such. . . . There are divers things in this blue country I like better than Ohio; for example, Thanksgiving dinner.

The holiday that appealed to the future president appealed to other Americans as well, and a steadily increasing number of governors issued Thanksgiving proclamations for their states.

Jonn Munn, a Connecticut Yankee by birth, ran a store and a bank in Canton, Mississippi, when the first Thanksgiving Day ever observed in that state was proclaimed for November 25, 1847. He recorded the event in his journal:

> An unusual scene has been witnessed in our village and state this day. By appointment of Governor Brown it was selected as a day of "Thanksgiving"—and for the first time in this state has such a date been set apart for such purpose. This good old New England custom was a long time confined to those states—in time it was adopted by the Western and middle states and for the last few years had gradually come to be observed in many of the Southern states, and on this day and this year about two thirds of the states unite in rendering thanks for the mercies and benefits received during the year now drawing to a close. There is something grateful and pleasant to the feelings of any man of right thought and mind in contemplating such a scene, but how much more so to one who was born on the soil of New England as he sees state after state adopting so advisable a custom. Far away from that birthplace, the observance of the day here brings a flood of early recollections. . . .
>
> In our village the day has been observed in a manner that would have given ample satisfaction to the most rigid observer of such days in the times of its earliest appointment. All business was suspended and quiet prevailed in our streets. There was a general attendance at church to listen to the Rev. Mr. Halsy of Jackson, and seldom have I listened to a more interesting and appropriate sermon. It was well adapted for a people who were assembled for the first time for such a purpose, and those listening attentively could not but have been instructed in the objects of those who first established the custom and the reasons that demand its observance.

New Englanders were not shy about instructing their fellow Americans in the reasons that demanded the observance of Thanksgiving. They were, in fact, accustomed to arrogate to themselves the prerogative of instructing their fellow citizens on whatever topic they chose. Boston was the cultural center of early nineteenth-century America. Virtually every reform movement of the era was born either in new England proper or in the New England–settled areas of upper New York State. Abolition, women's suffrage, the movement for free public schools, the campaign to establish public insane asylums, and America's first health food crusade were among the movements led by Yankees. A people who felt free to tell their reluctant fellow citizens to educate their children, free their slaves and give women the vote were unfettered in their eagerness to suggest that other regions join their home states in celebrating Thanksgiving Day.

Governor Thomas Drew proclaimed the first Thanksgiving Day in Arkansas for December 9, 1847. Newspapers throughout the state reprinted the governor's proclamation. The Arkansas *Gazette* also printed a poem written for the occasion in its December 2 issue:

> Th' appointment's gone forth from the Halls of the State,
> Inviting all ranks to the Church to repair,
> And the bountiful goodness of GOD celebrate,
> In the rapture of praise and the fervor of prayer . . .

Thanksgiving Day was officially proclaimed in California even before that state was admitted to the Union, and observed by individual Californians well before it was officially proclaimed. A New England forty-niner noted in his journal that, "We celebrated Thanksgiving Day (or what we supposed to be so) . . . by an extra dinner. . . . " In the burgeoning cities of the territory, the first official Thanksgiving Day, November 29, 1849, was celebrated with somewhat greater formality.

Since California was not admitted to the Union until 1850, that first Thanksgiving proclamation was issued over the signature of Military Governor General Riley, at the urging of his New York–born adjutant. Although the proclamation was issued in both Spanish and English, Spanish inhabitants seem to have ignored the holiday, probably wondering what all the fuss was about. The day was observed by eastern immigrants with services in the handful of churches that then existed. Reverend Albert Williams and the congregation of the First Presbyterian Church of San Francisco, not yet having constructed a church building, held their worship service in a tent. In Monterey, Reverend Samuel H. Willey commented on the day in his journal:

> A clear, bright, beautiful day. But only a beginning to Thanksgiving Day keeping in Monterey, where so small a proportion of the inhabitants care for any Protestant observance. There are fewer Americans in this town than were expected to be here

when the rains came. But who ever saw Americans leave places
where they can make money. . . . A few attend worship and
seem to remember their education and principles even in California.

Undaunted by the meagerness of the turnout, Reverend Willey held services and preached a Thanksgiving sermon, a sermon
of gratitude for the abundant resources and bright future of the
territory, that nevertheless expressed a wistful longing for old
New England.

> Though very few can procure the luxuries and delicacies or
> even the substantial comforts of life to compare with the loaded
> tables in New England homes, the very absence of these things
> will make the sacred memories of the day more vivid in their
> minds.
>   The mention of Thanksgiving calls up each one's home,
> with its antique structure, the venerable halls, rooms, windows
> all as we left them years ago. The same elms spread out their
> branches to shade them. The little brook comes leaping down
> over the stones merrily as ever. Though thousands of miles
> away, it seems as if we could hear the measured tick of the old
> clock in the corner.

Reverend Willey was not alone in his homesick ruminations.
Although those eastern families that had set up housekeeping prepared Thanksgiving dinners as traditional as resources allowed
and invited their acquaintances among the many single men of
the community, Thanksgiving Day was a lonely time for many
pioneers. Reverend R. F. Putnam confided to his diary in
1863:

> Thanksgiving, which was here as in Massachusetts, on the 26th
> of November, was a solemn and unsatisfactory day. In the
> morning we had services at church, but the congregation was
> very small. After the services we returned to our homes and
> spent the remainder of the day in quietness. We thought of
> home and longed to be there.
>   Our dinner was plain and simple, for we had no heart for a
> sumptuous repast. We had been invited to dine out, but
> declined all such invitations, preferring to remain alone and
> think of the dear ones who gathered around the Thanksgiving
> table at home.
>   We felt a sense of relief when the day was over. Holidays

in California are to us homesick days of which we have an instinctive dread. Commonly, they are the gloomiest days of the year.

Granted that Reverend Putnam seems to have been a gloomier character than the average Californian, his holiday depression was at least partially induced by circumstances. The good reverend's Christmas entry for the same year was cheerful enough, noting the attendance of a "large congregation" at morning services, but Thanksgiving was a newly transplanted holiday, with shallow roots in the West and South. Years would pass before Thanksgiving was as joyfully and spontaneously celebrated in other states as in New England.

As long as the western states remained a young land of new immigrants, one of the fixed customs of the day was for as many citizens as could manage the trip to return East to spend the holiday with family. Even after the railroads came through, the trip from Washington State or Minnesota back to New York or Connecticut was long and expensive, but almost everyone wanted to go home at least once before the old folks would be there no longer, and every year some westerners made the trip.

Among New Englanders settled in the cities of the mid-Atlantic states, the pilgrimage home to Thanksgiving became an annual ritual. The custom was acknowledged by Horace Greeley, Vermont-born editor of the New York *Herald Tribune,* who printed this poem addressed "To All New Englanders" in 1846.

> Come home to Thanksgiving! Dear children, come home!
> From the Northland and the South, from West and the East,
> Where'er ye are resting, where'er ye roam,
> Come back to this sacred and annual feast.

From Greeley's perspective, and from that of many Americans, Thanksgiving was a holiday that Yankees went home to New England to enjoy. Franklin Benjamin Hough, a New Yorker who wrote a history of *Proclamations for Thanksgiving* in 1858, estimated that upwards of 10,000 people left New York City each year to return to New England for Thanksgiving. The holiday these pilgrims sought on Vermont farms and in Connecticut villages was the traditional one of family gatherings and church services, turkey dinners and village socials.

This popular Currier and Ives lithograph is taken from a painting by George H. Durrie, a Connecticut native who specialized in picturesque New England scenes. The family arriving at the grandparents' tidy farm via a one-horse open sleigh epitomizes the journey home to Thanksgiving.

It was the New England model of Thanksgiving Day that Sarah Hale knew, loved and promoted in her magazine. Each year, along with Thanksgiving poems, recipes and editorial admonitions directing governors to proclaim the last Thursday in November as Thanksgiving Day, short stories about Thanksgiving appeared. Many a story featured a family gathered on Thanksgiving Day in a spacious old New England home when, miraculously, just as the family prepared to say grace, a son who had gone to sea and was presumed drowned, or who had gone west and not been heard from for many years, or who had stormed out in anger a decade before would reappear to great rejoicing and—thanksgiving.

Alternate plots featured spoiled city youngsters who learned virtues of charity, humility and gratitude by visiting country cousins for Thanksgiving, or girls who met their true loves while at home on Thanksgiving Day. Sometimes these girls wanted to be in New York at the opera or at a ball, but they were dragged off to the country by old-fashioned parents and, while rusticating, met young men handsomer, wealthier and more virtuous by far then their city beaus.

Mrs. Hale was joined in her campaign to make Thanksgiving a holiday familiar to the nation by the popular pictorial magazines of the day. These oversized periodicals, featuring pen and ink drawings of news events, interesting places and famous people, found in "An Old-Fashioned Thanksgiving Day" the perfect feature for their November issues. Magazine articles were instrumental in teaching Americans how to celebrate Thanksgiving Day at a time when growing numbers of governors were proclaiming the holiday for their constituents.

Governor John Gaines issued the first Thanksgiving proclamation for Oregon Territory in 1852, stating that he did so, "In conformity to a usage in most of the States of the Union," and this was true. By that year, the Northeast and Midwest, along with many parts of the South and several territories, celebrated Thanksgiving as an annual holiday. Oregon did not have another Thanksgiving until it achieved statehood in 1859—and a most begrudgingly proclaimed Thanksgiving it was. The economy was bad, Indians were attacking and burning settlements in the southern part of the state and the threat of civil war hung over the nation. "For what," complained the Oregon *Statesman,* "should the people of Oregon especially give thanks?"

Seventy-six Oregon City women knew the answer: the time for Thanksgiving had come and there were always sufficient blessings to encourage a God-fearing people to offer thanks. Accordingly, they petitioned Governor John Whiteaker for a Thanksgiving proclamation. In response, he issued one of the most niggardly proclamations on record: "Be it known that in conformity with the wishes of many citizens of Oregon," not, apparently, including his own, "I appoint and set apart Thursday, the 29th of December, 1859, as a day to be kept for PUBLIC THANKSGIVING, to be observed throughout the state in such manner as the good people thereof may deem appropriate."

Governor Whiteaker did not list any of the many causes for which the people of Oregon might give thanks, nor suggest, as other governors usually did, that they should suspend their regular activities and spend the day at prayer and family gatherings. But the people of Oregon knew how to celebrate Thanksgiving. They prayed and feasted and enjoyed the holiday that soon became a regular part of Oregon life.

Nebraskan editors appear to have been cast from a more optimistic mold than the Oregonian variety, for when the state's first Thanksgiving Day was proclaimed, Nebraska's only newspaper, the *Bellevue Palladium,* commented that, "Although we have, as in all new countries, comparatively little to be thankful for, we have sufficient to inspire our gratitude and blessing." The editor of the *Bellevue Palladium* noted that he was a guest "at an excellent Thanksgiving dinner," but we do not know whether anyone thought to invite the grumpy editor of the Oregon *Statesman* to Thanksgiving dinner.

Acting Governor Thomas Cuming set the first Thanksgiving Day in Nebraska on November 30, 1854, just six months after Nebraska Territory was established by the Kansas-Nebraska Act. The settlers were Yankees moving into the new territory from nearby Iowa and other northern states, and they would keep their old New England holiday in this new free-soil territory. The introduction of Thanksgiving to Kansas would prove more controversial and bloody.

Settlers in territories where Thanksgiving was not yet a holiday grew impatient. "November passed and week by week New Englanders looked for the announcement of their ancient and beloved festival," wrote Mrs. Isaac Atwater, a Minnesota pioneer, "but even the sacred last Thursday went by without it, and dismay and homesickness filled all hearts. Our good governor must have been of Scotch or Dutch pedigree to have overlooked a duty of such importance; but at last a hint was given him, a brief proclamation was forthcoming, and the day duly celebrated."

On that first Thanksgiving Day, December 26, 1850, St. Paul was a frontier village of about 225 buildings, and St. Anthony was the next largest town with but 115 houses; indeed, the entire Minnesota Territory, including both Dakotas as far as the Missouri River, held only 6,000 settlers. New and sparsely populated though the territory was, a "magnificent ball" was held in St. Paul in a hall decorated with "paintings, pictures, transparencies and chandeliers in a style of superb elegance," while the three hotels in town "each served elaborate dinners of buffalo, bear, and venison."

Such gaudy celebrations fit badly with our more stereotypic images of sturdy pioneers leading the way west in buckskin shirts. But typical immigrants to a young western city had not come west to enjoy the simple life—they had come in the hope of getting very rich, very fast. Founders of town sites surveyed land and laid out grid-patterned streets on acres of vacant prairie, hoping that theirs would be a new Chicago, making them overnight millionaries by land speculation alone. Even before their fortunes were made, these would-be millionaires aspired to live in style. Thanksgiving entertainments were arranged to demonstrate that society in the territories lacked none of the refinement of Philadelphia or Boston. An 1854 visitor to tiny Excelsior, Minnesota, recorded his pleasure in the Thanksgiving exercises held by the local lyceum during which ladies and gentlemen offered "addresses appropriate to the occasion" and "music upon the piano," all of which, in the visitor's flattering opinion, compared well with "the most selected gatherings in many portions of the east."

Governors of the young Minnesota Territory proclaimed Thanksgiving every year, a practice regularized by the first legislature after Minnesota became a state in 1858. A statute was enacted providing that, "The governor shall by proclamation set apart one day each year as a day of solemn and public thanksgiving to Almighty God, for his blessings to us as a state and a nation."

Edward J. Pond recalled his family's simple celebration of Minnesota's first Thanksgiving in their home at Chief Shakopee's village on the shore of Lake Harriet, where his father was a missionary to the Indians. "I know that we had venison we got from the Indians. We had cranberries too." High-bush cranberries grew wild in Minnesota; picked and boxed, they earned important cash for the early settlers. "We always had pumpkin pies. Then we had bread and butter and that was about all."

The simple fare of the Pond family is probably representative of what Minnesota farm families ate, both on Thanksgiving and on other days. Simple food, hard work and faith in God marked these pioneers, circumstances that led Reverend Edward D. Neill, in his well-received sermon on that first Thanksgiving Day in Minnesota Territory to a congregation of 38 worshipers, to compare "the infancy of our favored territory with that of the Puritan colonies."

Settlers throughout the West compared themselves with the Puritan colonizers of New England as self-consciously as New England settlers had once compared themselves with the biblical children of Israel. Perhaps no group of pioneers took these comparisons more to heart than the 5,000 Latter-Day Saints whom Brigham Young led over the Rocky Mountains in 1847 to settle the Great Salt Basin of Utah. No crops had ever been raised in this desert with its late spring and early autumn frosts; many believed that none could be grown here. That first harvest, then, was like the first harvest of the Pilgrims at Plymouth—it proved that land could be farmed and settlements planted where no Englishmen had lived before. To these pilgrims, driven from home by religious prejudice, it meant new homes and the opportunity to worship in the wilderness according to their own beliefs.

When the harvest was gathered, Utah, or Deseret as the first settlers called it, held a celebration very like the 1621 harvest Thanksgiving at Plymouth.

On the tenth of August [1848] we held a public feast under a bowery [bower built of poles and branches] in the center of our fort. This was called a harvest feast; we partook of a rich variety of bread, beef, butter, cheese, cakes, pastry, green corn, melons, and almost every variety of vegetables. Large sheaves of wheat, rye, barley, oats, and other productions were hoisted on poles for public exhibition, and there was prayer and thanksgiving, congratulations, songs, speeches, music, dancing, smiling faces and merry hearts. In short, it was a great day with the people of these valleys, and long to be remembered by those who had suffered and waited anxiously for the results of a first effort to redeem the interior deserts of America, and to make her hither-to unknown solitudes "blossom like a rose."

The Mormon pioneers who founded Utah were from many states and from England, but their leader, Brigham Young, was a son of Vermont. Before long, he began to issue Thanksgiving pro-clamations as other governors did, but in a style unique to the Latter-Day Saints. In one proclamation, issued in 1851, Gover-nor Young gave thanks for the harvest, good health, general pros-perity and peace, but went on to incorpoate uniquely Mormon concepts of priesthood and to emphasize such Christian virtues as brotherhood and charity.

Territory of Utah
Proclamation
For a day of Praise and Thanksgiving

It having pleased the Father of all good to make known His mind and will to the children of men, in these last days; and through the ministrations of his angels, to restore the Holy Priesthood unto the sons of Adam . . . and influencing them to flow together from the four quarters of the earth, to a land of peace and health; . . . reserved of old in the councils of eter-nity for the purposes to which it is now appropriated; a land choice above all others; . . .
I, Brigham Young, Governor of the Territory aforesaid, in response to the time-honored custom of our forefathers at Ply-mouth Rock . . . DO PROCLAIM . . . A Day of Praise and Thanksgiving . . . in honor of the God of Abraham . . .
And I recommend to all the good citizens of Utah . . . that they rise early in the morning . . . and wash their bodies with pure water; that all men attend to their flocks and herds with carefulness; . . . while the women are preparing the best of

food for their households . . . ask the Father to bless your food; and when you have filled the plates of your household, partake with them, with rejoicing and thanksgiving. . . . I also request of all good and peaceful citizens, that they refrain from all evil thinking, speaking, and acting on that day; that no one be offended by his neighbor . . . that all may cease their quarrels and starve the lawyers. . . . I further request, that when the day has been spent in doing good; in dealing your bread, your butter, your beef, your pork, your turkeys, your molasses, and the choicest of all the products of the valleys and mountains . . . to the poor; . . . that you end the day . . . on the same principle that you commenced it . . . preparing for celestial glory.

One after another, the western states proclaimed Thanksgiving, welcoming, as the Iowa City *Standard* put it in 1844, "the good old Pilgrim custom to our midst." The widespread acceptance of the idea that the Pilgrims founded this nation at Plymouth Rock and that Thanksgiving was worthy of adoption by every state in the Union because it was first observed at Plymouth was a triumph of Yankee persuasiveness. English colonists with a variety of motivations founded several colonies along the Atlantic seaboard in the 1600s. Jamestown, of course, was the first to become permanently established. Pennsylvania was the true haven of religious freedom. But it is the footfall at Plymouth Rock that American schoolchildren are taught to venerate.

The landing of the Pilgrim Fathers did not become the honored myth of our nation's birth because of a realistic understanding of who these people were—after all, they themselves were intolerant religious fanatics—but because of who their descendants became. Virginia grew into a prosperous, hierarchical colony led by aristocratic slave owners. Massachusetts became an almost pure democracy, inhabited by freeholding, self-sufficient farmers. Virginia gave the country great statesmen. New England produced teachers, ministers, lawyers, men and women of letters and merchants. The New England ideals of free education and respect for learning, citizen participation in government, equality of opportunity and centrality of religious faith became the ideals of a nation. For these reasons Plymouth, and not Jamestown, became our national myth.

When the republic was young, the creation of a national

mythology was a deeply felt necessity. Washington, the father of his country, assumed the status nearly of a demigod. His portrait hung in parlors and schoolrooms, adulatory biographies sold tens of thousands of copies and myths grew up around his every action and utterance. Lafayette, returning in 1824 to visit the nation in whose revolutionary army he had served as a young man, was hailed by worshipful crowds of thousands. The states needed heroes, myths and legends to make them one nation. To fill this need, New England offered the Pilgrims and the first Thanksgiving. Here was a third holiday for the nation to celebrate together along with Washington's birthday and the Fourth of July. Here was a new constellation of mythic Pilgrim heroes to place in the firmament alongside Washington and Lafayette. Just as Thanksgiving had been created to fill a need for holidays in Puritan New England, so it was adopted by western and southern states that needed national myths and nationwide holidays.

Yankee
Abolitionist
Holiday _____ 9

The long-standing practice of delivering political sermons on
Thanksgiving Day, which made Thanksgiving both a revolutionary holiday and the occasion of Federalist era political contention, now made Thanksgiving the tool of free-soilers and abolitionists. Thanksgiving was, above all, a New England holiday,
and New England was abolitionist territory; but the association
was broader than this.

Thanksgiving as Politics in the North

Throughout the middle and western states, Thanksgiving
was taken to heart by those same evangelical Protestant denominations that made abolition a religious cause. Antislavery and
abolitionist positions were the political beliefs of a small group of
citizens in colonial America and during the early years of the

republic; but in the 1830s and 40s, antislavery sentiments became an article of faith for northern Protestants, causing denominations to split into northern and southern branches. Many ministers who preferred to deliver strictly spiritual sermons on the Sabbath felt impelled to speak out against the evils of slavery on Thanksgiving.

Ministers did not take a unified position on slavery. Some were free-soilers, opposing the extension of slavery into new territories, without urging abolition in the South; others urged immediate emancipation for all slaves. Many grew stronger in their opposition as time passed, and the abolition movement gathered strength. Reverend Henry Ward Beecher, brother of Harriet Beecher Stowe, opposed slavery in his Thanksgiving sermon of 1847 more on the grounds that it degraded white Americans than out of direct sympathy for the slaves. Slaves, Beecher told his fashionable congregation at the Plymouth Church in Brooklyn, "cannot enlighten themselves, but they can darken those around them, they cannot preserve their own moral purity, but they can make others participants of their degradation."

It was this arrogant northern eagerness to tell southerners that slavery was not merely wrong, but bad for them as well, this facile northern tendency to condemn all southern society and not slavery as a discrete institution, that made southerners hate Yankees. Southerners regarded themselves as law-abiding pillars of society whose institutions were under attack by a lawless band of radical extremists.

Many northerners, fearful that pressing the South too hard on the question of slavery would lead to civil war, urged patience, moderation and compromise. The Fugitive Slave Law of 1850 was part of the last great compromise aimed at averting civil war. Southern congressmen agreed to admit California as free territory, but they demanded an honest northern effort to return fugitive slaves. To abolitionists, such a demand was anathema, but other citizens thought the price ought to be paid if it would buy national harmony. "The question," Reverend Icabod Spencer, of the Second Presbyterian Church of Brooklyn, said in his Thanksgiving sermon, "*is not* whether slavery is right, or the Fugitive Slave Law right. . . . The question is, shall Law be put in force; and the government of the country stand; or shall Law be resisted, and the government of the country disobeyed, and the nation plunged into all the horrors of civil war?"

Slavery was the burning issue of the 1850s. Abolitionists, slaveholders and the majority of people who hoped that somehow the question could be settled without bloodshed, were alike in their unremitting need to confront the issue. Should the Fugitive Slave Law be enforced or righteously violated? Should western territories be settled as free soil or slave? Was voluntary or peaceable abolition possible? Did the North have any right to question the slavery compromises enshrined in the Constitution itself?

On Thanksgiving Day, when the nation paused to count its blessings, the questions posed by slavery could not be overlooked. They were, in the words of Texas Governor P. Hansborough Bell's proclamation for Thanksgiving Day 1850: "The vast and perplexing questions which have agitated and divided the public councils."

In fact, the governor of Texas was not terribly perplexed by the proper solution to the slavery question. It lay in "maintaining our great charter in its original form, [the Constitution allowed both slave states and free] undefiled by false interpetations, unscathed by the unworthy attacks of ignorance or fanaticism. . . ." In the North, however, a growing number of "fanatics" were unwilling to abide the injustice of slavery merely because this evil institution was written into the Constitution. "Pray for the hastening of that day when all the oppressed shall go free . . ." urged the Cleveland *Daily True Democrat* in its Thanksgiving editorial of 1852, and in most northern churches, the faithful gathered to do just that.

Despite the strident tone of many Thanksgiving sermons, there were people of both North and South who felt that Thanksgiving Day could be a useful tool in the effort to preserve the Union in harmony and compromise. The hope, expressed by Sarah Josepha Hale, editor of *Godey's Lady's Book,* was that a national holiday on which all Americans gathered to count their blessings would encourage a feeling of national unity and make all parties more willing to compromise. By the 1850s, governors of most northern, southern and western states were in fact pro-

claiming Thanksgiving Day on the last Thursday in November—
but not the governors of Virginia.

Thanksgiving as Politics in the South

Many Virginians did celebrate Thanksgiving Day. Members
of the Episcopal church observed the first Thursday in November
as Thanksgiving, and the Presbyterian Synod annually proclaimed a Thanksgiving Day for its communicants. In 1853, Reverend John Knote wrote to Governor Joseph Johnson urging him
to declare Thanksgiving Day for Virginians. Johnson declined,
citing the opinion of Virginia's most illustrious governer, Thomas Jefferson, who believed that separation of church and state
proscribed the governor from making such a declaration. In
refusing to declare Thanksgiving, Governor Johnson garnered
the political support of a group of pro-slavery Virginia gentlemen
angered by the increasingly close alliance between abolitionists
and the Protestant clergy. These men wrote to praise Johnson for
refusing "to gratify and serve the base purposes of the hypocriti-
cal clergy and their blind and base followers."

In the summer of 1855, Virginia was devastated by an epidemic of yellow fever that killed 2,000 citizens. As the plague
lifted with the coming of cool weather, Governor Johnson
acceded to demands that he declare a day of Thanksgiving. He
wrote, "A portion of the people of this Commonwealth having
been afflicted by the ravages of a pestilence scarcely paralleled in
the annals of history. . . . I . . . earnestly recommend that all,
without distinction of creed or party, with one accord, unite in
rendering homage and thanksgiving to God for his blessings. . . ."

This was a special thanksgiving, however, held expressly in
gratitude for the end of the epidemic, not the importation of a
Yankee holiday to Virginia; and, to underscore the distinction,
Johnson set November 15 as Thanksgiving, while the other governors who issued proclamations ordered celebrations on November 29.

In Richmond, the *Daily Dispatch* reported that shops and
businesses closed, churches were full and most people said they

favored an annual Thanksgiving. Virginians, however, now elected Governor Henry H. Wise, a slave-owning, fire-eating advocate of states' rights who wanted nothing to do with a Yankee holiday. His first autumn in office, Wise received, as each governor did every year, a polite letter from Mrs. Sarah H. Hale, who, like Wise, supported Democratic candidate James Buchanan for the presidency. "I am aware," wrote Mrs. Hale, "that Virginia has not often joined in keeping this Festival; but this year, when, as I trust, the Democratic party will gain such a victory as will insure the perpetuity of our beloved Union, surely the 'Old Dominion' will gladly keep the Day of Thanksgiving—and *lead* in the Festival of the States."

In no uncertain terms, Wise told Mrs. Hale what he thought of her pet holiday: "This theatrical national claptrap of Thanksgiving has aided other causes in setting thousands of pulpits to preaching '*Christian politics*' instead of humbly letting the carnal Kingdom alone and preaching singly Christ crucified." By "other causes" Governor Wise meant abolition, and Wise was not a man to abet a Yankee abolitionist holiday.

Left to their own resources, Norfolk, Portsmouth and several other Virginia communities celebrated Thanksgiving Day in 1856 without a gubernatorial proclamation. An editorial in the Richmond *Daily Dispatch* regretted the governor's decision, noting that "Such a day would, at this season, be peculiarly appropriate in the Southern States, not only on account of the continued blessings of peace and plenty, but for the preservation of that Union in which the liberties and happiness of the South, the North, and the whole human race are involved." But even this editor, who longed to see Thanksgiving Day proclaimed, admitted that in many churches "the prevailing peculiarity of the Thanksgiving worship [was] embodied in the language of the Pharisee—'God, I thank thee that I am not as other men, as publicans and sinners, and, above all, as slave holders.'"

On Thanksgiving Day, 1857, Reverend Samuel T. Herron delivered to the Associate Presbyterian Church of New Lisbon, Ohio, just such a sermon as Virginia's Governor Wise reviled: "In an evil hour," Herron told his congregation, "slavery, like Ahab with Naboth's vineyard, looked upon Kansas. She saw her beautiful prairies and her fertile valleys, and coveted them. But she could not enter there, like Eden; a cherub and flaming sword kept the way of that land for the hardy sons of freedom."

Attempts at Compromise

Under the terms of the Kansas-Nebraska Act of May 25, 1854, both territories were opened to settlement; whether they would become free soil or slave would depend on the decision of the settlers, under the principle of popular sovereignty. It was widely assumed that Missourians would immigrate to secure Kansas as slave territory and that Iowans would move to make Nebraska free soil. Nobody except old Sam Houston in Texas chose to recall that the entire territory had already been given to the Indians for "as long as grass shall grow and water run." The North was outraged by this repeal of the Missouri Compromise of 1820, which had barred the extension of slavery into new territories lying north of the 36° 30′ parallel, as all of Kansas did. New England responded by making the Fugitive Slave Law a dead letter. "As easily," wrote a southern visitor in Boston, "could a law prohibiting the eating of codfish and pumpkin pies be enforced."

As expected, Missiourians poured over the border to secure Kansas as a slave state; but they had not reckoned with the depth of feeling in New England on the issue of free soil. Massachusetts abolitionists immediately formed the Emigrant Aid Company and sent thousands of new Englanders streaming westward toward Kansas in a high-spirited antislavery crusade, armed with a precise, new, breech-loading weapon, the Sharps rifle.

When the first free-soilers reached Kansas in 1854, the situation was far too tumultuous for any politician to issue a Thanksgiving proclamation. But, in the words of Mrs. Levi Gates of Lawrence, Kansas, "Why, we can have Thanksgiving every bit as well out here and a Thanksgiving Dinner that will be second to none. I'll cook it myself and there'll be plenty of men folks to eat it. Poor things. They haven't had much sure enough cooking since they come out here." Mrs. Gates set to cooking for her family and for everyone else in Lawrence hungry for some "sure enough cooking," but her hospitality did not extend to the native inhabitants.

> That day a lot of Indians filed into the tent and sat on the ground, pointing to the mince pies and then to their mouths. Fanny, my little girl, laughed and clapped her hands when she saw their gay blankets and headdresses and their odd gestures but I was frightened. My husband wasn't there. Still, I couldn't let those Indians eat up my precious mince pies so I caught up the gun and, pointing it at them, ordered them in my gruffest voice to go away. And so we saved the pies.

Open warfare broke out in Kansas in 1856 between free-soil and pro-slavery settlers, but abolitionists willing to move west outnumbered slaveholders, and Kansas entered the Union in 1861 as a free state. A prelude to that victory was the Thanksgiving Day proclaimed for December 25, 1855, by Colonel James Lane, chairman of the Free State executive committee of Kansas Territory, which met in Topeka in the confusing days when Kansas had two rival territorial governments. By 1856, Kansas again had a single government led by Governor John Geary, who proclaimed the territory's first official Thanksgiving. It is not to be imagined that many slaveholding southern settlers joined in the celebration. The partisan nature of the holiday was made clear in the words of the proclamation:

> While insult, outrage, and death has been inflicted upon many of our unoffending citizens by those whom we desire to recognize as brothers, while the attempt is being made to inflict upon us the most galling and debasing slavery, our lives have been spared and a way pointed out by which without imbuing our hands in blood, we can secure the blessings of liberty and good government.

The time for compromise had already passed when the fighting began in Kansas, but northerners and southerners alike continued to pray, to hope and to work for peace. Reverend A. Hartpence spoke for many southerners when he cried out to his congregation in Franklin, Tennessee, on Thanksgiving Day, 1857, that

> Hallucination affects the ultrist. He seems blind to consequences. How else can he fail to see the dire results of his policy

as suicidal to all concerned? Though our hills become altars for
the sacrifice of brothers, and our rivers red with the blood of
slaughtered countrymen . . . some would dissolve this
Union! Let such fanatics everywhere be rebuked. The cry of
disunion is treasonable alike on the plains of South Carolina
and the hills of Massachusetts. . . . Shall the Union be dissolved? Forbid it, shades of Webster and Washington! Forbid
it, statesmen and Divines! Forbid it, Almighty God!

Seven hundred and fifty miles north of Franklin, in Oneida,
New York, Reverend Caspar Gregory in his Thanksgiving sermon spoke for many northerners who agreed with Reverend
Hartpence that the Union must be saved, but Gregory felt equally
strongly that slavery must end—and there lay the irreconcilable
conflict.

Looked at in one light, there is but one side to the question and
the wise and good both North and South agree. . . . Slavery
stands confessed a great and grievous ulcer upon the body pol-
itic, weakening to the South and a blot upon the whole.
    The party that will cure it soundly, shall have its name
enrolled on earth among the friends of the church and the benefactors of mankind, and its praise shall be wafted to heaven
upon the grateful thanks of TWO FREED PEOPLES, THE
WHITES AND THE BLACKS.
    But if either party, professing to heal her sore, shall kill this
fair republic, then its name shall be covered with all manner of
obloquy and contempt.

Reverend Gregory knew as did Reverend Hartpence that
only if the South would abolish slavery or the North refrain from
opposing this "evil institution" could the Union be peacefully
preserved. It was the urgent desire of most Americans that fall to
pray for such a miracle to maintain the peace.

Governor Robert Marcellus Stewart of Missouri was among
the politicians struggling to formulate a compromise position
capable of preserving peace. By backing the compromise plan of
his fellow border-state politician, Senator John Crittenden of
Kentucky, which would have extended westward the line set by
the Missouri Compromise, he threw his weight behind a political
attempt to save the Union.

In his Thanksgiving proclamation of 1859, Governor Stewart's effort was to inspire in others a patriotic desire to preserve the nation. Purposefully declining to proclaim Thanksgiving for November 24, when abolitionist parsons would preach their sermons in northern churches, Stewart urged the people of Missouri to "recur to the period in their struggle for liberty, when the people of Virginia, cherishing the tenderest sympathies of brotherhood for the inhabitants of the New England Colonies, after solemnly protesting against an oppressive Act to which they were subjected, appointed, in manifestation of sympathy, a 'day of fasting and prayer.' "

Stewart's reference to Virginia's defiant support of Boston during the Port Bill crisis was a timely reminder of a period when a day of prayer had unified Virginia and Massachusetts as Thanksgiving now divided them. To emphasize this erstwhile unity of the now quarreling states, Stewart called on the revered figure of Washington, appointing as Thanksgiving Day, Thursday, December 8, the day when "the venerated Patriot, Washington . . . at night successfully crossed the Delaware, thus saving the remnant of his force, whose achievements shortly after . . . made the Spartan band the nucleus of an ultimately victorious people. The appropriateness of that event as a day of Thanksgiving will suggest itself to every patriotic heart."

Actually, Washington's retreat across the Delaware, while skillfully executed and successful in saving his small army from a powerful foe, was not an action of the glorious sort that usually inspires patriotism. But just as General Washington had retreated across the Delaware to save his army, Governor Stewart was willing to retreat on some points of southern honor if it would save the Union. He urged the people to pray that "the baneful spirit of sectional jealousy may be allayed" and quoted Washington's farewell address urging "a cordial, habitual and immovable attachment to the Union."

Governor Stewart was not alone in invoking mythic heroes of the Revolution to save the Union in its hour of crisis. The Mount Vernon Ladies Association, which was founded in 1856, succeeded in 1860 in making Washington's home a permanent shrine to his memory. *Godey's Lady's Book* ran a series on heroines of the Revolution, carefully alternating tales of northern and southern heroism and not so subtly highlighting colonial cooperation between the sections. In the November 1859 number of the *Lady's Book,* Mrs. Hale made one more editorial effort to hold the Union together, invoking the Constitution, Washington and God's mercy to save the republic.

OUR THANKSGIVING UNION.

This last Thursday in November—will it not be a great day in our Republic? Seventy years ago the political union of the United States was consummated; in 1789, the thirteen individual States, then forming the American Confederacy, became, by the ratification of the Constitution, over the forming of which Washington himself presided, the United American Nation. The flag of our country now numbers thirty-two stars on its crown of blue, and some half dozen or more additional starlets are shining out of the depths of our wilderness continent, soon to be added to our system of independent and united government of the People. God save the United States! He has saved, enlarged, blessed, and prospered us beyond any people on this globe. Should we not be thankful, and keep high holiday of gratitude and gladness in acknowledgment of these national blessings? Seventy years ago, there were only about three millions of people under our flag; now it waves its protecting folds from the Atlantic to the Pacific, and nearly thirty millions of souls are enjoying its blessings. If every State should join in union thanksgiving on the 24th of this month, would it not be a renewed pledge of love and loyalty to the Constitution of the United States, which guarantees peace, prosperity, progress, and perpetuity to our great Republic.

Regardless of the love of the Union felt by millions of Americans, no compromise could accommodate both southern conviction that slavery was an institution the South was entitled to maintain and northern demands that this evil system be abolished. In December 1860, following the election of Abraham Lincoln, outgoing President James Buchanan, noting the "panic and distress . . . and dangerous condition of our country," proclaimed January 4, 1861 as a day of fasting and prayer.

Let us, with deep reverence beseech Him to restore the friendship and goodwill which prevailed in former days among the people of the several states, and, above all, to save us from the horrors of civil war. . . . Let our fervent prayer ascend . . . that He would not desert us in this hour of extreme peril, but remember us as He did our fathers in the darkest days of the Revolution, and preserve our Constitution and Union.

It was already too late. Even as the faithful fasted and gathered to pray, the first volunteer units were being recruited for the Union army.

Years of Sorrow— Days of Thanks _____ 10

North and South rushed into arms in the spring of 1861, ready for a 90-day war that each side felt certain would conclude in glorious victory. By early July, Washington, D.C., held a volunteer army of 25,000 eager to lick the rebels. Throughout the North, overconfident editors, politicians and citizens urged immediate action to quash the upstart Confederacy. The Confederate Congress was meeting at Richmond, and "On to Richmond" became the popular cry in Washington.

General Irvin McDowell led the half-trained Union volunteers toward the small Virginia stream called Bull Run, where on July 21 they met the equally unseasoned Confederate volunteer army under General Pierre Gustave Toutant Beauregard. So confident was the North of victory that McDowell's troops were followed by an army of reporters, sightseers and congressmen escorting ladies in carriages with picnic hampers.

Battle raged in a bloody confusion of untrained troops, novice officers and uniforms so varied as to be unidentifiable.

For hours neither side could organize its forces or gain the upper hand. Then the combination of Confederate reinforcements sent by General Joseph Johnston, the charge of the Thirty-third Virginia Regiment under Colonel Arthur Cummings and General Thomas Jackson's famous "stonewall" stand sent Union forces scurrying back to Washington in an infamous rout. All day, on July 22, soldiers and sightseers straggled into Washington, spreading rumors that Beauregard's army was in pursuit. Beauregard's army, however, was left in such disarray by victory that pursuit was impossible. Richmond was jubilant, as Confederate officers tripped over each other rushing to claim credit for victory. The population greeted their makeshift army as heroes.

Both Sides Celebrate Days of Thanksgiving

Saved from the invading Yankee horde, the Confederate Provisional Congress acted in accord with tradition by resolving, in recognition of the hand of God in the "glorious victory," that the following Sunday, July 28, be observed as a day of thanksgiving. Victory thrilled the rebel states into believing that theirs would be a successful war for independence. Defeat put the North on notice to expect a long, difficult and expensive war.

When November came, governors throughout the North proclaimed Thanksgiving Day, and President Lincoln gave federal employees a holiday. The date occasioned the first Thanksgiving proclamation from the governor of the new state of West Virginia. Thursday, November 28, was the date chosen in all states except Massachusetts and Maine, which selected November 21, also a Thursday. November 21 was also the anniversary of the signing in 1620 of the Mayflower Compact. In that famous document, settlers aboard the *Mayflower* set out a framework for the government of their new society—the first such voluntary constitution of government in the colonies.

The symbolism was apt, for although the dispute that led to secession was about slavery, the war between the states was being fought by the North for the principle of constitutional Union.

Southerners had declared the nation to be made up of independent states, voluntarily associated, and gambled that the North would not fight to hold the Union together. But far from professing indifference, northerners patriotically prepared to fight for nationhood.

The war was, in the view of the North and the words of the governor of Connecticut in his Thanksgiving proclamation of 1861, a "rebellion . . . against our national union." "A fratricidal war," the governor of Nebraska called it, "threatening to sink the sunlight of our nationality into eternal gloom."

Thanksgiving sermons that year focused on the importance of lawful, constitutional government. They considered the justifiability of defending such a government by the use of arms and attempted to define the rare occasions—the southern rebellion emphatically not among them—when citizens might be justified in rebelling against their government.

Reverend Ebenezer Cutler of Worcester, Massachusetts, followed a typical line of reasoning in his "Thanksgiving Discourse—The Right of the Sword." The American Revolution, according to Reverend Cutler, was justifiable for many reasons—because of the many and deliberate oppressive actions taken by George III, because the colonists had been patient and had first exhausted peaceful avenues of redress, because they were forced to defend both life and liberty against attack, and "because of unmistakable indications that revolution was the will of Providence."

Reverend Cutler did not explain what those "unmistakable indications" were, or how one discerns them while a revolution is in progress. But no matter—both North and South agreed that the American War for Independence was fought in a righteous cause. The question of the hour was whether the "War for Southern Independence" was justifiable. Reverend Cutler and most northerners, of course, thought not:

> The States that are now at war with the national government . . . are not engaged in legitimate revolution, but in foul rebellion. . . . The principle of secession is the principle of perjury, treachery and anarchy. . . . This rebellion of the Southern States is obviously . . . *resistance against the ordinance of God.*

Cutler's condemnation of the "foul rebellion" as "treachery" and "resistance against the ordinance of God" fit the northern mood on Thanksgiving Day 1861. Northerners were fighting mad that the Confederate States had seceded from the Union, and the ignominious defeat at Bull Run had merely lengthened the timetable of the anticipated northern march to victory. "Truly, we have cause for Thanksgiving," crowed the Cleveland *Leader*. "The National army is advancing into the stronghold of the rebels, and the Stars and Stripes wave where they have not been seen before since the bastard flag of the rebellion was hoisted by degenerate hands."

Although the *Leader* exaggerated Union success on the battlefield, it quite accurately reflected the broad northern support for a quick and glorious campaign to crush the rebellion. Governor John Andrew of Massachusetts expressed the mood of the nation in a lengthy proclamation that achieved its climax in these words, quoted in newspapers and magazines around the country:

> And with one accord, let us bless and praise God for the oneness of heart, mind, and purpose in which he has united the people of this ancient Commonwealth for the defense of the rights, liberties and honor of our beloved country. While our tears flow in a stream of cordial sympathy with the daughters of our people, just now bereft by the violence of the wicked and rebellious, of the fathers, husbands, and brothers and sons, whose heroic blood has made verily sacred the soil of Virginia, and, mingling with the waters of the Potomac, has made the river now and forever ours; let our souls arise to God on the wings of praise, in thanksgiving that He has again granted to us the privilege of living unselfishly, and of dying nobly, in a grand and righteous cause.

The South had counted on northern disinclination to fight, and there had been fear in the North that "long and uninterrupted years of material prosperity" might, as the governor of Maine put it in his proclamation, have "sap[ped] the virtue or waste[d] the strength of the people." But "when the hour of duty and trial came . . . the practice of exalted patriotism became at one the rule. . . . "

Americans reveled in exalted patriotism. To be fighting and

expecting to win a just war for a glorious cause was exhilarating for everyone and rich in rhetorical opportunities for Thanksgiving proclamations, sermons and editorials. In the camps of the Union army, however, the war was viewed on a more mundane level.

"We are assembled this morning . . . far from our peaceful, happy homes, and in the midst of all the dreadful realities of civil war." Reverend B. W. Chidlaw spoke to the men of the Thirty-ninth Ohio Volunteers in Camp Todd, Macon, Missouri, celebrating Thanksgiving Day as proclaimed by the governor of their home state for November 28. Like other northern ministers, Chidlaw told his men that they fought to "restore the Union," but speaking to men who had seen the reality of war, he compared the desolation that was being visited on Missouri with their "distant homes," where all, thankfully, was "peace and harmony." While civilian ministers exhorted congregations on the glories of fighting for a just cause, this army chaplain assured his regiment that the war was being fought to "bring peace in all our borders."

Reverend Chidlaw also took advantage of the large turnout for Thanksgiving services to admonish the men to beware the temptations of strong drink, gambling, "lust-inflaming books," "vile conversation" and "debauched reviling in guilty pleasure . . . with strange women." It has ever been the chaplain's duty to issue such warnings and the soldier's prerogative to ignore them.

Belying the jingoistic spirit of the first wartime Thanksgiving, the war started badly for the North. Fall and winter passed, and General George McClellan accomplished nothing in the eastern theater. Northern enthusiasm splintered into partisan bickering over the direction of the war effort. Finally, on February 13, 1862, Ulysses S. Grant led Union troops to their first substantial victory, the capture of Fort Donelson on the Tennessee River. Dubious northerners and even southern chauvinists now began to believe that northern men could hold their own against southern soldiers in battle. On April 7, Grant won a second victory at Shiloh, a real, if costly, triumph for the victory-starved North.

Southerners had expected that the North would not really care to fight over secession. Failing that, they believed that Britain would come into the war on their side; for both northern and southern pragmatists expected that England might fight to secure a cotton supply for English mills. Through the fall and winter of 1861–62, northerners awaited apprehensively and the South eagerly anticipated, a British alliance. However, the skillful diplomacy of American ambassador Charles Francis Adams helped Britain's cautious ministers to restrain their government from recognizing the Confederacy, a restraint that probably saved the Union.

Although the threat of British intervention continued throughout the war, the first crucial decision not to intervene was made in December 1861. That, and Grant's victory in Tennessee, led President Lincoln to proclaim a day of thanksgiving.

Like Jefferson Davis, who proclaimed a thanksgiving after the southern victory at Bull Run, Lincoln acted in the tradition of proclaiming thanksgiving days for special events. Sunday, April 13, was designated a day of thanks for signal victories of "the land and naval forces engaged in suppressing an internal rebellion, and" for having averted "from our country the dangers of foreign intervention and invasion."

The date chosen fell precisely 47 years after the last presidential Thanksgiving proclamation, issued by James Madison for April 13, 1815, in gratitude for the Treaty of Ghent, which ended the War of 1812. The reflected prestige was badly needed by the president of half a republic, who had more critics than supporters during the difficult, early years of the war.

Confederate forces under Robert E. Lee and "Stonewall" Jackson held firm against the mighty Union Army of the Potomac in the early summer of 1862, suggesting to observers in both America and Europe that the Confederacy was too strong for the Union to conquer. While the South basked in renewed optimism, northern strategists regrouped their forces under General John Pope and again sent the army south to attack Richmond. At the Second Battle of Bull Run, on August 29, 1862, the Union army was outflanked and defeated by rebel forces under Lee, Stonewall Jackson and James Longstreet.

The Union—blessed with superior resources and a great president—was still losing the war. Endowed with generals who had led them to victory, the Confederate Army of Northern Virginia turned north to invade Maryland and Pennsylvania.

Confederate President Jefferson Davis acknowledged this hour of triumph by proclaiming a day of thanksgiving for Thursday, September 18, 1862, in gratitude for the victories at Bull Run and at Richmond, Kentucky, on August 20. Southern Thanksgiving sermons were as proud and militant as their northern counterparts had been at times of triumph for the Union army. "The blows at Manassas [Bull Run] demolished the enemy's toils of a year," gloated Reverend H. A. Turner of Washington, Georgia. "Blessed be the name of the Lord, He has thus far been on our side." But on September 14, four days before this Thanksgiving, the southern advance had been repulsed by General George McClellan at the battle of Stone Mountain. Henceforth, President Davis would several times set aside days of fasting and prayer, but there would be no more Confederate Thanksgiving Days.

When the season for Thanksgiving proclamations came around in the North, many Confederate sympathizers, savoring the heady scent of Confederate victory after Bull Run, confidently waited for the Union to give up the war. These "cooperheads," as southern sympathizers were called, found insufferable the Thanksgiving rhetoric expressing gratitude for Union victories. The Visalia, California *Expositor*, a copperhead newspaper, published a satire of the typically pious, militaristic Thanksgiving proclamation as its Thanksgiving editorial for 1862.

> O Lord, we thank thee for letting the rebels wallop us at the battle of Pittsburg Landing—for letting them smite us hip and thigh, even unto the destruction of 9,600 of our good loyal soldiers, and 463 of our officers; and for giving speed to their legs through the awful swamps of Chickahominy; and, O Lord, most especially do we thank thee for the licking they gave us at Bull Run the second, and assisting our flight from the fatal field; and, O Lord, never while we live will we forget Antietam, where we had 200,000 and they only 70,000—if they, O Lord, had a happened to a had as many men as we, we'd have been a done gone in—and that friendly creek between us, the mountain that kept our men from running—and, O God of Isaac and Jacob, your special providence in sending night to our aid saved us. For the battle of Perrysville, O God, when we lost 20,000 and the rebels only 2,500, we thank thee also.

*Union soldiers gather for the
holiday meal.*

On September 22, 1862, Lincoln fulfilled a personal covenant with God. He issued the Emancipation Proclamation, pumping renewed enthusiasm into the Union cause and winning liberal support in Europe that precluded the English and French governments from entering the war or officially recognizing the Confederacy.

In retrospect, it is clear that the Union's industrial strength and larger population were beginning to overwhelm the blockaded, weakened Confederacy; but this was not discernible on Thanksgiving Day 1862. The Thanksgiving editorial of the Cleveland *Leader* described citizens "shaking their heads over the aspect of national affairs, profess(ing) to see nothing to be thankful for."

In the army, soldiers still waiting for a general willing to fight and able to win, enjoyed a holiday from their usual routines. Each regiment observed Thanksgiving Day by authority of the governor of its home state. Regiments assembled on Thanksgiving morning to hear the proclamation read, followed by a speech by the commanding officer or a sermon by the chaplain, if the regiment had one. Relieved from routine duties, soldiers spent the day relaxing or playing ball. Those fortunate enough to be encamped near northern population centers were treated to "sumptuous dinners."

Resourceful soldiers sometimes managed to eat well even in unpromising circumstances. Colonel Charles Wainwright, camping with the Army of the Potomac near Fredericksburg, Virginia, enjoyed the services of an adjutant who somehow had managed to prepare and cook canvasback ducks, leg of mutton, cranberry sauce, pumpkin pies and "Green turtle soup, a la tin can" for the colonel's Thanksgiving dinner.

This often well-fed and luxuriously appointed Union army was no match for the 75,000 ill-fed, ill-clad southerners who marched across Virginia under the command of Robert E. Lee. On December 13, the Confederates attacked and defeated 113,000 Yankees at Fredericksburg. The defeat began a season of gloom for northerners, who had grown weary of war. May 1 brought another Union defeat at Chancellorsville, which revealed Lincoln still to be without a capable commanding general after two years of war.

The Turning Point—The North Gives Thanks

That summer, Lee invaded Pennsylvania. Northern and southern armies met at Gettysburg, and a resounding Union victory sent Lee hurrying south with the remnant of his once invincible army. In the West, Confederate General John Pemberton surrendered to Grant at Vicksburg on the Mississippi. President Lincoln found his general.

Patriots throughout the North noted that Pemberton's surrender was tendered on the Fourth of July and regarded this fact as a token of victory to come. A grateful president addressed the nation in words that reflected the depth of his own religious belief:

> It has pleased Almighty God to hearken to the supplications and prayers of an afflicted people, and to vouchsafe to the army and navy of the United States victories on land and on the sea so signal and so effective as to furnish reasonable grounds for augmented confidence that the Union of these States will be maintained, their Constitution preserved, and their peace and prosperity permanently restored.
>
> These victories have been accorded not without sacrifices of life, limb, health, and liberty, incurred by brave, loyal, and patriotic citizens. Domestic affliction in every part of the country follows in the train of these fearful bereavements. It is meet and right to recognize and confess the presence of the Almighty Father, and the power of his hand equally in these triumphs and these sorrows.
>
> Now therefore be it known that I do set apart Thursday, the 6th day of August next, to be observed as a day of national thanksgiving, praise and prayer, and I invite the people of the United States to assemble on that occasion in their customary places of worship, and, in the forms approved by their own consciences, render the homage due to the Divine Majesty for the wonderful things he has done in the nation's behalf, and invoke the influence of his Holy Spirit to subdue the anger which has produced and so long sustained a needless and cruel rebellion, to change the hearts of the insurgents, to guide the counsels of the government with wisdom adequate to so great a

national emergency, and to visit with tender care and consolation throughout the land all those who, through the vicissitudes of marches, voyages, battles, and sieges have been brought to suffer in mind, body and estate, and finally to lead the whole nation through the paths of repentance and submission to the Divine Will back to the perfect enjoyment of union and fraternal peace.

With this proclamation, Lincoln declared, and a weary nation agreed, that here, at last, was something to be grateful for. The Confederacy was beaten; its final collapse seemed only a matter of time. In cities from San Francisco to the Atlantic seaboard bells rang out, fireworks exploded and salutes were fired to celebrate the victories that ensured the continuation of the Union. The New York *Times* gloated over the symbolic date of Grant's victory: "the surrender on . . . the nation's birthday . . . of the master-key of that great rebellion which (aimed) to prove the destruction of the Republic. When Vicksburgh was given up, the Confederacy, in its defensive relations, was ruined."

Churches were filled with jubilant Yankees mindful of the propriety of taking time from self-congratulatory celebrations to render thanks to the Almighty. Sermons touched on all aspects of the war and on every current political topic, but most ministers and congregations wanted especially to offer thanks for the emancipation of the slaves, for the salvation of the Union and for peace, which nearly everyone expected (prematurely, as it turned out) would come very soon.

Thanks, in the words of Reverend Henry Smith, who delivered the Thanksgiving sermon on "God in the War" before the U.S. Christian Commission were due for "God's Providence in this War," both in helping the North learn from its defeats and in finally leading Union forces to victory. Ministers acknowledged that war was bad in itself and that in this war both good and evil could be found on each side. In the final analysis, though, "God, who sees bad enough on each side to damn a continent, prefers our side to the other." Few northerners doubted it; for beyond being a civil war and a war to save the Union, this war was a holy crusade against slavery.

*Black men, though no longer
slaves, served at an elegant banquet
given by the press corps for the
Union Army officers in the
garlanded Masonic Hall on Folly
Island in Charleston Harbor on
Thanksgiving Day, 1863.*

A National Thanksgiving Is Proclaimed

Thanksgiving Day, August 6, 1863, like the Thanksgiving of April 13, 1862, and the two Confederate thanksgivings, was a special day of thanksgiving proclaimed by the government in grateful celebration of victory on the battlefield. On September 28, 1863, indefatigable Sarah Josepha Hale sat in her Philadelphia office and wrote a letter to President Lincoln as "Editress of the 'Lady's Book,' . . . laying before you a subject of deep interest . . . even to the President of our Republic. . . . This subject is to have the *day of our annual Thanksgiving made a National and fixed Union Festival. . . .* "

Thanksgiving was already an annual holiday proclaimed by every northern governor. What Mrs. Hale wanted was an annual proclamation by the president fixing a uniform date and legal enactment of Thanksgiving as a national holiday whose observance could not be omitted by the whim of some future chief executive. And she finally found a president willing to cooperate.

On October 3, Lincoln proclaimed a nationwide Thanksgiving Day for the last Thursday of November 1863—a Thanksgiving proclaimed not in celebration of military victory but in gratitude for a "year filled with the blessings of fruitful fields and healthful skies." It was a Thanksgiving in the New England tradition of setting aside a Thursday in autumn to give thanks for "general causes." Counting the many blessings for which Americans could be grateful, Lincoln reminded his fellow citizens that "No human counsel hath devised, nor hath any mortal hand worked out these great things. They are the gracious gifts of the most high God, who, while dealing with us in anger for our sins, hath nevertheless remembered mercy."

The actual proclamation was drafted by Secretary of State William Seward, who brought considerable experience to the task, having issued four Thanksgiving proclamations during his tenure as governor of New York. But the proclamation was issued over the signature "A. Lincoln." "I do, therefore, invite my fellow citizens in every part of the United States, and those who are sojourning in foreign lands, to set apart and observe the last Thursday in November next as a day of thanksgiving and praise to our beneficent Father who dwelleth in the heavens." For a nation about to be reunited, this truly was a day of Thanksgiving.

Thanksgiving Day fit the mood of a war-weary nation, feeling hopeful for the first season in nearly three years. Soldiers in the field and their families back home worshiped and celebrated in faith that the war would soon end, the Union would be restored and the nation could resume peaceful pursuits.

Weary but hopeful northerners tried to ensure a good Thanksgiving dinner for those who carried the burden of war. In Richmond, Indiana

> There was preaching in the different churches in the morning, and about 12 o'clock the farmers along the national pike and 12 miles into Ohio came in town with their wagons filled with wood and provisions for the soldiers' families. It was a *great curiosity* to see the train coming in, especially one wagon, there was a stove in it and a large kettle filled with "pot pie." They marched down Main Street and stopped at the Starr Hall, an old lady dished up the pot pie and it was carried up in the hall for dinner. They together with the citizens prepared a dinner for themselves and all the soldiers' families.

For soldiers in the field, holidays are a lonely time. "Here were Connecticut boys," wrote Reverend H. Clay Trumbull, chaplain of the Tenth Connecticut Volunteers, "in the field, doing picket duty in front of the enemy's lines, with no possibility of going home, seriously requested to celebrate Thanksgiving Day. It seemed hardly less than a mockery."

The holiday nevertheless came off successfully for these soldiers, thanks to "friends of the soldiers in Connecticut (who) sent to the regiment a good supply of turkeys and cranberries, of apples and hickory nuts. . . . " There was also a church service at which Reverend Trumbull preached on the very apt text from the Twenty-third Psalm: "Thou preparest a table before me in the presence of mine enemies; thou annointest my head with oil, my cup runneth over."

In an Indiana regiment the story was the same. "We had an excellent dinner here Thanksgiving Day, Turkey, Chicken pies, cakes, nuts, apples, and every thing nice. We have the best kind of

Football in the Army, as portrayed by Winslow Homer, appears to have been a free-for-all with few rules and good chance of serious injury.

Donations arriving at Number 24 Trinity Place, New York City for the special Thanksgiving Dinner to be sent to soldiers and sailors.

times. We have a foot Ball and we have a good deal of fun with it. The boys are taking a game now."

The End in Sight

The North was now ready to end the war and return to peaceful pursuits, but the South was not yet ready to quit. The war dragged on for another cruel year, northern armies advancing, slowly, and at staggering cost in human life, into the heart of an exhausted but defiant South. The Union was winning, but winning so painfully that many northerners would gladly have sued for peace on terms favorable to the South. Other northerners thought the railsplitter from Illinois unequal to the task he had been elected to perform and supported General McClellan for the presidency—a general, they believed, would know how to win. Even Lincoln thought himself likely to lose the election of 1864.

Then, on September 3, a dispatch wired by General William Tecumseh Sherman made headlines around the world: "Atlanta is ours and fairly won." The words rekindled hope in northern hearts. President Lincoln immediately requested that thanks be offered in church services the following Sunday. The Reverend J. P. Thompson, visiting the president on September 6, spoke of the pleasure people would take in a Thanksgiving proclamation for the next Sunday, and a jubilant president playfully replied that he would "be glad to give you such a proclamation every Sunday for a few weeks to come."

In the proclamation he issued for Thursday, November 24, 1864, Lincoln counseled his "fellow citizens . . . that on this occasion they do reverently humble themselves in the dust and from thence offer up penitent and fervent prayers and supplications to the Great Disposer of Events for a return to the inestimable blessings of peace, union, and harmony throughout the land."

Without doubt, many citizens followed this reverent advice, but for others the mood that November was one of triumphant jubilation, devoid of sympathy for the nearly defeated South.

Cooks preparing hundreds of turkeys for the ovens at Baker's Bakery, Battery Barracks, New York. Patriotic New Yorkers sent fully cooked Thanksgiving dinners to the Union Army and Navy.

*Two homesick soldiers perform the
ritual of pulling the wishbone at an
army camp far from home.*

*This Thomas Nast drawing
captures the glory of victory.*

Committees in northern cities dispatched turkeys and trimmings to sailors at sea and soldiers in camps throughout the nation. Northerners sat down to Thanksgiving dinner that year confident that the feast was shared by nearly every Yankee soldier and triumphantly aware that even as they ate Sherman was marching through Georgia at the head of 25,000 troops, administering a death blow to the Confederacy.

Unable to restrain its excitement, the New York *Times* painted this extravagant picture of Thanksgiving Day in the army:

> The glorious host under SHERMAN, which is sweeping through Georgia, bearing aloft in the sunlight the flag of the Union. It is not impossible that as they marched along, cutting the wide swathe of which we read, they they took occasion to pick up and bear aloft on their bayonets all the turkeys, geese and chickens of Georgia to furnish themselves with a Thanksgiving feast to-day.

1864 was the second year in which Lincoln set the final Thursday in November as a national day of thanksgiving. Before another November came around, this noble man had been murdered, but his successors respected the precedent he set. They have proclaimed Thanksgiving Day every autumn since.

Victorian
Holiday   11

Andrew Johnson proclaimed December 7, 1865, Thanksgiving Day for a nation at peace, but the long task of reconstructing the Union was just beginning. Devastated by the war and struggling to escape starvation, few southerners celebrated Thanksgiving in 1865. Even out West, in the gold fields of Montana and on the cattle ranges of Texas, prosperous Confederate sympathizers abstained from feasting on turkey and cranberries. Thanksgiving was still very much a Yankee holiday.

President Johnson's Thanksgiving proclamation created a legal holiday only for federal employees and residents of the District of Columbia. Elsewhere, Thanksgiving depended upon proclamations issued by state governors. Although southern governors in 1865 and since have generally ordained days of Thanksgiving to coincide with presidentially proclaimed days, some of them felt as Oran Milo Roberts, governor of Texas from 1879 to 1883, did when he refused to proclaim Thanksgiving Day for Texas, declaring that, "It's a damned Yankee institution anyhow."

Damnably Yankee though Thanksgiving was, southern governors did not hesitate to use it to promote their own political beliefs. December 23, 1875, was proclaimed a special thanksgiving in Alabama to honor the replacement of a reconstruction constitution by a new document that restricted black participation in state government. Governor Houston's proclamation claimed that the new constitution "promises to . . . maintain civil and religious liberties." Louisiana skipped Thanksgiving several times during its tempestuous reconstruction, then celebrated a special thanksgiving on May 10, 1877, when an all-white government was restored.

In Georgia, the return of white supremacy was celebrated by observing Thanksgiving Day one week earlier than the date set by President Ulysses S. Grant for the rest of the nation. The Atlanta *Herald* suggested that Georgians "make next Thursday the fullest and most complete day of Thanksgiving that this state has ever witnessed. . . . Let praise be given to God that he delivered the South from her bondage, and the republic from its danger." The Yankee editor of the Cleveland, Ohio, *Leader* believed that God had delivered the South from bondage when Lincoln freed the slaves and the republic from danger with Lee's surrender at Appomattox Court House, not when a lily-white government came back into power in Georgia. "Georgia," read his editorial, "will not hold her Thanksgiving on the 26th because President Grant suggested that day. It would be acknowledging the authority of a 'Yankee President' which, poor, ragged, ignorant, benighted Georgia is too ostentatiously rebellious to do. 'I can't lick that big fellow,' said the schoolboy, 'but I can throw stones at his dog.' "

Despite its Yankee provenance, Thanksgiving gradually became popular in the South. Proclaimed by both president and governor, the holiday was observed by the closing of government offices and by Thanksgiving services in the churches. But family reunions, pumpkin pies and turkey dinners were customs that southerners had to be taught.

Eager to instruct them were the editors of the many women's magazines of the day, mostly published in the Northeast for a nationwide readership. Southerners now read articles of the kind

A matron carefully considers the purchase of the Thanksgiving turkey as the family look on.

that had taught Americans in the mid-Atlantic and western states how to celebrate Thanksgiving in the 1840s and 1850s. Instruction was given in stuffing a turkey, baking pumpkin pies, preparing mincemeat, decorating the dining room with a harvest motif and using leftover meat in turkey hash. Southern newspaper editors recognized such advice as good copy and began printing stories on "How to Prepare Thanksgiving Dinner" during the last week of November.

In November 1897, the New Orleans *Daily Picayune* commented that "Down here in New Orleans Thanksgiving is not the great festival that it is in the northern and eastern states. . . ." Nevertheless, the *Picayune* was running domestic advice columns on "Decorations for Thanksgiving Day," "Our Thanksgiving Menu," "The Day After Thanksgiving Menu," "Thanksgiving Left-Over" (suggestions included turkey salad and turkey gumbo) and a "Daily Fashion Hint" displaying a stylish outfit to wear on Thanksgiving Day. Other sections of the paper offered lists of Thanksgiving church services and a full-page, illustrated spread polling prominent citizens on causes for which they were thankful.

Religion and Thanksgiving

In North and South alike, on Victorian Thanksgiving mornings, the churches opened for services. Many pious folk remembered that Thanksgiving had its beginning as day of grateful prayer and went to church to offer thanks for the many blessings they enjoyed. But it seemed that some people had other, less admirable reasons for attending services.

On Thanksgiving, with stores closed and everyone at leisure, city avenues leading to the fashionable churches witnessed stylish promenades of well-to-do ladies and gentlemen. One might well wonder whether piety or style was foremost in the minds of these worshipers, who, wrapped in velvet and draped in furs, strolled or rode in carriages to church. The churches these well-to-do worshipers entered were decorated for Thanksgiving in opulent Victorian style. Pittsburgh's fashionable Trinity Episcopal boasted grape-leaf garlands and bunches of grapes "suspended at every projection" in the Gothic style building. Sheaves of grain were tastefully arrayed throughout the sanctuary, and the baptismal font "over-flowed with an abundance of vegetables and fruits." After services, the produce was distributed to hospital kitchens.

Leaders of society and pious working folk alike attended Thanksgiving services according to their individual beliefs in synagogues, Mormon temples and churches of every variety except Catholic. Thanksgiving originated, in part, as a Puritan reaction against Catholic holy days. In turn, once Thanksgiving was established, the Catholic church refused to observe this Puritan holy day. Catholic churches existed in America from early colonial times, but there were so few in the northern states where Thanksgiving began that Catholic participation did not become an issue until the mid-nineteenth century. The Catholic church had been willing to hold services on the civilly mandated days of thanksgiving proclaimed for special victories and for peace after the Civil War, but the idea of saying mass for an annual holiday proclaimed by civil authority—not to mention one that had been started by Protestants—was unacceptable.

For some years, the church hierarchy discouraged Catholics from observing the day, although individual priests sometimes acknowledged Thanksgiving during regular weekday Mass. Those who did attend on that Thursday might hear homilies like that delivered by Bishop Bernard John McQuade at St. Patrick's Cathedral in Newark in 1872, urging gratitude for the "manifold blessings" the congregation enjoyed, especially for the civil and religious liberty granted to Catholics in America. In 1884, the Plenary Council of Catholic Bishops, meeting in Baltimore, commended the holiday to their fellow churchmen.

Cardinal Gibbons, archbishop of Baltimore, brought Catholic Thanksgiving services into harmony with the practice of other denominations by recommending to the clergy that mass on Thanksgiving Day be followed by a prayer for the government and "a few words of exhortation." Catholics could now hear the same sort of Thanksgiving sermon as did descendants of Puritans.

In the second half of the nineteenth century, however, fewer and fewer descendants of the Puritans were troubling themselves to attend church on Thanksgiving, or on any other day. Earlier, during the 1840s, the country had witnessed one of the periodic flood tides of religious enthusiasm in American Protestantism. Interest in religion was widespread and fervent and churches were filled on Sundays and on Thanksgiving Day as well. When this religious enthusiasm ebbed in the 1860s and 1870s, the Thanksgiving service, with its happy associations of home and family, retained its hold longer than other forms of devotion. As the *Telegraph* in predominantly Presbyterian Pittsburgh put it in 1878, "Men who have cast aside the observances which bound them in youth in such matters, and who, perhaps, have not entered a church for a twelvemonth, do not as a rule forget to enter the house of God on Thanksgiving Day, because (if for no other reason) it is so generally the custom."

The custom, however, was fading rapidly, and on Thanksgiving Day in the 1880s, churches of the rival denominations of Methodists, Presbyterians, Baptists and Congregationalists stood half-empty on Thanksgiving morning. Some anonymous person cleverly turned this embarrassment into an asset by inventing the Thanksgiving union service. Several denominations, emphasizing on this occasion the beliefs they held in common, would unite on Thanksgiving Day for a joint service. Virtually every city in America held union services, some encompassing two or three congregations, and others, like the annual union servie at the Detroit Opera House, embracing most of the Protestant congregations in a large city. Union services reflected the mood of the times. In the 1840s, when interest in religion was keen, Protestant denominations had engaged in intense rivalry. Engulfed by the secularism of the 1880s and 1890s, the old rivals eagerly united to assert their faith and the religious nature of this traditional holy day.

The Family Still Comes Together

The ideal Thanksgiving was delineated so regularly in the press that it became permanently embossed on the American consciousness. The image was epitomized by President Benjamin

Harrison's 1891 Thanksgiving proclamation which advised the citizenry that "Among the appropriate observances of the day are rest from toil, worship in a public congregation, the renewal of family ties around our American firesides, and thoughtful helpfulness toward those who suffer lack of the body or of the spirit." A great many families did enjoy precisely this type of Thanksgiving Day. Family reunions were a hallmark of boyhood Thanksgivings recalled by E. T. Powell, who grew up in upstate New York at mid-century.

> There were no railroads then, or at least they were far away and few in number. There was no noise of steam roaring and whistling up and down our valleys; and we did not rush about the world as if there were no such thing as space at all, until we lost all power to rest. But once a year we came together, with our ox teams and on horseback; and we came as families, taking our time about it; and it was a great event. All the morning we had gone to the windows, looking down the street and wondering when the uncles and aunts would get there; for they were to come from Chuckery and from Herkimer, and from Oriskany; and we would give our thanks together to our Common Father. It was half way to noon before the tired teams were all in the barns; and the grandmothers were the center of a restless group, in the spare room that opened off the huge kitchen, and was never opened except for occasions of state. There were nine of the cousins, two of the aunts, two of the uncles and there were the grandmothers. Besides these were our uncles George and Sam, who were part of our own family. This was our little world, and we had it all to ourselves. Indeed! but we did not hear in those days every morning from Bombay and New Zealand, or even from New York or London: nor had we got to calling all sorts of heathen brothers! The family was an institution and it was not easily broken up.

Thanksgiving secured its place in the affections of Americans by providing a reason, and a mandate, for families to assemble. "This week is our festival of Thanksgiving," wrote John Greenleaf Whittier. "It is a beautiful institution, gathering under the old rooftree scattered and divided families."

The tendency of Victorian families to scatter across the map made holiday reunions important. Grown children might be living on prairie homesteads, in eastern cities or in midwestern

This little girl, barely tall enough to reach the table top, is finding it very difficult to wait for the feast to begin.

towns. Railroads made it possible for families to travel substantial distances to be together on Thanksgiving, although the most common journey was from any major city to the villages and farms of the surrounding countryside. Thousands of homeward-bound travelers jammed the railroad stations on Thanksgiving Eve, while extra trains were added to the schedules and extra cars to every train. Steamboats that plied the inland waterways and steamships that carried passengers between seaport towns were full of travelers heading homeward in the pampered luxury of these "floating palaces."

From every direction, people headed home for Thanksgiving, a journey that often neared its destination at the railroad depot of some little country town like Kingston, Rhode Island, where young Mary Tirrell of Providence spent Thanksgiving on her grandparents' farm.

> Grandfather met the train at the small station in Kingston, ten miles from the farm. White houses and red barns were strung out along the winding road and as we rounded the last bend we could see our grandparents' farmhouse with its outbuildings grouped beneath a low hill. I still think of it as the most beloved place of my childhood.
>
> Aunt Ida and Aunt Mary Eliza rushed from the house with outstretched arms; Grandmother came smiling, wrapped in a shawl. The matriarch of our family, Great-grandmother, leaned on her cane in the doorway. Aunt Dorcas stayed at the stove; her whole attention was needed to make at least four dozen johnny-cakes for the two dozen relatives who were expected.

Family reunions maintained their popularity despite the element of truth in the apocryphal story of a young lady who, when told that they would have a family dinner on Thanksgiving, exclaimed, "Yes, and let us have any family but our own." Nor were family reunions confined to New England. Americans in every section of the country gathered on Thanksgiving Day, whether the setting was a Rhode Island farmhouse sheathed in white clapboards and standing beside a tidy red barn, or a rambling adobe ranch house in Arizona Territory that Freddie Hanson recalled from his childhood. The pleasure families took in being together was the same.

> During my childhood the population of northern Arizona was

so scattered that Thanksgiving was an extra special day. It meant getting together with friends and relatives whom we hadn't seen for weeks, sometimes months. It was the day the whole clan gathered at Aunt Katheryn's huge old ranch home for the annual home-coming. It was a rambling western style house, up steps and down, with no set pattern except that of need.

Twelve-inch adobe walls made it a haven of coolness on any summer day, but in November fires crackled in countless fireplaces. The very word Thanksgiving brings back memories of such a lot of sights and smells, love and laughter, fun and fellowship, that it crowds out all thought of other holiday gatherings.

Very often we travelled the four miles on horseback, the six of us imbuing even our indifferent mounts with joy. Or, if the skies were overcast, or snow was already falling, we used a two-seated surry with a fringed top. We arrived early and remained late.

We children hung back in uneasy consciousness of our unaccustomed holiday garb, eyeing each other, making mental notes of obvious changes in stature and bearing. There were always the first feelings of embarrassment as kisses and exclamations were exchanged in a tumult of excitement, happiness, and good will.

Many families augmented the pleasure they took in being together for Thanksgiving dinner by inviting guests. Visitors to a city, elderly people without families of their own, students and young working people unable to return home for Thanksgiving were among the more popular invitees. The prodigious appetites that young folks accustomed to dormitory or boardinghouse food could display at the Thanksgiving dinner table was legendary.

A story making the rounds in Keokuk, Iowa, in 1874 told of a physician who was called to treat a young man who "worries hash at a fourth-class boarding house" but had been invited to dine out on Thanksgiving Day. The doctor asked the patient what he had eaten and the young man, noting that he might not be able to recall everything, recounted that he had consumed: "Three dishes of oyster soup, two plates of fish and two of turkey, two dozen fried oysters, and a dozen raw; some gherkins, four slices of roast pig, a quart of coleslaw, two cups of coffee, four stalks of celery, a liberal supply of boiled cabbage, six hard boiled eggs, some turnip, a glass of milk, apple dumpling, a bottle of native wine, two dishes of plum pudding, two mince pies, some fruit cake, and three dishes of ice cream." The doctor, it was said, listened to this recital, pronounced the case to be hopeless,and left to call the undertaker.

Thanksgiving Festivities

After dinner, while the elders talked or napped, the young folk enjoyed some of the popular parlor games of the era. Charades was always a favorite, but there were also card games, chess, checkers, blind-man's buff and many others. Without benefit of television, radio or even a Victrola, families devised their own entertainment. Albums and scrapbooks were brought out for guests to admire. Those talented in the fashionable art of elocution might recite a piece of memorized poetry or declaim some dramatic bit of prose, but music was the most popular form of entertainment.

Every young lady could play the piano, or, if she could not, she had probably wasted years of her life attempting to learn. By evening, family and guests were sure to gather around the piano and ask one of the young women to play. Singing might begin with solos or duets that the young ladies, in expectation of being asked to perform, had practiced ahead of time; and the whole group would soon join in singing popular tunes and old favorites. Since this was Thanksgiving Day, some familiar hymns were sure to be included in the program, and the holiday would end quietly as the family sang together.

Although this peaceful, family Thanksgiving remained the American ideal, it steadily gave ground to the lively diversions of modern society. Playing charades, for example, lost its appeal in cities where holiday merrymakers could see the productions of professional theater companies. Thanksgiving matinees soon achieved such popularity that they became a Thanksgiving tradition in their own right. Every large town had its theater or opera house visited by touring players, singers and musicians. There might not be shows scheduled every week, but theater owners

Family Party Playing at Fox and Geese, a popular parlor game that provided after-dinner entertainment. A more sedate group in the background is playing cards.

tried to book performers for Thanksgiving, when they were assured of a large audience.

Even more popular than the Thanksgiving matinee was the Thanksgiving ball. Balls were sponsored and attended by every segment of society. Debutantes danced in mansion ballrooms and country girls danced in farmhouse parlors. The Elks had a ball, as did the German Barber's and Hairdresser's Association, the Independent Grocer's Guard, the Masons, the Knights of Macabees and the Steuben Rifle Society.

Thanksgiving Abroad

Around the world, colonies of homesick Americans gathered together to celebrate Thanksgiving. Even in the years before 1863, when Thanksgiving was proclaimed by state, and not federal, authority, American ambassadors would sometimes issue Thanksgiving proclamations for their own staff and for any Americans who chose to join them in observing the holiday. In 1860, when the number of Americans resident in Japan was quite small, the American minister at Yeddo (Tokyo) and the counsel at Kanagawa proclaimed November 29 Thanksgiving Day. On the appointed day, the American colony gathered at Yokohama, heard a sermon by an American missionary and ate Thanksgiving dinner.

Americans in Berlin gathered annually at a Thanksgiving banquet hosted by the American ambassador. There was a Thanksgiving morning service in the American church, but abroad, as at home, dinner was the high point of the day. Seated in a grand hotel banquet hall along with the ambassador and his wife were members of the German nobility and several hundred homesick Americans. Decorations featured fruit and flowers arranged in a harvest theme, but also included a bust of Washington and standing suits or armor holding American and German flags.

Every effort was made to provide an authentic Thanksgiving dinner, even though this entailed importing sweet corn, cranberries, sweet potatoes and pumpkins from the United States. Tur-

*Ambassador and Mrs. White and
Consul and Mrs. Mason are shown
along with other Americans who
have gathered for the annual
Thanksgiving Dinner at the
Kaiserhof Hotel in Berlin.*

keys were stuffed and pies baked as nearly as possible like those
being prepared back home. Alas, some things were not possible.
In 1860, the American women tried to instruct their German
cooks in the baking of pumpkin pies, but the cooks thought the
dish described to them too outlandish to attempt. Under no condition would they bake so *"ausgezeignet"* a concoction in their
ovens.

Despite the absence of pumpkin pies, dinner was a success. A
collection was taken up for the poor, toasts were drunk to empe-
ror and president, and homesick Americans feasted on home-
style food and on the company of other Americans. Some of them
were homesick indeed. A German guest, Professor Holsendorf,
rose to say that he wished he could introduce Thanksgiving to
many Germans who had never heard of anything about America
except Bowie knives and steamboat explosions. Immediately, an
American student jumped to his feet, declaring that he loved all
American institutions, even steamboat explosions; for "who
would not rather be blown half way from New York to Albany
than never get there?"

Thanksgiving was an emotional holiday for those forced to
spend it away from home, especially in a foreign country. One
traveling American wrote of spending the last Thursday in
November wandering morosely through London streets longing
for some token of the holiday back home, before settling into an
armchair in the library of the British Museum to read the
Thanksgiving entry in the *Encyclopaedia Britannica.* Cold comfort indeed on a holiday that counted the gathering of families
among its chief pleasures.

Other expatriate Yankees gathered at the annual Thanksgiving banquet of the American Society in London. Every year this
elite group of Americans feasted on turkey and cranberries,
toasted Queen Victoria and the incumbent president and sang the
American national anthem. Red, white and blue bunting was festooned around a hall dominated by a portrait of George Washington, flanked by both British and American flags. Sheaves of
wheat, stalks of Indian corn and pumpkins were imported from
the States to portray the American harvest. One year, the pumpkins included a 175-pound prizewinner from a New York county
fair. Another year, hovering over the head table was a canopy

made of dozens of pumpkins, atop which was perched a model of the Statue of Liberty.

All of this decorative excess was for the delectation of gentlemen only. In the style of fashionable men's clubs, members of the American Society made their banquet a stag affair. Ladies were permitted only to peek at the assembly from a balcony overhanging the banquet hall.

A Time of Sharing

Banquets replete with pretentious ritual were dear to Victorian hearts, and while Americans resident on this side of the Atlantic bowed to tradition and ate Thanksgiving dinner at home with family and friends, they indulged their love of public display by sponsoring elaborate Thanksgiving feasts for objects of charity. Thanksgiving dinners were given at prisons, almshouses, hospitals, orphanages, settlement houses and insane asylums amidst great self-congratulation over the fact that on this day no one went hungry. Prisoners at Sing-Sing prison in New York were regaled with turkey and mince pie and then presented with two cigars each. Inmates of Massachusetts prisons could hope for something even nicer, for governors of the commonwealth traditionally chose Thanksgiving Day to pardon prisoners.

Inmates of public institutions were provided with holiday dinners at public expense, but serving Thanksgiving dinner to poor people at private missions, settlement houses, schools and hospitals was a fashionable form of philanthropy. One year, the ladies of each Episcopal parish in New York undertook to sponsor Thanksgiving dinner for 100 settlement house waifs with food they prepared and served themselves; and Mrs. Grover Cleveland "played the part of waitress to perfection" for the benefit of young charges of the New York Kindergarten Association. The poor often ate their dinners in front of an audience of complacent benefactors, and in many institutions, Thanksgiving Day was the occasion for formal programs in which charity students performed for the institutions' donors.

In 1895, 750 young pupils at New York's Five Points Mis-

*Children in orphanage uniforms
are served a holiday meal.*

At a Thanksgiving dinner in New York City's impoverished Five Points district, wealthy donors watch poor children eat the meals that their gifts have provided.

sion put on a Thanksgiving recital that featured rhythmic calisthenics—the boys waving dumbbells and girls wands tipped with red, white and blue ribbons. The children sang in chorus, solos and duets, then some of the smallest children stood to recite mottoes. Among the more memorable: "Wine is a mocker and strong drink is raging." Following this performance, the children filed upstairs to a dinner seved from tables marked with the names of each donor.

Self-congratulatory displays were the incentive and prerogative of the philanthropist, but one Chicago department store surely overstepped the bounds of good taste with its 1884 Thanksgiving dinner. Inspired by competition with a rival store across the street, which had set wax mannequins in the window arrayed to represent "Thanksgiving Dinner at the White House," the store in question filled its windows with dining tables laden with good food. Street urchins were then invited to come and eat the food—a spectacle that, brilliantly lit up by newfangled electric lights, attracted an audience of hundreds.

All charitable enterprise on Thanksgiving Day was approved by the world of fashion, but it was more fashionable to feed children than adults and, among children, the most fashionable objects of charity were newsboys. Newsboys were singled out by society because they were perceived to be poor but enterprising, in true Horatio Alger style. In Buffalo, former President Millard Fillmore presided over the newsboys' Thanksgiving banquet. Owners of the Cleveland, Ohio, *Leader* invited their newsboys to dine at the Bethel restaurant. But in New York City, only the reigning queens of society, Mrs. John Jacob Astor and Mrs. William Waldorf Astor, were privileged to donate the annual Thanksgiving dinner at the Newsboys' Lodging House. Not to be outdone, Mrs. Frederick W. Vanderbilt invited the newsboys of the summer resort of Newport, Rhode Island, to dinner. Since there were not enough newsboys in Newport to fill the hall, Mrs. Vanderbilt included the rest of the town's poor children in the feast, which was served by members of the exclusive social club, the King's Daughters.

Charity banquets reflected the affluence of upper-class Americans, who could afford to provide ample feasts for the poor as a grand holiday gesture. Traditionally, families had filled bas-

A little street waif has been called into the home of a wealthy family to be given her first luxurious Thanksgiving dinner; the family has already finished eating.

kets with their leftovers to carry to poor neighbors after the feast, and this custom was still widely practiced. In Cleveland, in the 1870, orphans living in city institutions celebrated Thanksgiving a day late, "so that the crumbs swept up from the bountifully laden tables can fall to the lot of those hungry little ones."

In the Victorian era, Thanksgiving completed its transition from a regional holiday to a national one. From coast to coast, Americans dined on turkey and pumpkin pie, made charitable gifts and enjoyed family reunions. The religious core of the holiday, however, was lost in the transition.

Thanksgiving Kicks Up Its Heels 12

Thanksgiving began as a holy day, created by a community of God-fearing Puritans sincere in their desire to set aside one day each year especially to thank the Lord for His many blessings. The day they chose, coming after the harvest at a time of year when farm work was light, fit the natural rhythm of rural life.

Between the seventeenth and nineteenth centuries, these two circumstances changed. Far from being uniformly pious, many nineteenth-century Americans paid mere lip service to religion or ignored it completely. Moreover, whereas the founders of New England had worked to the rhythm of planting time and harvest, Victorian Americans worked to the ringing of factory bells. Workers put in 12 hour days, six days a week, with no paid vacation, and had only four legal holidays: Christmas, Washington's Birthday, Independence Day and Thanksgiving. With so little time for recreation, it is no wonder that they turned the holy day of thanks into a holiday frolic of football and parades.

The transformatioan began when Thanksgiving expanded

beyond the borders of New England. New Englanders, after all, understood from childhood that decent people went to church on thanksgiving morning and dined at the old homestead in the afternoon. When New York made Thanksgiving an official holiday in 1817, New Yorkers of New England descent understood this as well. Alas, in the great metropolis at the mouth of the Hudson were many New Yorkers unexposed to the strictures of Puritan religion in childhood and unfamiliar with the proper observance of the New England holiday. These revelers made the quiet old holiday the occasion of parades, picnics and an exuberant public masquerade.

New York's Fantasticals

Just as New Orleans has Mardi Gras and Philadelphians become mummers on New Year's Day, for the century stretching from the 1840s until the years just before World War II, New York had parades of "fantasticals" on Thanksgiving Day. The fantasticals were neighborhood-based organizations of young men whose sole purpose for existence was so that their members could dress in flamboyant costumes and parade through the streets on Thanksgiving. It has been suggested that these fantasticals had their origins in the celebration of the final evacuation of British troops from New York on November 25, 1783, the costumes perhaps suggesting the varied rags and odd bits of clothing worn by the Continental soldiers who marched into the city as British troops left. Others have written that the fantastic costumes were a remnant of European Mardi Gras customs, suppressed by Dutch and English Protestants and somehow transposed to Thanksgiving.

To this author, it seems most likely that the fantasticals were a high-spirited extension of Guy Fawkes Day customs. Guy Fawkes was observed in New York throughout the colonial period, and a quieter version of the day continued to be observed by the Episcopal Church in New York as an annual day of thanks until New York governors began to proclaim Thanksgiving in 1817. The young masqueraders who accosted New Yorkers beg-

ging "something for Thanksgiving" were cousins of the English
children who beg "a penny for the Guy." Thus, the fantasticals
most likely began as adult versions of these Guy Fawkes/Thanks-
giving Day ragamuffins.

The fantasticals awakened their fellow citizens every
Thanksgiving morning with loud blasts on their chosen instrument, the fish horn. "At daybreak yesterday morning, the slum-
bering citizen was startled by the loud report of a fish-horn
beneath his window and the sound of horse's hoofs rattling over
the cobblestones. Springing to the window, . . . (he) recognized
his favorite ash-cart man arrayed in the garments of Henry V,
and astride a powerful horse that had evidently become furious at
the music which burst from his master's fish-horn."

Although the Original Hounds of Eighth Ward long claimed
to be the oldest of the fantastical companies, the Hamilton Rangers of the Fulton Street district, fishmongers by trade every man
of them, succeeded in making the blare of the fish-horn the most
prominent sound of early Thanksgiving morning on the streets of
New York. At the 1885 celebration, one of the Hamilton Rangers
took a few minutes to explain the motives of his organization to a
reporter: "You see, sorter explanation like, we's Ninth Warders
and kinder likes to get away from the fish once in a while. We
belongs to the Fulton market and sells fish, but to-day we are
doing the actor and dude act, and it means fun, you bet!" The
"actor" segment of that act consisted of a masquerade parade.
The "dude" part came in the afternoon, when these workmen
regaled themselves with a bountiful picnic, and in the evening
when, still resplendent in outlandish costumes, they danced at
gala balls.

By police department estimate, more than 50 fantastical
companies paraded each year through the streets of Victorian
New York—Ham Guard Warriors, Gilhooley Musketeers and
the Oli Bolis competing with the Sleetville Slenderfoot Army, the
Gentlemen's Sons of the Eighteenth Ward and the Secondhand
Lumberdealers Association for originality of name as well as
splendor of costume. Reviews of their efforts appeared in the
morning *Times.*

First in rank among the organizations out yesterday [Thanksgiving Day 1881] were the Square Back Rangers who live in the Fourth and Sixth Wards. Cherry Hill is the rendezvous of this organization, the members finding sweet comfort in saloons kept by Pat Davis and Steve Haley. The hill was alive with grotesquely attired men at an early hour, and the bandwagon stood in front of Davis's saloon with a party of musicians who nearly bursted blood-vessels trying to make people in Harlem hear them play "Marching Through Georgia."

Captain Kyd sat in a coach with Bismarck, Wah Kee, and the Duke of Cherry Hill. Behind them was a man wearing a woman's riding habit whose face was (painted) as black and shining as a stove-pipe, and whose character was shown in the books of the organization as "Miss Vanderbilt." About 150 persons were in coaches or on horseback, all in fancy costumes, and many of them such as to create much merriment among the crowds that flocked to see them. Patrick Foster, a City Prison keeper, was the recognized Captain of the Squarebacks. He wore a black satin costume supposed to represent him as Sir Walter Raleigh.

When the procession started, the people on the sidewalks set up a yell and the bands of musicians worked with a will. . . . After them came a fantastic and picturesque array, in all the costumes of the ancient and modern history of every country—there were robbers, pirates, fiends, devils, imps, fairies, priests, bishops, gypsies, flower girls, kings, clowns, princes, jesters—all in variegated and bewildering attire, and last, but not least, Jimmy Cavanaugh and Daniel Finn brought up the rear in a dog cart. Mr. Cavanaugh was dressed as a bewitching maiden and carried a gay parasol and a fan. After wandering all over the lower portion of the city, they reached Sulzer's Harlem River Park, at 3 o'clock in the afternoon. There the banquet was spread.

The public parade was over, but for these fantastical revelers the fun was just beginning at rowdy picnics in parks and amusements halls on the city's edge. In 1885, the Hamilton Rangers paraded to Riverview Park at Eightieth Street and the East River, once there

truly making the Park howl. On the outside lads . . . played leap frog and blew horn blasts that made the roaring wind ashamed of itself . . . Men of all ages, a majority of whom must have learned to ride on rails rather than Kentucky thoroughbreds, bobbed about on horseback in a style anything but serene.

The mass of moving, shouting beings, whose costumes were as varied as the whims of a coquette, dazzling the eye with the variegated brilliance of a kaleidoscope, flitted about on the dancing platform with a quick step. . . . [The crowd] vanished when the band began to play a march to Turkey Hall below. . . . The procession struggled for the first snatch at the Thanksgiving bird. Heads were hit and noses punched, but the Rangers got there all the same, and the way gobblers were gobbled would have made England's best and fastest pie-eater ashamed of himself.

It was in the midst of this exciting scene that one character approached another whom he termed a sleuth hound, a remark which caused the one addressed to quickly draw a dangerous-looking sword with the retort that someone was a bloody villain. A fierce sword fight followed, the excitement being intense as the blades clashed, sparks flying at a lively rate from steel arms. Suddenly, amid screams and terrible yelling generally, one of the fighters was observed to fall prostrate, apparently stabbed through the heart or at least a vital part. A policeman who rushed forward, club aloft, asked: "Is he killed?"

"Nah, you old guy; can't you see it is all in the acting. One of 'em is Macduff and one is Macbeth. We all seed it on de Bowery long ago!"

Late in the afternoon, the fantastical processions retraced their steps from the picnic grounds to their home wards, where they danced until dawn at gala balls, finally breaking off to change their clothes and get to work on time.

This wild carousing of working-class youth met, alternately, with smiling indulgence and stern disapproval from the respectable middle class. The exuberant energy with which they disported themselves awakened admiration in many who preferred to spend their own Thanksgivings more sedately; but all respectable shook their heads at the excessive drinking and fighting in which the revelers indulged.

There is no evidence that the fantasticals cared in the least what others thought of them. This was their day, their choice of pleasures, their choice of companions. Bylaws and custom restricted membership in fantastical companies to adult males; women were invited to watch or wait at home until it was time for the ball. These young men planned their parades for weeks in advance and enjoyed themselves so thoroughly that they marched even in the cold, snow and rain that New York often suffers on late November days. Only a snide New York *Times* reporter would suggest, as one did in 1881, that "whether they awake in Police stations, ashbarrels, or in their own beds with their boots on, they will no doubt scratch their heads and wonder whether, after all, they had 'lots of fun on Thanksgiving Day.' "

The Target Companies

New York's second, unique Thanksgiving custom was the target company. These quasi-military clubs of men, more restrained than the fantasticals and a cut above them in social class, existed for the sole purpose of parading on Thanksgiving morning toward the edge of the city, where they engaged in target shooting for prizes. Dressed in shiny, high-topped boots, black pants and uniform jackets in company colors, these soldiers-for-a-day cut a fine figure. Each group had a name, often chosen in honor of their captain, like the Delaney Light Guard, led by Mr. Delaney, superintendent of Gould's Hotel on Fulton Street, or for their trade, like the Carpet and Furniture Guard.

In parks at the city's edge, they set up targets. By all reports, the marksmanship of these men, who took their guns out only on this one day in the year, was abysmally poor. But they pleased themselves with their soldierly holiday pastime, and one of the company would take home a pewter tankard, proof that he was the least unskillful marksman of them all. A few of the target shooters remained in the parks to carouse with the fantasticals, but target companies were largely composed of respectable family men who, after a few rounds of beer, marched home for Thanksgiving dinner with the family.

The Ragamuffins

Running along the sidewalks cheering on the fantasticals and

A uniformed target company parades toward their shooting grounds on the outskirts of New York. The last marcher bears aloft the target at which they will shoot.

*These outlandishly costumed
children are taking part in a New
York Thanksgiving tradition.
Dressed as gaudily as they can
manage, they beg coins from
passers-by asking "Anything for
Thanksgiving?"*

target companies, the boys and girls of New York had special Thanksgiving customs all their own. Black youngsters, faces whitened with talcum, and white children, faces blackened with coal dust, scurried through the city streets in gay costumes accosting passersby with their time-honored demand, "Anything for Thanksgiving? Got anything for Thanksgiving?" Whereupon the grownups gave them pennies.

Not as elaborately costumed as their elders, the Thanksgiving "ragamuffins" often "borrowed" a hoop-skirt and dress from mother or older sister. Thanksgiving costumes were made, and sometimes masks were purchased, by fond middle-class parents who recalled their own youthful forays into the streets on Thanksgiving Day. Just when the custom began is uncertain, but the last of the ragamuffins were seen on New York streets about 1940. How the custom started is also unclear, except that children have always loved to dress up and to beg for treats.

About 1900, Progressive era reformers made the ragamuffin the target of a campaign of eradication. What had seemed to Victorian Americans a harmless childhood sport had, in twentieth-century eyes, a dangerous implication: it was teaching children to beg. For three decades teachers lectured, guardians of public behavior scolded and the police banned the practice—to no avail. Children liked to become ragamuffins on Thanksgiving and the custom flourished. Then, in the 1930s, it declined and vanished, a victim of hard times and modern notions of child-rearing.

Military Parades

Fantasticals, target companies and ragamuffins were unique to Thanksgiving in New York and such nearby places as Brooklyn and Jersey City. The young men of other American cities, as well as a great many New Yorkers of less flamboyant inclinations, turned out in spotless uniforms and well-polished boots to march in military parades. The Second Regiment of the National Guard of Pennsylvania paraded in Philadelphia, and the DuQuesne Greys, scions of the city's upper class, marched in Pittsburgh. The San Francisco Blues and Honolulu Rifles formed

From coast to coast firemen's
parades were popular Thanksgiving
events.

tanks and marched up the avenues of their cities. "Negro military companies" paraded in Savannah, Georgia, and Fenian partisans of Irish independence from Britain paraded in Philadelphia. Police and firefighters donned their dress uniforms and paraded in nearly every city and town in America.

Military Thanksgiving parades were known before the Civil War, but the war gave the custom impetus. Some of the military companies on parade were composed of Civil War veterans; some were militia units. In many cities the paraders also included military clubs of young gentlemen. These upper-crust boys' clubs drilled their young members in horsemanship, military protocol and target shooting and, the parents hoped, instilled character in the process. On Thanksgiving and other holidays they marched up the fashionable boulevards in their elegant uniforms.

On Thanksgiving morning in any particular city anywhere from one to 100 military units might march, but there was no coordinated Thanksgiving parade. Groups simply informed the police department of their intention to parade, then selected the route and time to suit themselves. They marched around the streets of their own neighborhoods, up a major boulevard or along a public park, and traffic, which was light on a holiday morning in any case, waited for the parade to pass.

Bonfires

The young men of Norwich, Connecticut, faithfully observed a unique custom of lighting Thanksgiving bonfires. Every hilltop in Norwich was the site of a fire lit with keen rivalry by companies of youths from each Norwich neighborhood. Flammable debris was collected for weeks in advance, stashes of old barrels and broken washtubs closely guarded against raids by partisans of rival companies. Saturated with turpentine before they were ignited, the bonfires could be seen for miles. By the end of the nineteenth century, this custom was found only in Norwich, and no one could say how it had begun, although local memory did trace its existence as far back as the 1790s.

It is quite possible that the Norwich bonfires originated during the revolutionary war when both New England's annual Thanksgiving and special thanksgivings for military victories were celebrated—celebrations that frequently included fireworks, the firing of salutes by musket or cannon and military parades.

Military Thanksgiving parades in New York may have had their origins in military exercises celebrating the national Thanksgiving Day in 1815, in gratitude for victory in the War of 1812. When Thanksgiving became a New York State holiday in 1817, individuals with no church tradition of Thanksgiving celebration may have modeled their observances on this special thanksgiving for victory in war. Similarly, the special thanksgiving days observed during the Civil War, by both northern and southern governments, fostered the military Thanksgiving parade and fireworks displays found in many cities after the war.

The popularity of parades and sports on Thanksgiving can also be explained simply. Here was a new holiday introduced to people who had no traditional customs for its observance, many of whom were not particularly religious. They adopted the most attractive Thanksgiving customs presented to them, feasted on turkey and enjoyed family gatherings. Sermons and church services, however, were dispensed with in favor of more diverting activities. By the 1870s, with the grip of religious faith weakening in America, even descendants of the Puritans began to celebrate Thanksgiving in a livelier fashion. Theaters were packed for evening performances in Boston and Hartford. Even the more old fashioned were willing to spend the evening at the opera house or symphony hall, provided the morning had been spent in church and the afternoon at a family dinner.

Sports

While some Americans marched in military parades and many stayed home with the family, there were others engaged in nearly every sporting activity known to civilization. On Thanksgiving Day, athletes raced thoroughbreds, pitched quoits, rode to the hounds and engaged in the two sports that Americans favor above all others—football and baseball.

*At Thanksgiving time turkeys
could be won by rolling dice or
playing other games of chance in
bar rooms.*

Late November weather is ideal for outdoor sports in the southern states, but bad weather was only a slight deterrent even in cities where Thanksgiving Day characteristically brings snow or icy rain. Wherever it was cold enough, children and adults alike carried ice skates to the ponds and rivers. Where there was sufficient snow, the children coasted downhill on sleds, and young people rode out in horsedrawn sleighs. Sleigh rides were a favorite of courting couples, partly because in an open sleigh driving through town no chaperone was deemed necessary, which made intimate conversation possible, and partly because frosty air made it imperative to snuggle close in order to keep warm.

Nothing could be more traditional than hunting before Thanksgiving, aiming to bag a main course for the great feast, but there were more than a few sportsmen who chose to spend Thanksgiving Day itself in the hunt. Every Thanksgiving Day, come fair weather or foul, the New York Hare and Hounds Club harried an unfortunate rabbit over the byways of Westchester County. Hunting of a more serious sort took place in many county districts where men with a day of leisure took to the fields in pursuit of game.

Not precisely hunting, although it involved shooting a game bird with a gun, was the turkey shoot. In one popular format, a live bird was tied to a block of wood while marksmen fired at it in turn as long as the besieged bird could "stand up or fly a rod." A less bloody system involved firing at paper targets, with the gobbler designated as prize a mere spectator. Nonmarksmen could enter a turkey raffle and win a bird for the price of a five-cent ticket, or they might work for a magnanimous boss who gave every employee a turkey for Thanksgiving. Turkeys were also used as merchandise promotions. In Pittsburgh, in 1888, Smaller & Co., Clothiers, offered to "give a nice, large dressed Turkey" free to anyone who bought a men's suit or overcoat during the three days before Thanksgiving. If all of these options failed, gobblers sold at the city markets, in the 1880s, for about 20 cents a pound. Poultry was the luxury meat of the era; poor folk made do with beef for Thanksgiving dinner.

Victorian shooting was sometimes an actual quest for game, sometimes a contest to determine who was the best shot. On Thanksgiving Day 1888, Al Bandle of Cincinnati challenged R.

O. Heikes of Dayton to a match in which each would shoot at 100 live birds for a $1,000 purse. Members of the Squirrel Hill Gun Club met representatives of the Herron Hill Gun Club in the Oakland section of Pittsburgh to shoot at clay pigeons and 500 live sparrows. Scores in the sparrow shoot were kept low when the sly birds refused to fly from their cages and allow contestants to get a clear shot at them. The bloody sport of cockfighting drew crowds, especially in the South, while Clevelanders witnessed a match between a bull terrier and a racoon. Both animals weighed 24 pounds, and each owner had put up $25. It took the racoon 16 gruesome minutes to destroy the dog. Most Thanksgiving Day sports were gentler, but bets were placed on every possible event.

Velocipedes, perfected by the Frenchman Pierre Lallement just as the Civil War ended, came into widespread use only after a Scotsman, John Dunlop, invented the pneumatic tire in 1888—buffering the bone-rattling experience of bumping along on solid tires. Bicycles quickly became the rage of the era. By 1893, one company of outlandishly garbed New York fantasticals turned out for its annual parade riding bicycles. Elsewhere, mounted young people peddled away from dull family parties, and bicycle clubs took advantage of the holiday to attract crowds to bicycle races.

Promoters staged both bicycle and foot races. The peculiar Victorian sport of the walking race was often staged on Thanksgiving Day, when promotors could draw a big crowd. Walking very fast, contestants took care never to lift both feet off the ground simultaneously, which would have constituted running and grounds for disqualification.

Balloon ascensions were another novelty of the age. An advertisement in the New York *Times* of November 24, 1859, informed the public that "Professor Love will celebrate Thanksgiving Day by making a balloon ascension in the Pioneer, at the Crystal Palace grounds at 2 o'clock."

Despite such diverse offerings, most Americans who went out on Thanksgiving, went out to the ball game. Baseball was a Thanksgiving Day tradition in the 1860s and 1870s. Local teams held grudge matches on the holiday, sure of a good turnout. A match with a visiting team was often the day's principal outdoor entertainment in a small town.

In the 1880s baseball retreated to the summer months, giving way to legions of schoolboy and college football players who chose Thanksgiving Day for the "big game." Great battles were staged on campus gridirons from coast to coast. With no national media to spotlight games, attention in every city focused on the local game—Case versus Western Reserve in Cleveland, the University of Kansas versus the University of Missouri in Kansas City, Tulane versus Louisiana State in New Orleans.

Everywhere, nattily dressed fans turned out wearing chrysanthemums in their school's colors. When this was a problem—chrysanthemums do not grow in the Tulane colors of blue and olive—enterprising florists tinted the flowers or tied them with ribbons of the correct shade. In New York, the correct colors were blue or orange.

There was a time in the mid-1880s when Harvard played Yale at the Polo Grounds in New York every Thanksgiving Day, and Harvard fans wore crimson corsages. This tradition came to an end when undergraduates enjoyed their trip to New York City for the 1887 game with such uproarious enthusiasm that the Harvard faculty put its foot down: no more Thanksgiving football trips to the big city. After that, New Yorkers watched Yale play Princeton for the honors of Thanksgiving Day.

> On this day New York was full of students from Yale and Princeton, the two most celebrated universities in America (according to Guiseppe Giascosa, an Italian dramatist who visited the United States in 1898), assembled for a football match which divided the whole city into two factions. . . . The immense metropolis seemed transformed into a little college town altogether wrapped up in the life of its students. All the New Yorkers, of whatever state or condition, men and women alike, carried on their hair, arms, cravats, or elsewhere, the colors of one of the two universities as a sign of sympathy and support. Before the houses, the hotels, and the clubs, immense open carriages, their four horses bedecked with garlands, waited to take spectators direct to the playing field. Troops of students marched like conquerors through the crowds which burst into cheers to wish them well. This was a pleasant occasion dedicated to the flower of American youth.
>
> The game follows, a stupendous and elaborate exercise of

In its early years, football was a free-wheeling sport in which players took their knocks unencumbered by protective gear of any kind.

strength and skill. In the evening the streets and theaters [were] jammed with students, but the flower of American youth [had] begun to fade and [gave] forth the odor of alcohol.

Traditionalists lamented the shift of emphasis from worship to football and the displacement of Thanksgiving dinner itself to a starting hour after the final touchdown. Some clergymen gave in and announced that services would conclude promptly at 11:30 to enable the faithful to arrive at the game on time, but the Reverend Doctor John Paxton took the bull(dog) by the horns, calling it a "scandal and a shame that two professedly Christian colleges (Yale and Princeton) should combine to possess the town on this day to the practical exclusion of religious observances." The New York *Times*, more easily reconciled to the inevitable, facetiously suggested dropping the designation "Thanksgiving Day" from the holiday in favor of the more accurate "Football Day."

Families around the nation struggled with the necessity of accommodating both time-honored Thanksgiving rituals and youthful enthusiasm for sport.

"It's only a dinner," said Charles Maynard, Jr., in tones of impatience. Charles Maynard, Sr., stood over against him on the hearth-rug.

"I tell you it's a good deal more than that, young man!" he returned emphatically. "It's a sacred rite, is Thanksgiving dinner, commemorating all the fortitude and trust of our forefathers; and it isn't going to be kicked into oblivion by a lot of sporty rascals with more muscle than reverence; not in my house, anyway."

Charles junior's lips twitched.

"We only want to kick it along from one o'clock to six; not into oblivion," he replied. "This football game is a matter of local pride," he added.

"And Thanksgiving dinner is a matter of national pride and loyalty," retorted Mr. Maynard.

"Wouldn't do away with it for the world," said Charles. "Altogether too many fond memories cluster around it."

Maynard senior raised himself up on his toes and shook his head. "The trouble with the rising generation is that they have too many turkeys and too much plum pudding. You're all *blasé*. You little know what it is to look forward for weeks to the

Americans in the gay nineties lamented loudly about the displacement of the family Thanksgiving dinner by the fashionable Thanksgiving football game. Here, an illustration shows a family having the proper sort of Thanksgiving dinner.

Here, an illustration depicts gay nineties New Yorkers cheering a Thanksgiving contest on the gridiron.

annual feast that was such a treat in my young days."

This was too true. Charles junior took a new tack. "The Lansings are going to dine at six," he hazarded.

Mr. Maynard snorted contemptuously.

"Yes, and you inquire into it and you will find that they'll have ice-cream for dessert. Ice-cream," he repeated with fine scorn, "on Thanksgiving Day! I tell you it has come to this: It's Manhattan Field versus Plymouth Rock, and I'm for Plymouth Rock if I have to sit down to my one o'clock dinner alone!"

Things did not come to such a pass, at least not in this story by Clara Louise Root Burnham. The son, a proper Victorian boy, understood the value of duty, tradition and family. If he could not persuade dad to accompany him to the game, he would do the noble thing and miss the game to dine with his father. Charles Maynard, Sr., however, had other ideas. He sent Charles, Jr., and his date, Miss Lansing, to the game while he took the train home to Thanksgiving dinner with cousins in the small New England town where he was born. This resolved the issue for the Maynard family, but for other Americans the contest between Plymouth Rock and Manhattan Field continued, unresolved, a century later.

Outlaws and Turkey in the Wild West 13

The notion of celebrating Thanksgiving in the Old West con-
jures up incongruous, almost comic images: Thanksgiving dinner
washed down with whiskey in a frontier saloon; Butch Cassidy
and the Sundance Kid inviting neighbors to a Thanksgiving dinner and dance; the U.S. Cavalry hunting turkey to eat at the fort
on Thanksgiving Day; a harvest feast menu featuring buffalo
meat, beans and coffee; church services in Tombstone, Arizona,
the year of the shoot-out at the O.K. Corral. True images, every
one.

During Thanksgiving week, 1881, the year of the famous
O.K. Corral shoot-out, the Tombstone *Epitaph* ran an editorial
urging that the day "be scrupulously observed by our citizens,
and that the good name of Tombstone be redeemed." Westerners
were, after all, not so unlike folks in Massachusetts, Ohio or Missouri. Among the cowboys, cavalrymen, outlaws, Indian traders
and pioneers were God-fearing men and women with blessings to
count, frontier dwellers glad to pause once a year and enjoy a

holiday like the Thanksgiving days remembered from childhood—that is, as much like the Thanksgivings of childhood as
conditions permitted.

"We're going to have Thanksgiving dinner on these," an
Erie, Kansas, woman told her neighbors as she unpacked a barrel
of new dishes sent by loving relatives back east. "I know what
you're thinking and I know it's true. We've got almost nothing to
eat but buffalo meat, same as you, but we'll eat it together—
maybe I can think up another way to cook it. Even if we don't
have anything else, we'll have it on these new dishes." Thanksgiving traditions were maintained by pioneer women who kept
the familiar holiday in new homes, often without turkey, cranberry or pumpkin—often, indeed, without an abundance of anything
except gratitude.

A pioneer woman from Kittitas County, Washington,
recalled during her childhood a "grand" Thanksgiving spread of
"three deliciously stuffed wild prairie chickens, baked a golden
brown; mashed potato and lots of gravy, dried corn and winter
radishes." This pioneer Thanksgiving dinner was a far cry from
the multicourse repasts of oysters, fish, meat, poultry, exotic
fruits and imported wines that many easterners enjoyed in 1870.
But wholesome and adequate food was blessing enough on the
frontier. "The prize dish," of that Thanksgiving feast "was mother's apple dumplings"—unremarkable enough in Washington
State, except that the writer goes on to explain that the dumplings
were made from dried apples imported from The Dalles, Oregon,
since "at that time no one thought apples could grow here (in
Washington)."

Bagging Thanksgiving Dinner

Hunting wild game for the Thanksgiving table was quickly
established as a western Thanksgiving custom. One Lieutenant
Jordan and five enlisted men from Fort Washakie, Wyoming
Territory, brought ten elk, six black-tailed deer and one buffalo
back to the fort from their Thanksgiving hunt in 1881. Although
hunters would settle for prairie chickens, buffalo or elk, wild turkey was the prize bag.

Frederick Remington captures two hunters returning to the ranch with game for the Thanksgiving feast.

The soldiers at this lonely campfire will at least enjoy turkey for their Western Thanksgiving dinner, supplied by their comrades returning from a successful hunt.

General George Crook, commander of the U.S. troops in Arizona, made a ritual of his Thanksgiving turkey hunt. A dedicated sportsman, Crook was man who regularly rode ahead of his troops, deep in hostile Apache territory, hoping to get off a shot at a deer or game bird. In November 1880, the general arrived at Fort Apache from his headquarters in Prescott, Arizona, to begin the annual turkey hunt. Accompanied only by two junior officers, he had ridden 150 miles on rough trails through Indian country to bag Thanksgiving dinner.

The mountains around Fort Apache teemed with game; turkeys were especially abundant because Indians did not favor them as food. Accompanied by several junior officers, General Crook rode into the grassy mesa where oak and pinyon groves swarmed with turkeys. Two days later the hunting party was back at the fort with more than 100 big gobblers and some two dozen mule deer, all killed with regulation army rifles (no shotguns for the sporting general). Loading their kill on pack mules, the hunters trekked back to Prescott, the meat kept fresh by the cool November weather. It was a fine sport, and so popular did hunting turkey become that by 1900 almost none was left in the wild. Twentieth-century forest rangers have restored the turkey to its range and hunters to their Thanksgiving sport.

Well north of General Crook's hunting grounds, in Montana Territory, in November 1868, preparations were being made by the men of the new Fort Browning trading post, on Milk River, to treat the local Indians to a Thanksgiving feast. Hunters had brought in four buffalo for Thanksgiving dinner, and Captain D. W. Buck, the post trader, was mixing "Indian whiskey" for the celebration. A keg of straight alcohol was the base of the drink. To this were added several bottles of Perry's Pain Killer and several of Hostetter's Bitters with enough red ink to give the mixture a good color. Then half a dozen bars of castile soap and three plugs of blackstrap chewing tobacco were stirred in along with sufficient Milk River water to give the whole Indian camp a three-day drunk. There was a purpose to this wining and dining of Indians. Traders who had seen pouches of gold nuggets in the Indian camps planned to trick some drunken Indian into telling them which creeks and hills were gold-laden.

Trading for buffalo hides, wolf skins and muskrat and beaver pelts was suspended on Thanksgiving, while the Indians drank and the traders feasted and planned how they would spend their gold. In the kitchen of the two-room trading post, Indian women married to some of the fur traders cooked a Thanksgiving dinner of roast haunch of venison, antelope steaks, buffalo liver, fried dough served with a carefully hoarded tin of jam, coffee, tea and a steamed pudding of flour, suet and raisins served in brandy sauce. But the prize dish and centerpiece of the feast was not turkey, not meat of any kind—it was potatoes. Captain Buck had broken a small patch of land near the fort and managed to raise a small crop of the tubers. The biggest was no larger than a golf ball, but potatoes were a luxury to people accustomed to a diet of meat and flour.

Dinner was a success; the Indians got properly drunk, but they had been warned by Catholic missionaries never to reveal the source of their gold lest the white men take away their land and, drunk though they were, not one would talk. White prospectors would not discover pay dirt in the Little Rockies until 1884.

Some Indian tribes had become so assimilated to the white man's ways that they issued Thanksgiving proclamations of their own. J. B. Mayes, principal chief of the Cherokee Nation, proclaimed Thanksgiving for his people in 1884 with a unique blend of traditional Indian phrases and Victorian ideas:

> As our forefathers when nature's children of the forest in pursuit of game around the council fire in simplicity did give praise and thanks to the Great Spirit in their yearly mystic "green-corn dance" for the return of His great gift to them—the "indian" corn—now to-day, as a Christian nation of people, it is but meet that the Cherokee people should give thanks to the Christian's God for his continued protection of our tribe.

Citizens of Clay County, Texas, turned Thanksgiving hunting into a unique holiday party. The week before Thanksgiving, popular belles divided the young men of Clay County into two teams that spent Wednesday hunting. The bag was tallied on a point system that awarded a wolf 500 points, a raccoon 250 points, an opossum 250 points, a polecat (skunk) 250 points and fish 5 to 10 points each. Dinner was served at the schoolhouse.

The ladies cooked and sat at tables for dinner with members of the winning team. Members of the losing team waited table.

City dwellers lacking either skill or inclination to ride through Indian country in search of Thanksgiving dinner could fix a gobbler in their sights at a turkey shoot, like the one set up on the Santz Cruz River bottoms in Tucson on the day before Thanksgiving 1883. Contestants lined up on the dry Arizona riverbed and took aim from a distance of 60 yards at 30 turkeys, 12 chickens and 3 geese buried in dirt up to their necks. When the first round was over, the birds were disinterred and the marksmen had a go at whole birds from 200 yards. Winners of this grisly event got to roast the targets for Thanksgiving dinner.

Tucson residents also seized on Thanksgiving to indulge their love of sports. Horse races and baseball and football games were scheduled on Thanksgiving Day. In 1879, the big game was a baseball contest between two local newspapers, neither of which had reporters who could cover the outfield beat—final score: Tucson *Star* 30, Tucson *Citizen* 31. By 1899, football had come west, and sports fans witnessed a doubleheader at Carrillo's Gardens. In the morning, Tucson beat Tempe at baseball. After dinner the Tempe Normal School (now Arizona State University) trounced the University of Arizona at Tucson in a football match, 11 to 2.

Thanksgiving evening was devoted to balls in western cities as in eastern ones, but frontier dance parties could encounter difficulties unheard of in the East. The Fireman's Ball was to be the great event in Helena, Montana, in 1866. Young America Hall was gaily lit as fashionably dressed women of the town were escorted in. Unfortunately, the ball ended in disaster shortly after it began when the women of Helena noticed that some rebel against Victorian social mores had escorted to the dance two young milliners known to ply another trade after hours. The respectable ladies pulled on wraps and left.

Some Lavish Spreads

Festive dinners and fashionable balls were popular Thanksgiving events, so one year Butch Cassidy and the Sundance Kid decided to put on a dinner and evening dance for their friends, respectable and otherwise.

Brown's Park is a deep valley in the mountains where Utah, Colorado and Wyoming meet. In the 1890s, the valley was a stop on the daily stage coach route from Rock Springs, Wyoming, to Fort Duchesne, Utah, and the home of several respectable farming families. It was also the home of two outlaw gangs, when they were not busy elsewhere. Butch Cassidy, Elza Lay and their boys, known as the Wild Bunch, were on friendly terms with the Powder Springs gang whose leaders, Billy Bender and Les Megs, claimed the fealty of such notorious outlaws as the McCarty boys and Harry Longbaugh, the Sundance Kid.

Since folks in the valley had had the courtesy, or perhaps the good sense, not to try to turn anybody in, the Powder Springs boys and the Wild Bunch decided to show their gratitude by throwing a Thanksgiving party more elegant than anything Brown's Park had ever seen. Isom Dart, a black cowboy, held sway in the kitchen, amply provided with turkeys, pumpkins, vegetables and such unaccustomed winter luxuries as bluepoint oysters, fresh lettuce, ripe tomatoes and Roquefort cheese.

Butch Cassidy and Harry Longbaugh stood out front on Thanksgiving Day to hand the ladies down from their horses, then donned white butcher's aprons to wait table and assist Chef Dart, who was dressed in resplendent white from his tall chef's hat to his shoes. Brown's Park gentlemen wore their Sunday best for the occasion, and all the ladies had new dresses.

Thirty guests attended the outlaw's Thanksgiving. Farm families and outlaws sat at tables spread with fine china, linens and silver lent by valley families, and heard old John Jarvie make a blessing before enjoying the five-course meal. Dinner was the eptiome of refinement. Between courses Ann Basset, dressed in powder blue silk taffeta, recited a piece on the meaning of Thanksgiving, Ada Morgan and Tom Davenport sang "The Last Rose of Summer" and a trio on zither, guitar and fiddle played "The Tennessee Ploughboy."

Butch Cassidy broke the elegant mood by lugging in a big, old black coffee pot from the kitchen, leaning over a lady clad in a stylish silk gown and sloshing some coffee into her cup. His horrified companions hustled the Utah farm boy into the kitchen for a quick lesson in refined table service. Butch reemerged to gracefully pour the rest of the coffee at a side table. After the plum pudding with brandy sauce was finished, the party rose from the table and danced until sunrise.

Westerners lacking the financial resources of this gang of bank robbers and highwaymen celebrated Thanksgiving less lavishly. Many men ate in the saloons that offered hard-drinking cowboys free lunches, featuring sliced turkey on Thanksgiving Day. Diners were, of course, expected to pay for their whiskey. Sober folk could lunch at the Thanksgiving dinners sponsored by the Women's Christian Temperance Union in many western towns. The WCTU menu for Elko, Nevada, in 1888 was appetizing—turkey, ham, sweet potatoes, lobster salad, pumpkin pie, mince pie, coconut cake and jelly roll and many more dishes. Beverages were limited to coffee and tea.

Oysters and lobster were the two luxury seafoods favored for the Thanksgiving feast in those days before refrigeration. Both could be purchased canned or, packed in barrels with seaweed and saltwater, could be shipped inland live. Some western families were in the habit of purchasing a barrel of oysters in the fall to be kept in the basement and used for special dinners throughout the months with an "r" in their names.

Bringing in barrels of oysters was, of course, the privilege of well-to-do westerners in established settlements. The first pioneers celebrated Thanksgiving with whatever was at hand. One Washington State pioneer recalled a Thanksgiving dinner made up primarily of salmon—fresh and dried. Established city folk might have oysters, turkey, mince pie and ice cream; ranchers, cavalrymen and Indian traders dined on whatever prizes their rifles could bring down; and homesteaders just getting established were grateful for what little they had.

Sometimes, however, a westerner, even in a new settlement, wanted to put on lavish spread. Henry Plummer was such a man. Plummer was sheriff of Virginia City, Montana, a lawless mining camp that sprang up overnight when gold was found in nearby hills. On the side, he ran a ring of highway robbers whose technique was to waylay prospectors on their way into town with gold and to ambush gold shipments being sent out of Virginia City. It was the dapper sheriff's belief that if he behaved like a respectable gentleman, the citizens of Virginia City would never suspect that their personable sheriff was really head of a notorious gang of highwaymen.

Accordingly, on Thanksgiving Day 1863, Sheriff Plummer invited the most prominent citizens of Virginia City to dinner; he even spent $40 to have a turkey imported from Salt Lake City for the feast. But, then, $40 wasn't much when someone else worked to dig it out of the hills. Plummer's guests were impressed with his hospitality, but local vigilantes were even more impressed with the weight of suspicion against him. Two months after his Thanksgiving dinner party, Henry Plummer was dead, hanged by the neck by a vigilante posse.

Thanksgiving celebrations in the wild West often included an element of adventure missing from the holiday in more settled parts of the country, but the basic themes were familiar. There was the desire to feast at an ample table, to entertain family and friends and enjoy the dishes and customs remembered from childhood. At the same time, there was an urge to celebrate the holiday with sports, dancing and amusements of all kinds. This tension between longing for a quiet, old-fashioned Thanksgiving and desire for a gay and lively holiday would continue as Thanksgiving entered the twentieth century.

All-American
Thanksgiving___ 14

Fashionable Thanksgiving Days at the turn of the century
began with services in a Gothic style Episcopal church, the
denomination that status-conscious, upper-class Americans be-
longed to. After church, the wealthy returned to homes built to
look like French châteaus or Italian villas and enjoyed a seven-
course repast of dishes with French names served on Louis XVI
style dining tables. In the evening, the well-to-do sought amuse-
ment by attending Italian operas. But while European operas and
architecture were the rage, Italian, Polish and Irish immigrants
were decidedly déclassé.

Immigration, and fear of immigrants, have been a great
underlying theme of American history from the colonial period
to the present. Victorian Americans, watching the ever-increasing
flow of Irish, German, English, Scandinavian, Canadian, Chinese, East European and Italian immigrants, worried that these
strangers with their foreign ways would alter the character of the
American nation. Two methods were proposed to avert the

threat. First, there was the recurrent political impulse to prohibit immigration and eliminate the problem completely. Second, America hoped to assimilate the immigrants as rapidly and completely as possible, encouraging them to behave like native-born American Prostestants.

Nineteenth-century America dealt with immigrants primarily by assimilation. Chinese were the only group legally excluded from immigrating to America in the nineteenth century—apparently, they were viewed as too different to be assimilable. European immigrants were allowed unrestricted entrance until after World War I.

Americans Seek Their Roots

Fear of immigrants and the cultural changes they might foment led to a growth of interest in America's cultural history during the last decade of the nineteenth century and the first decade of the twentieth. Books about life in colonial times enjoyed tremendous popularity, and for the first time many Americans eschewed European architectural styles to live in houses built in American colonial style. Above all, Americans seeking to assert their connection with historic American values joined patriotic societies.

The Daughters of the American Revolution (DAR) was founded in 1890, the Colonial Dames in 1891, and the General Society of Mayflower Descendants in 1894; these three are merely the best known of the dozens of social and patriotic organizations founded at the turn of the century by descendants of the founders of particular towns or colonies or of particular colonial groups, such as the Descendants of Colonial Governors, founded in 1896. There was a pecking order among the societies. For example, the National Society of Old Plymouth Colony Descendants (1910) was easier to join than the Mayflower Society, membership for which required your having had ancestors on the first boat. There were also societies for the descendants of soldiers in the colonial wars, the Revolution and the War of 1812.

Almost any old American family could prove its eligibility to

An immigrant family that has just landed at Castle Garden, on the Battery at the tip of Manhattan, eats dinner on a park bench on Thanksgiving Day—unaware of the holiday.

Residents of Plymouth, Massachusetts dressed in period costumes parade through the streets of town in the 1921 edition of the traditional Pilgrim's Progress. Each participant represents one of the original Pilgrims walking to services at the First Parish Church.

join one or another of the patriotic societies. What they all had in common was that recent immigrants could not join.

Beyond their exclusivity, the patriotic societies endeavored to amplify and venerate the acts of the founders. If immigrants were to be turned into Americans, it was necessary to define the hallmarks of Americanism and to impart them to the new arrivals. The legend of the Pilgrims and the holiday of Thanksgiving seemed tailor-made for the purpose. The Pilgrims, refugees from religious persecution in Europe, were perfect models for new immigrants. In legend and in fact, the Pilgrims were sober, hardworking, God-fearing Protestants; moreover, they were the authors of America's first democratic constitution, the Mayflower Compact. Promulgators of the Pilgrim legend hoped or wished that the "wretched refuse" of Europe's "teeming shore" immigrating to America would become as sober, hardworking, democratic and—God willing—Protestant as were the Pilgrim role models.

In the words of one member of the Allied Patriotic Society, interviewed at a meeting called in 1926 to protest the intrusion of department store parades onto Thanksgiving: "Thanksgiving Day was the suitable day for worshipping (the) memory . . . of the Pilgrim fathers." "Worship" fairly well describes the attitude taken toward the Pilgrims. There were paintings of the Pilgrims, odes to the Pilgrims and stories about the Pilgrims. There were innumerable institutions, buildings, streets and businesses named "Mayflower" and interminable pageants portraying "The Pilgrims at the First Thanksgiving." Americans, in short, were force-fed Pilgrims until it was said that many wished Plymouth Rock had landed on the Pilgrims instead.

The legend of the Pilgrims and the first Thanksgiving became so important a part of American folklore that Jamestown, although first in the history books, became a clear second in the hearts and minds of America. Indignant Virginians reasserted their claim to primacy by proclaiming loudly that Virginia, not Massachusetts, was the site of the first Thanksgiving, and it was also at this time that partisans of Popham, Maine, staked their claim to have had the first Thanksgiving. But nobody paid much attention; to Americans, Thanksgiving indelibly meant Pilgrims.

Thanksgiving and the Americanization of Immigrants

Many efforts to Americanize immigrants were of the gentlest kind. The commissioners of immigration in New York City, for example, annually provided turkey dinners for immigrants at Castle Garden and, later, Ellis Island on Thanksgiving Day. But the primary instrument of Americanization was the public school system. Pupils learned the story of the first Thanksgiving, participated in school Thanksgiving pageants and urged their parents to celebrate the holiday the way "teacher" told them that Americans celebrated.

Pearl Kazin wrote of an immigrant schoolgirl's introduction to Thanksgiving in a short story that appeared in the *New Yorker*:

. . . at P.S. 125 . . . , as soon as October was folded back on the calendar, we began paying intense, if somewhat baffled, homage to the glories of Thanksgiving.

Most of us were the children of immigrants from Vilna or Minsk or Odessa, who rarely budged from Brooklyn, and we had to sing our praises for the gathering of the harvest and the prodigal bounty of the land as the trolley cars clanged by under the windows. Day after day, whether our schoolwork took the form of history or geography, drawing or music, we devoted ourselves to that old American holiday first conceived, we were told, in a bleak place called New England, by the Pilgrims, also known as ancestors. These ancestors spoke English without an accent, did not have to pass through Ellis Island when they reached the golden land, and had come to these shores to escape from religious persecution. Something about their religion, I assumed, accounted for their strange and stern addiction to brown—brown hats and long brown shirts, brown trousers, square-buckled brown shoes, in which they tramped through the brown wilderness.

This passion on the part of the Pilgrims for one drab color was commemorated by us with particular vigor and abundance during our drawing class. Down came the multicolored autumn leaves that had festooned the blackboard molding, and now, bending over our slanting, ink-faced desks, we labored intently, fingers deeply stained and arms splotched to the elbow with brown paint, making the first Thanksgiving—the huge Pilgrim family, at an enormously long table, in the clearing they had courageously hacked out of the ominous New England forest. With crayons and paints we smeared a lavish feast. In the lower grades, I tried to be faithful, in my art work, to the historybook pictures, but later my idea of the turkey and feast came to be inspired less by those lifeless line drawings than by the November issue of the *Ladies' Home Journal.* Sometimes I snipped out the full-color-photograph turkeys and mounted them on drawing paper. Then, in the fanciest "Old English" lettering I could devise, I labelled them proudly "We Gather Together" or "Our Country in Olden Times."

There was a song we sang only in November—"We gather together and ask the Lord's blessing. He chastens and hastens His will to make known." We sang it with loud and cheerful assurance as Miss Johnson thumped away on a piano whose keys were as stained as smoker's teeth. Like Christmas carols and making the sign of the cross, this Thanksgiving hymn had the lure of the forbidden. I would come home on November afternoons, my face hectically pink from the autumn air and the grandeur of Thanksgiving, and sing "We Gather Together" until my mother, who would be working on a dress for me or one of her customers and never seemed to be listening, would suddenly hear "the Lord's blessing" and exclaim, "What kind of a song is this for a Jewish girl to sing! Stop this minute, it's not nice somebody should hear you."

For weeks before the holiday I brought the same lament home from school every afternoon, as though it were tucked in among the schoolbooks buckled together with the thick leather strap I inherited from my brother. "But Mama, *why* can't we have turkey for Thanksgiving like everybody else?"

"Who's everybody?" my mother would say, without taking her eyes from the sewing machine. "The Feins eat turkey Thanksgiving? Doris Levine's mother goes on the subway to buy a turkey God knows where Thanksgiving?"

"Oh, honest to God, Mama. You're always making believe you don't understand one single word I'm saying. I meant like *Americans* have on Thanksgiving, not that dopey Doris."

"What's the matter, they're giving you a vacation in school all of a sudden? They forgot to give you homework, you have to bother me with stupid things when I'm busy?" And then, as her fingers guided the twittering needle down to the end of the seam, "We don't have enough *our* holidays for you? Eh, who knows even where to buy a turkey, how much it costs. An

arm and a leg it wouldn't surprise me. Go, *mamaleh*," she
would say, with sudden tenderness, stopping the machine and
holding the dress material to her breast, "go do your homework, please, do me a favor. Headaches she has to give me with
her turkey yet."

"I knew it was useless to argue. I knew it before I began to
try. But something urged me, every November, to try just this
once more. How easy it seemed, how easy and beautiful and
right, as I pictured it, mooning in my room and smoking an
orange crayon with melancholy puffs: the round table in the
living room swelled with the two leaves we dragged out from
behind the sofa only at Passover time. Though we didn't have a
dining room, on this day it could be called that. At four in the
afternoon, all the guests would assemble—my Uncle Harry
would be there, and my Uncle Morris, who on this day would
forget to pinch my cheek black and blue as he said, "And how's
the world treating you?" And their wives would for once not
squabble, my two aunts both named Frieda—the good Aunt
Frieda and the bad Aunt Frieda, the one I liked and the one
who never let you sit on the sofa in her house because she kept
the pillows puffed up like soufflés. This day would differ from
other days because on Thanksgiving my brother and I would be
glad to see our cousins, who for a change would not say, "What
do you have take dopey violin lessons for?" And after we had
all kissed each other sweetly, we would sit down with cheerful
smiles, around the jolly table set exactly the way they showed in
the *Ladies' Home Journal.* After we had sung 'We Gather
Together," my mother would march in from the kitchen at just
the right moment, holding the enormous, steaming brown bird
aloft on a silver platter, which she placed reverently in front of
my father, poised and ready with a carving knife handed down,
of course, by ancestors. Then Papa would begin to carve, with
magnificent effortless skill, an art taught him by his father, who
had learned it from *his* father.

Immigrant children wanted desperately to be "real" Americans. Many adults were nearly as eager to assimilate, as long as
this did not entail exchanging their ancestral religion for American Protestantism—an ideal promoted by not a few American
Protestants who sought to convert Catholic, Jewish and Eastern
Orthodox children in the public schools, at summer camp, in settlement houses and in a variety of institutions for delinquents,
orphans, invalids and other unfortunate youngsters.

Thanksgiving: A Nonsectarian Holiday

Catholic parents suspected Thanksgiving of being a Protestant holiday, and Jewish parents regarded it as a Christian holiday. In truth, the boundary between things Protestant and things American was not terribly clear in the minds of many American Protestants who celebrated Thanksgiving along with Americanism and encouraged immigrants to do likewise.

George Washington had been very careful to invite Americans of "all religious societies and denominations" to join in giving thanks, and later presidents followed his example by referring to the deity with such phrases as "Creator of the Universe," "Heavenly Father" or "Almighty God," names that would be acceptable to people of every faith. Only Grover Cleveland broke with tradition by including a distinctly Christian doctrine in his 1896 proclamation, which urged Americans to implore forgiveness "through the mediation of Him who has taught us how to pray. . . . " The ensuing letters and editorials agreed on the value of proclamations designed to include all religious groups, and no president ever repeated Cleveland's mistake.

Occasionally, a governor would issue an overtly Christian proclamation, only to be corrected by the press or by a Jewish constituent, but most gubernatorial proclamations were as careful to include all religious groups as were presidential ones. Gradually, Catholics, Jewish and Orthodox Christians began to celebrate Thanksgiving Day, often mixing holiday foods from their homeland with American Thanksgiving traditions.

Danny Thomas, the popular actor, was raised in Toledo, Ohio, by Lebanese immigrant parents. For Thanksgiving dinner his mother prepared the finest holiday dishes she had learned in the old country: tender, boned chicken mounded on honeyed, raisin-studded rice; breast of lamb stuffed with sautéed meat, onions, pignolia nuts and rice; stuffed grape and cabbage leaves and zucchini squash. Danny's father made sure that his nine sons and one daughter understood the spiritual meaning of the day by inviting each to write a prayer. The author of the best prayer "could stand and recite it before dinner on Thanksgiving Day.

For the rest of his life, Danny Thomas recalled the prayer that won for him as a sixth grader:

> For the air we breathe,
> and the water we drink,
> For a soul and a mind
> with which to think,
> For food that comes
> from fertile sod,
> For these, and many things,
> I'm thankful to my God."

The tone, if not the menu, of this Thanksgiving Day would have pleased the most xenophobic member of the DAR or the Mayflower Society, because Danny Thomas's family kept Thanksgiving as a religious and family holiday. For the patriotic societies, and for many who sympathized with them, constant vigilance was required to preserve Thanksgiving Day against assaults by hedonist revelers and heedless modernizers.

The Old-Fashioned Thanksgiving Reinstated

The urge to modernize Thanksgiving Day was part of the general Victorian urge to innovate, renovate, update and improve everything they touched. It was an impatient, forward-striving age, quite ready to replace pumpkin pie with vanilla ice cream.

> "Shades of our grandmothers!" exclaimed the editor of the *Delineator* in 1910. "Only the turkey left as an apology for the original dinner. Think of biscuit tortoni and angel cake usurping pumpkin and mince pie and raised doughnuts! Think of tomato salad, Bermuda potatoes and stuffed peppers taking the place of the home-grown vegetables of the farm!'
>
> "Would it not be worthwhile for those who stand for Americanism to cherish and resurrect with other antiques the original Thanksgiving dinner with its traditional menu?"

The campaign to restore old-fashioned customs was supported enthusiastically by middle-class homemakers fearful of the foreign customs brought by new immigrants and weary of the ceaseless mimicking of European customs by the well-to-do. Women who chose to have their homes, their food, their children's education, their religion, their books and their world view be all-American desired to have their Thanksgivings be American style as well. For turn-of-the-century Americans, the authentic Americanism of a custom was proven by establishing an origin no later than the Federal period. This was the first generation to make "old-fashioned" a synonym for "fashionable." Magazine editors and patriotic ladies searched for certifiably old-fashioned Thanksgiving recipes, menus and customs in an effort to enhance their enjoyment of Thanksgiving Day by closely linking its celebration with the generation of the Founding Fathers.

French dishes gave way on Thanksgiving tables to pumpkin and mincemeat pie and to such all-American novelty items as corn soup garnished with popcorn. Centerpieces featured turkey or Pilgrim figurines, and hollowed-out pumpkins did service as fruit baskets. During Thanksgiving week, churches, schools and other organizations sponsored Thanksgiving pageants featuring a play depicting a colonial or revolutionary era Thanksgiving Day, followed by the recitation of Thanksgiving poems and singing of harvest hymns.

Thanksgiving and International Affairs

The arena in which the patriotic societies emphasized Americanism and American traditions was a complex society comprising many groups, issues and ideas. Pan-Americanism, a belief in the value of cooperation among the nations of the western hemisphere, enjoyed popular support as a diplomatic policy, but it ran into difficulties when it encroached on Thanksgiving Day.

In 1909, Monsignor William Russell of Saint Patrick's Church in Washington, D.C., has the novel idea that a Thanksgiving Day Mass attended by President William Howard Taft and the ambassador of each of the American republics would be an appropriate expression of the spirit of Pan-American unity.

Each year of Taft's term in office, the president and the Washington diplomatic corps responded to Russell's formal invitations by attending Thanksgiving Day Mass at St. Patrick's Church in full diplomatic dress. In honor of the occasion, the sanctuary was hung with the flags and crests of the American nations, and diplomats were carefully seated according to the protocol of rank and station.

The Pan American Mass, as it was called, was such a success that in 1912 the Pan American Union congratulated itself on the "dignified and official character which the occasion has now assumed." Labeling the Mass "official" was a fatal mistake because American Protestants were ill-disposed to hear that the Catholic church had abrogated to itself the role of host of the "official" celebration of this American holiday. Even though the government had never designated an official national Thanksgiving service, the attendance of President Taft for four years and of President Woodrow Wilson in 1913 did give the Pan American Mass the aura of an official observance.

Representatives of the Protestant clergy and of the American Federation of Patriotic Societies urged President Wilson to remove his official sanction from the Mass by attending his own church on Thanksgiving Day. Evangelical ministers expressed a greater degree of concern, calling Wilson's attendance a "great danger to civil and religious institutions." But the most ardent protests were those incited by the virulently anti-Catholic weekly *The Menace*, which used the issue of the Pan American Mass as an opportunity to fan the anti-Catholic prejudices of members of such nativist patriotic societies as the Guardians of Liberty, Select Circle of True Americans, Daughters of America and Order of the Knights of Luther. These working class organizations gave crude expression to the same xenophobic sentiments that the well-to-do members of the DAR and the Colonial Dames politely expressed. Surprised by the furor, Wilson declined to attend in 1914, and the Pan American Mass withered.

World War I

Although they would have preferred not to, Americans were

forced to pay attention to world affairs when war began in Europe in the summer of 1914. Upper-class Americans were immediately ready to intervene on behalf of England and France, but most Americans wanted no part of this European conflict. Many immigrants, after all, had come to America preciely to escape Europe's endless wars. Irish-Americans opposed any British alliance, and German-Americans, who would have liked to have sided with their fatherland, strove to maintain American neutrality. For three years, America stayed out of the stalemated war, until the German policy of unrestricted submarine warfare brought the country into the war in April 1917, on the side of the Allies.

Once the die was cast, America embarked on a short, glorious march to victory. Twenty months after Congress declared war Germany surrendered, making America the most powerful nation on earth. Americans, however, were more apprehensive than ever about threats to their way of life from foreign immigrants and from such foreign ideologies as bolshevism.

While the boys were fighting in Europe, patriotism flourished at home. There was only one wartime Thanksgiving Day, and Americans used it to display their national eagerness to beat "the Hun." At 4 o'clock, Eastern Standard Time, on Thanksgiving, patriotic citizens under the auspices of the National Council of Women assembled in towns across the nation to sing "The Star-spangled Banner"; George M. Cohan went to the Brooklyn Navy Yard to sing "Over There" for the sailors; and all of the boys in uniform feasted on traditional turkey dinners. In France, specially detailed officers had scoured the countryside for two weeks before the holiday to find enough turkeys to feed the troops.

On the home front, Thanksgiving was "Hooverized." Herbert Hoover made the Food Administration one of the great success stories of the war. Under his guidance, Americans reduced consumption of such key foodstuffs as wheat, meat, fats and sugars needed to feed the troops and the hungry civilian population of Europe. Wartime food exports reached three times the ordinary volume. Patriotic Thanksgiving tables in 1917 and 1918 were set with rye and corn bread instead of wheat and with vegetables grown in backyard victory gardens. Housewives avoided tomatoes, oysters, oranges and other food stuffs that would occupy space in railroad cars that were needed to move war supplies to Europe. Americans dining on homegrown string beans, potatoes, pumpkins and corn bread congratulated themselves on having achieved a really old-fashioned Thanksgiving menu of homegrown produce just like the Pilgrims ate at the first Thanksgiving.

Parades and Sports Intrude on Thanksgiving

After the war, America rushed headlong into the twentieth century. The values of religious faith, rural life, home and family that Thanksgiving represented were eclipsed by new ways of thinking and living. Victorian standards of behavior, which had lingered in the first two decades of the twentieth century, collapsed in the 1920s. Thanksgiving lost prestige in a society where the trend setters sneered at religion, farm life was derided as fit only for rubes and hayseeds and young people regarded their elders with disdain.

But the most direct blow to Thanksgiving Day came from retail merchants and advertising copywriters. After three centuries as a holiday in its own right, Thanksgiving was rudely demoted to serve as the official opening day of the Christmas shopping season. The idea of giving Christmas gifts was far from new—it had been observed even in American Protestant families since the mid-nineteenth century when descendants of the Puritans had abandoned their opposition to the celebration of Christmas. But it took Madison Avenue advertising techniques to expand the custom to epidemic proportions, and Madison Avenue saw Thanksgiving as a handy way to promote Christmas sales.

In 1921, Gimbel's Department Store in Philadelphia sponsored the first Thanksgiving parade designed to kick off and promote the holiday buying season. The idea caught on, and by the end of the decade, Thanksgiving Day-Christmas parades were sponsored by department stores in cities across the country. They usually featured Santa Claus himself waving at the children from the last float. Along with Santa's workshop and displays of new toys, floats included depictions of scenes from children's literature, and nursery tales and popular cartoon characters. And, in 1938, as America prepared for another war, Uncle Sam made his debut as a giant balloon in the Macy's parade in New York. There were also turkeys, Indians, replicas of the *Mayflower* and depictions of the first Thanksgiving; but such gestures to Thanksgiving traditions failed to appease critics of the parades.

In 1926, the Allied Patriotic Societies objected to the parade on the grounds that it would interfere with church attendance and was an undesirable commercialization of an important American holiday. The charge of commercialization could not be rebutted. Macy's responded to the cliam of interference with churchgoing by scheduling the parade for 1:00 P.M. that year, but it was soon back in its morning time slot. The afternoon schedule would conflict with Thanksgiving football games and by the 1920s, that was the more serious conflict for many families.

Football, played by college and high school teams before local fans, gripped the nation more firmly than ever. The dinner hour, once set to coincide with the return of the faithful from morning church services, was now scheduled to avoid conflict with the football game.

Prosperous and gay, Americans paid little heed to tradition in the 1920s. Old-fashioned was a term of opprobrium. Traditional Thanksgiving dinners were still served, Thanksgiving sermons delivered, Thanksgiving pageants performed and Thanksgiving charity given—but the young and modern viewed these activities with restless impatience. Loyal members of the patriotic societies had made real headway in teaching immigrants to conform to American mores and to celebrate this American holiday, but their own children preferred football and parades to church services and family dinners. It would take hard times to bring renewed dedication to the traditional values of the holiday.

The Fourth Thursday in November 15

A decade of prosperity ended aburptly in October 1929 with a stock market crash that ushered in the Great Depression, bringing years of hunger and poverty to a nation that had believed itself immune to destitution. At the height of the depression, one-third of the labor force was unemployed, leaving millions of American families without homes, jobs, money or any hope of obtaining them.

Thanksgiving Day was a sad holiday for families struggling just to keep ahead of hunger. Generous individuals increased their charitable activities, but private charity was wholly unequal to the task of feeding half a nation. In 1932, Americans voted to elect a president who promised them a "new deal"—Franklin Delano Roosevelt, a great leader in an hour of great need. He implemented bold new programs designed to restore economic health, and did not hesitate to change hoary traditions in order to address the problems at hand.

Beginning in 1869, and following Abraham Lincoln's exam-

ple, an unbroken chain of presidential Thanksgiving proclamations had been issued for the last Thursday in November. There
was no legal requirement that presidents choose this date, not
even any legal mandate that Thanksgiving be declared at all—the
proclamation was issued wholly at the president's discretion. But
just as surely as Independence Day fell on July fourth and Christmas Day on December twenty-fifth, the last Thursday of November was Thanksgiving Day. And so it was for three-quarters of a
century, until, in 1939, Franklin Roosevelt reshuffled the
November calendar, dealing out a new date for Thanksgiving—
seven days early.

Roosevelt's Controversial Proclamation

The year 1939 was one of hope that the depression was ending at last, mixed with apprehension that some false step might
delay progress on the road to recovery. Economic health seemed
to have returned to the nation's factories and shops. But, retail
merchants warned, with the last Thursday in November scheduled to fall on the 30th, there would be only 24 days, and only 20
shopping days between Thanksgiving and Christmas—not
enough time for a strong holiday selling season. So the National
Retail Dry Goods Association did the logical thing: it asked President Roosevelt to move Thanksgiving.

Although no president had ever complied with such a
request, the request itself was not unprecedented. Knowing that
before the Civil War Thanksgiving had been observed on varying
dates, a number of groups had requested such a change. For
example, in 1935, the Sea Food Advisory Committee noted that
once in seven years Christmas, Thanksgiving, New Year's Day,
Washington's Birthday and the Fourth of July all fall on a Thursday or a Friday, putting a major dent in seafood consumption for
the week. Therefore, the committee recommended that Thanksgiving Day be permanently shifted to the last Tuesday in November.

Small numbers of veterans and shopkeepers were allied in the 1920s and 1930s in suggesting that Thanksgiving Day and Armistice Day be combined. The veterans urged such a move because they saw the holiday commemorating the end of the First World War fading from the national consciousness. Merchants concurred because two holidays in one month generally caused a falloff in retail sales. The national Retail Dry Goods Association's 1939 appeal was actually its second request of the kind; in 1933, when the last Thursday also fell on November 30, the association had asked President Roosevelt to move Thanksgiving up a week. He had refused, citing the confusion that such a move would bring.

It is true that an occasional post–Civil War governor had set Thanksgiving on other than the traditional last Thursday, mostly for flagrantly political reasons. Several southern governors made political hay by proclaiming the celebration on other than the presidentially appointed day during Reconstruction. In 1893, at the height of agrarian agitation protesting currency policy and favoring free coinage of silver, Oregon's Populist governor Sylvester Pennoyer emphasized his disagreement with Democratic president Grover Cleveland by proclaiming November 23 Thanksgiving Day in Oregon when Cleveland proclaimed November 30 for the nation.

But these proclamations of untraditional dates were so few and so long ago as to be forgotten in 1939 when Roosevelt jolted the nation by selecting November 23 as Thanksgiving Day. A vacationing president made the announcement at an informal press conference at the family summer home on Campobello Island. President Roosevelt explained that retailers wanted a longer Christmas shopping season, and said he hoped that the extra week gained by moving Thanksgiving would boost sales.

The announcement made front-page headlines around the nation, as a storm of protest swirled, led by Republicans and traditionalists—not to mention football coaches who had scheduled the "big game" for what they thought would be a holiday. The National Retail Dry Goods Association estimated that the extra shopping week would increase sales by as much as 10 percent, but other Americans were not convinced that this was worth the price of displacing a national institution. The ensuing controversy pro-

*President and Mrs. Roosevelt
usually spent Thanksgiving at the
Warm Springs Foundation,
founded by the Roosevelts to help
polio victims. Each year, one young
patient was given the privilege of
sitting beside the President. Young
Robert Rosenbaum is shown
watching President Roosevelt carve
on Thanksgiving Day, 1938.*

vided a much needed field day for politicians, editorial cartoonists and Americans who had for too long been preoccupied with weightier problems.

In any direction one chose to look in August 1939, the world was in trouble. In Spain, a vicious civil war had just ended in victory for fascists. Germany was persecuting its Jewish citizens, seizing territory from Czechoslovakia and aggressively rearming. No one could be sure who Germany intended to attack, but when the Russo-German nonagression treaty was signed on August 23, it became clear that the West was vulnerable to a German threat. Italy, under the fascist Benito Mussolini, had already invaded and conquered Ethiopia, while Japan had invaded China and intended to conquer and rule much of the Pacific. It was a tremendous relief to have something as innocuous to worry about as the proper date for Thanksgiving.

No sooner had the president's intentions been made known than partisans appeared to argue both sides of the question. Walter Hoving, president of Lord & Taylor department store, predicted that as much as one billion dollars in additional business might be generated throughout the economy by the extra shopping week. Frederick A. Gimbel, of Gimbel Brothers department stores, concurred, stating, "We all know that it is an American tradition to begin Christmas shopping after Thanksgiving."

Governor Leverett Saltonstall of Massachusetts disagreed emphatically, "Not for revelry and sport, and not for the inauguration of Christmas shopping, is this day set apart." The governor declared: " The purpose of this proclamation is, without sham or pretense, to call upon our people to give thanks to the power that has made and preserved us as a nation."

"What in the name of common sense has Christmas buying to do with it?" thundered Reverend Norman Vincent Peale from the pulpit of New York's Marble Collegiate Church. "It makes no difference what day is set apart for Thanksgiving, but it is questionable thinking and contrary to the meaning of Thanksgiving for the President of this great nation to tinker with a sacred religious day on the specious excuse that it will help Christmas sales. The next thing we may expect Chirstmas to be shifted to May 1 to help the New York World's Fair of 1940."

Here the argument was drawn. On one side stood those who

would change a traditional date for commercial reasons; on the other, those who knew that traditions draw part of their value from remaining unchangable in a changing world. Thankful prayers are assuredly acceptable to the Almighty at any time of the year, but would not the holiday lose some of its meaning if the date were fixed in a conscious attempt to maximize department store profits? A shopkeeper in Kokomo, Indiana, who saw the humor in the controversy, hung a sign in his window: "Do your shopping now. Who knows, tomorrow may be Christmas."

Because President Roosevelt's proclamation officially set the date for Thanksgiving only for the District of Columbia, state governors faced the task of deciding whether to proclaim Thanksgiving Day on the traditional or New Deal date. Republican Governor Clarence A. Bottolfsen of Idaho promptly declared that he did not believe that a "tradition as sacred to Americans as Thanksgiving should be tampered with," and set the Idaho celebration for November 30. Republican Governor Lewis Orrin Barrows of Maine said that FDR could have Thanksgiving whenever he wanted to, "but we in Maine will continue to have our Thanksgiving the same time as we have down through the years." In South Carolina, however, Democratic Governor Burnet Rhett Maybank declared, "Surely I will issue (the) same proclamation as President Roosevelt."

Politician watchers, spotting a pattern, began to call November 23 the Democratic Thanksgiving and November 30 the Republican Thanksgiving Day. A New York *Times* editorial writer suggested that if the Republican and Democratic national chairmen would take up residence on opposite sides of the international date line, they could enjoy Christmas on different days, too.

While cartoonists and orators had a field day, state attorneys general were faced with deciding which of two Thanksgiving proclamations would create a legal holiday in states where some employees were legally entitled to a day off on all presidentially and gubernatorially appointed holidays. Attorney General Williamson of Oklahoma decided that banks in that state would close on the 23rd, although the governor had set Thanksgiving Day on the 30th. Williamson's legal opinion included this poem:

Thirty days hath September,
April, June and November;
All the rest have thirty-one.
Until we hear from Washington.

Colorado law required that the state observe both holidays, but Republican Governor Ralph Carr vowed to eat no turkey on the 23rd. Republican Senator Styles Bridges of New Hampshire said he wished that while he was at it, "Mr. Roosevelt would abolish winter;" and Republican Governor Nels Hanson Smith of Wyoming commended Roosevelt for finally instituting a change "which is not imposing any additional tax on the taxpayers."

Some mayors stepped into the controversy. The mayor of Atlantic City proclaimed November 23 as "Franksgiving" and November 30 as Thanksgiving and saw his city enjoy profitable holiday trade on both weekends. Up in Massachusetts, the Plymouth town council invited President and Mrs. Roosevelt to attend a "real" Thanksgiving dinner on November 30. Democratic Mayor William Pattern of Torrington, Connecticut, proclaimed November 23 Thanksgiving Day for his fellow townsmen, but they resolutely ignored his proclamation and celebrated instead on the traditional last Thursday as proclaimed by the Republican governor. Mayor George Leach of Minneapolis may have had the final word when he declared Thanksgiving to last from 12:01 A.M., November 23 until 11:59 P.M., November 30, and admonished the citizenry, "Let your conscience be your guide."

The nation that willingly backed Roosevelt on nearly every new program he proposed did not want its Thanksgiving timed to increase retail trade. Sixty-two percent of the people polled told George Gallup's Institute of Public Opinion that they disapproved of Roosevelt's plan to move Thanksgiving. Significantly, 79 percent of the Republicans, but only 48 percent of the Democrats, disapproved on the new date.

Even more upset than the politicians were college football coaches and athletic directors who had scheduled the "big game" for what would now be an ordinary Thursday. At the University of California at Los Angeles, the athletic director was philosophical: "Guess we will have to play on a nonholiday weekend and send the President the bill for our loss." But down in Arkansas, Coach Bill Walton of Ouachita College was fighting mad. He threatened that "We will vote the Republican ticket if he interferes with our football."

Dozens of college and high school teams traditionally played the last game of the season on Thanksgiving Day or Thanksgiving weekend, usually reserving the date for a contest with an arch rival. Teams tried desperately to juggle their schedules, but programs arranged months in advance could not easily be changed on short notice. In Texas, the annual contest between the University of Texas Longhorns and the Aggies of A&M was scheduled for the traditional date, November 30. Since the Longhorns were scheduled to play Texas Christian and the Aggies to meet Rice on November 18, moving the big game up to November 23 would leave the teams with only four days between contests, too little time to prepare for such an important game. Governor W. Lee O'Daniel played a hero's role in resolving the dilemma by proclaiming two Thanksgiving Day holidays for Texas, one to coincide with the presidential proclamation and one on the date of the Texas–A&M football match.

Most Texans were pleased, but the mayor of little McGregor, Texas, set an independent course. The McGregor High School football team was scheduled to play the team from nearby Gatesville High on Friday, November 24, so Friday, declared the mayor, would be Thanksgiving Day in McGregor. New Jersey's Democratic governor complied with President Roosevelt's choice of dates and the president of Rutgers State University obediently let the students go home to Thanksgiving dinner on November 23, but gave them a second holiday on November 30 to travel to Rhode Island for the Rutgers–Brown game.

When the dust settled, 23 states celebrated on November 23, 23 waited until November 30 and, in Texas and Colorado, Thanksgiving Day came twice.

Many individual Americans were dissatisfied with the gubernatorially selected dates. William P. Carroll, 77 years old, lived in Portland, Maine, which, along with the rest of New England, had held to the traditional date. Carroll, who was once Portland's town crier, was a Roosevelt man; so on November 23 he donned frock coat and silk hat and marched through Portland, followed by two bands of Democratic musicians. The little parade halted at intersections while Carroll made pro-Roosevelt Thanksgiving speeches to passersby who were hurrying about their weekday business.

Lewis O. Barrows, governor of the state of Maine, attended the annual banquet of the New England Conference on November 23 in Boston where a misguided chef prepared a turkey dinner for the assembled dignitaries. Governor Barrows grandly waved it away: "You wouldn't eat oysters in July," he said, "you wouldn't watch a football game in April, and you wouldn't eat a turkey on November twenty-third." Whereupon the governor ceremoniously drew a can of sardines from his pocket and ate them for dinner.

New York celebrated Thanksgiving on November 23, but on November 30 Federal District Judge Robert Inch adjourned court at 12:15, wished the federal grand jury "a very pleasant holiday" and went home to eat Thanksgiving dinner. Judge Inch was a Republican. Like the stalwart judge, many Republicans and nonpartisan traditionalists stubbornly celebrated Thanksgiving on the last Thursday in November.

Since Thursday was the traditonal "cook's day off," two Thanksgivings meant that hundreds of maids, cooks, chauffeurs and other domestic workers would go three weeks without a day off. Reasoning that one more Thanksgiving would hardly be noticed, domestic staff in Hollywood, California, declared a third Thanksgiving Day for November 16. A dinner dance was planned in a downtown ballroom with Arthur Treacher, famous for portraying butlers in the movies, as guest of honor.

There was genuine confusion when Thanksgiving Day arrived. Connecticut residents who commuted to work in New York had a holiday on November 23. Their children, however, had school that day, since Connecticut celebrated on November 30. Kansas City, Missouri, observed the New Deal date, while Kansas City, Kansas, held to the traditional last Thursday in November. Washington State observed the 23, but little Clarkston, Washington, celebrated on November 30 along with Lewiston, Idaho, its larger neighbor across the Snake River. Railroads and airlines tried to please everybody by serving turkey dinners on both Thursdays, with American Airlines covering its bet by serving turkey on all five Thursdays in November. In New York Broadway theaters held Thanksgiving matinees both weeks.

The War Intrudes

Despite controversy, rhetoric and confusion, most Americans enjoyed Thanksgiving Day in traditional style. There were family dinners, football games, charitable donations and church sermons. When Americans listened to Thanksgiving sermons or paused quietly to count their blessings in 1939, it was clear that the nation had a great deal to be thankful for. The long depression seemed to be over at last. More dramatically, although World War II had begun in Europe in September and Japan continued its aggression in China, Americans still considered themselves safe from war. President Roosevelt offered thanks in his Thanksgiving proclamation that "in a world of turmoil we are at peace," carefully respecting the strong neutralist sentiment in the nation by avoiding further reference to the international situation.

Americans looked with horror at the actions of the fascist governments of Spain, Japan, Italy and Germany—especially Germany—and found a theme for Thanksgiving Day 1939: thankfulness for the civil liberties that citizens of this nation enjoy under the Constitution and the Bill of Rights. Just as governors of Massachusetts had done during the Revolution and Civil War, Governor Leverett Saltonstall put the feelings of the nation into words when he proclaimed:

> Let us be thankful for democracy which holds that every person is valuable because he is a person.
>
> When we remember how autocracies enslave the bodies, minds and consciences of men; how ferociously they suppress criticism, how rigidly they censor speech and press, education and religion; when we remember their persecution and blood purges, then with utter sincerity we should thank God for the Bill of Rights incorporated in the Constitution of the United States.

Americans were increasingly preoccupied by events in Europe in 1940. Even isolationists found that opposing entry into the war took large amounts of time and energy. Roosevelt's announced intention to proclaim the third Thursday in November as Thanksgiving Day stirred up little controversy in 1940; it was overshadowed by the great question of America's proper role in the war.

President Roosevelt stepped up aid to England under his policy to do everything "short of war" to defeat Hitler and restrain Japan. Even the 1940 presidential election campaign aroused less interest than concern about the war. At the nominating conventions, Roosevelt defied precedent by running for a third term, while Republicans passed over prominent isolationist candidates to nominate Wendell Willkie, who, like Roosevelt, was a proponent of aid to the Allies. Willkie, casting about for issues to enliven a dull campaign, announced that, if elected, he would restore Thanksgiving Day to the traditional last Thursday in November.

November 1940 saw half a nation celebrate Thanksgiving on November 21 and the other half on November 28. While citizens of Plymouth, Massachusetts, celebrated Thanksgiving Day on November 28, Nazi warplanes dropped death and destruction on old Plymouth, England. Americans leaving the annual Thanksgiving pageant reenacting the first Thanksgiving at Memorial Hall, in Plymouth, were met by newsboys crying the headlines: "Germans bomb Plymouth! Two hundred tons of bombs fall on Plymouth." The time had come for America to worry about more serious questions; proponents of both dates for Thanksgiving were prepared to work out a compromise.

Government and business groups, surveying the effect of earlier Thanksgiving days on Christmas shopping in 1939 and 1940, agreed that there had been no increase in business; some even found that the ensuing confusion had hurt sales in their areas. At a news conference on May 20, 1941, the president announced that, since moving Thanksgiving up a week had not increased retail sales, he intended to restore the traditional date in 1942. Thanksgiving Day 1941, with calendars already printed and football schedules already made up, would be celebrated on the third Thursday.

Americans generally nodded in quiet approval of an end to two years of needless holiday confusion, but the conservative editors of *Time* magazine had a field day with the news:

President Admits Mistake
    At the start of the New Deal, President Roosevelt
announced that he would admit his own mistakes and correct
them. Last week, just eight years, two inaugurals and two
months later (a total of 2,986 days) he announced for the first
time that he had found one.

Even after the president agreed to restore Thanksgiving to its
traditional date, some feared that a holiday set by a politician's
proclamations was too vulnerable to future political abuse. Several congressmen, therefore, introduced bills to establish Thanksgiving as a national holiday, fix the date by statute, and put an
end to the potential for abuse in the fact that, in the words of
Ogden Nash:

> Thanksgiving, like Ambassadors, Cabinet officers and others
>   smeared with political ointment,
> Depends for its existence on Presidential appointment.

Thus on November 26, 1941, President Roosevelt signed a bill
establishing the fourth Thursday in November as Thanksgiving
Day. The choice of the fourth Thursday, which is the last Thursday in the month five years out of seven, was a compromise
between supporters of the traditional and New Deal dates.
    The Thanksgiving date controversy, which ought to have
been settled by this law, was revived when politicians noticed
that in 1944, 1945, 1950 and 1956, November would have five
Thursdays. Some congressmen wanted to change the law to set
Thanksgiving Day on the last Thursday, but most agreed with
Louisiana's Senator John Holmes Overton that the date did not
matter much, "Just so they have one, and tell me in time to get
myself a turkey." Still, a few governors preferred the traditional
date and exercised their prerogative of proclaiming it. Idaho,
Arkansas, Nebraska, Tennessee, Virginia and Texas celebrated
on November 30, 1944, although Fort Smith and Fayetteville,
Arkansas, preferred to break with their governor and join the
nation on November 23. Georgia, meanwhile, celebrated twice.
By 1956, the Lone Star State alone celebrated on the traditional
last Thursday. Since then, the nation has united in giving thanks
on the fourth Thursday in November.

Wartime Thanksgiving

Americans who paused to give thanks on November 20 and November 27, 1941, were grateful to be living in a land of freedom and plenty, but they were acutely aware that their world was not at peace. The United States was poised to fight a war that many still hoped it would not have to enter. President Roosevelt sacrificed his customary Thanksgiving holiday at Warm Springs, Georgia, to stay in Washington because of concern about the situation in the Far East. Their son and daughter-in-law, Captain and Mrs. James Roosevelt, joined President and Mrs. Roosevelt for dinner at the White House.

Many young people had already enlisted in the expectation that American entry into the war was inevitable. Soldiers and sailors in training camps throughout the nation and at bases in Hawaii, Greenland and Newfoundland feasted on turkey on Thanksgiving day, but troops stationed in Iceland did not. Officers there decided to postpone Thanksgiving dinner until a delayed shipment of turkey and cranberries reached the base. In New York, servicemen on furlough were given free tickets to theater matinees, football games and radio broadcasts. British Foreign Secretary Anthony Eden addressed the Thanksgiving banquet of the American Society in London, telling Americans that "Our faiths are one; our causes are one and our aims are one."

Still, American isolationists strove to keep America out of the war, while the president and others who saw the values that the nation stands for threatened by Nazi hegemony sought ways to help England resist the German threat. Any serious efforts to maintain American neutrality ended with the Japanese bombing of Pearl Harbor, Hawaii, at dawn on December 7, 1941. America was at war.

Clearly, this would be a long war, with Allied victory ensured only by harnessing American industrial might to war production. Munitions factories worked long hours, with no break for holidays. Metals, silk, gasoline and rubber were rationed to make these essential commodities available for war use. Americans backed the war effort by buying war bonds, working overtime and doing without materials needed by the armed forces. In

November 1942, Macy's department store contributed to the war effort by canceling its annual Thanksgiving Parade: trucks to pull the floats squandered scarce gasoline and moreover, the giant balloons were made of rubber, a precious material needed for the war. Santa Claus, Superman, the clown, the elephant and the other balloons contained 650 pounds of rubber, but before they were melted down the dragon was inflated one last time. In front of New York's City Hall, Macy's President Jack Struass presented the 60-foot balloon and a dagger to Mayor Fiorello La Guardia. The diminutive mayor, victor in many a political battle, circled the beast, grasped the dagger and slew the dragon.

Since midsummer 1940, Britain had stood alone against the Nazi onslaught. The arrival of American troops to relieve the beleaguered nation in 1942 meant that, high though the price would be, Allied victory was attainable. Hundreds of thousands of GIs were stationed in Great Britain during the war, and the English developed a genuine fondness for their casual, gum-chewing, slang-speaking allies. The people of the two nations "divided by a common language" regularly surprised one another with unfamiliar phrases, customs and ideas. When autumn came, England learned that its erstwhile colonies had invented a holiday. British interest was piqued when the American command announced that, at the request of enlisted men, the thousands of turkeys specially shipped from the United States for Thanksgiving dinner would be donated to British hospitals. American forces would dine on roast pork and apple sauce with old-fashioned plum pudding for dessert.

Alerted by the donated turkeys to the importance of Thanksgiving Day for their American allies, the British were inspired to make Thanksgiving Day the occasion for gestures of unity between the two peoples. King George and Queen Elizabeth invited 200 officers and 25 nurses to the first Thanksgiving party ever held at Buckingham Palace. Old Glory flew beside the Union Jack on buildings throughout London on Thanksgiving Day, and souvenir hawkers crying "Wear your colors" did land-office business in cardboard badges showing entwined American and British flags.

Other Englishmen and women, realizing that young Americans away from home on a holiday for the first time would miss family most, arranged for parties of GIs and British children to spend the holiday afternoon together. Catholic soldiers gathered for services at Westminster Cathedral and Jewish soldiers prayed at London's New West End Synagogue.

Hundreds of American soldiers gathered at Plymouth, England to pay homage to the Pilgrims who colonized Plymouth, Massachusetts, by praying at Saint Andrews, Plymouth's ancient parish church, on Thanksgiving Day. An American flag flew for the first time from Chorley, Lancashire, where an American officer prayed in the pew Miles Standish once occupied in the small parish church. At Boston, Lincolnshire, Americans toured the prison cells where the Pilgrim fathers were once imprisoned, and at Southampton, American troops stood at attention before the spot where the *Mayflower* was fitted out.

The dramatic highlight of that wartime Thanksgiving came when, for the first time in its 1,200-year history, Westminster Abbey was taken over by a foreign army. A quiet announcement had been made that a purely American Thanksgiving service would be held in the ancient abbey where English monarchs since the Norman conquest have been crowned and many lie buried. Soldiers began to arrive long before the service was scheduled to begin. Thousands filled every seat, blocked the side aisles and spilled out of the great doors where hundreds stood straining to hear snatches of the service and join in singing the hymns. Ambassador John Winant read President Roosevelt's Thanksgiving proclamation and four chaplains led the interdenominational Protestant service.

As the ministers and dignitaries filed down the center aisle toward the door, Corporal Heinz Arnold, who in civilian life had been organist of the Reformed Church of Patchogue on Long Island, struck up the opening chord of "God Bless America" on the organ. The combined voices of 4,000 young Americans rang out in the church and in the sunlight outside. To the hundreds of British gathered to see the American Thanksgiving, "It was marvelous to hear." As the soldiers emerged from the abbey, one young man paused on the threshold and remarked, "What a perfect football day! I wish I could see Cornell and Pennsylvania tee off."

At home, the crew of the light cruiser *Boise*, just returned

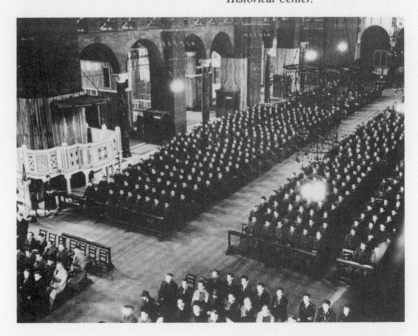

from the battle in the Solomon islands, were honored guests at the Cornell–Penn game in Philadelphia that day. After the game they were served dinner at a downtown hotel. Army camps around the nation served special Thanksgiving dinners, and soldiers on furlough were feted at service clubs, restaurants and private dinners. Plymouth, Massachusetts, bypassed its traditional Thanksgiving pageant to treat 300 servicemen and women to an old-fashioned Thanksgiving Dinner in Memorial Hall.

Maintaining old traditions seemed especially important in wartime, but some old Thanksgiving traditions gave way before the imperatives of defeating the Axis. Cooks were reminded to flatten tin cans for recycling, and the importance of conserving resources for war-related purposes meant that few Americans could travel home for the holiday. War plants kept up production with no holiday from work. General Dwight D. Eisenhower sent a message of thanks to workers who reported for their normal shifts, postponing Thanksgiving dinner until after quitting time. But, far from dampening spirits, wartime restrictions added to the national spirit of unity in the drive toward victory. On Thanksgiving Day Americans turned on their radios to hear a special broadcast from Independence Hall in Philadelphia, climaxed by the tapping out of the dot-dot-dot-dash victory code on the Liberty Bell.

Thanksgiving 1942 was the first of three Thanksgiving days that American soldiers would spend fighting the Axis powers. They fought for everything Thanksgiving symbolizes—for the bountiful homeland they loved, certainly, and to defend their homes and families, but also for a nation where people live in freedom, free to worship as they choose, free from tyranny and oppression. The effort to send home-style Thanksgiving dinners to soldiers at the front both symbolized the values for which they fought and demonstrated how thoroughly Americans at home backed the war effort. To Americans back home, it was terribly important to send real Thanksgiving dinners to the men and women overseas. That many civilians ate chicken for Thanksgiving Dinner seemed unimportant if only the troops used to K-rations and C-rations could have great helpings of hot turkey and cranberry sauce.

Thanksgiving Day 1942 found the American army slowly

advancing up the Italian boot from its base in Naples. The pressing work of clearing debris, repairing bridges and clearing roads for the heavy traffic of an advancing army could not stop for holiday celebrations, but the quartermaster resolved to provide a hot turkey dinner for every soldier in Italy. Army cooks sealed turkey, cranberry sauce, mashed potatoes and vegetables in special heat-retaining pouches and sent them into the mountains as far as jeeps and trucks could travel. When the roads became impassable, the dinners were loaded on pack mules. Where rainstorms had washed out bridges, Thanksgiving dinner was hurled across the freshets to soldiers waiting on the opposite bank, and where U.S. units had penetrated close to the enemy, Thanksgiving dinner was carried to the front lines under cover of night. Some units proudly heated their meals in captured German field kitchens.

Each Thanksgiving of the war, the Army made good on its promise that "nobody gets canned turkey," although 12-ounce cans of turkey were sent to prisoners of war in Japan and Germany under Red Cross auspices. Troops fighting to retake Leyte Island in the Philippines on Thanksgiving Day 1944, stood ankle deep in mud to eat turkey, mashed potatoes, giblet gravy and pumpkin pie. The meals, brought by a Navy refrigerator ship, were passed out with ammunition as units rotated back from the fighting.

Troops in the United States on ships at sea and on every battlefront were fed real Thanksgiving dinners. In Algiers, in 1943, a cynic nourished too long on army food kept a copy of the official menu issued several days before the holiday. It read: "Grapefruit juice, roast turkey with giblet gravy, dressing, mashed potatoes, string beans, corn, cranberry sauce, celery, olives, pickles, hot rolls, butter, pumpkin pie, apples, tangerines, candy, nuts and coffee." On Thanksgiving Day, the cynic lost his bet when the quartermaster delivered all that was promised.

In Cairo, in 1942, Major General Ralph Royce dined on turkey sent as a gift by King Farouk, while two soldier teams worked off their dinners with a game of football. Some senior officers remembered and contrasted the fare with what they had gotten in the First World War. At that time, officers and men ate separately, and although the officers ate better, none of the food was as

Corporal Leo L. Keller from Whitman, West Virginia munches a drumstick on the French front. On Thanksgiving Day, 1944, hot turkey dinners were sent all the way to the front lines.

good or as abundant as that being sent on modern ships with freezer units. The GIs shared their bounty with their Allies, inviting British friends to dinner and sharing shipments of turkey with British units.

On every front Thanksgiving Day was a time when those in uniform remembered and missed the folks back home. Alex Haley, the prominent writer, later recalled the lonely Thanksgiving Day he spent as a coastguardsman serving aboard the U.S.S. *Murzim* in the South Pacific in 1943. In his capacity as ship's cook, Haley put in a long day serving roast turkey to his 200 shipmates before he had a few minutes to himself to reflect on the day's meaning. The young sailor, ruminating on the afterdeck, suddenly realized that "there were *people* to thank, people who had done so much for me that I could never possibly repay them. The embarrassing truth was I'd always just accepted what they'd done, taken it all for granted. . . . At least seven people had been particularly and indelibly helpful to me. I realized, with a gulp, that almost half of them had since died."

Three were still alive, though, and Haley sat down at a table in the mess to write letters of thanks to his father, his grandmother and his elementary school principal. Writing the letters eased the young man's homesickness. His reward, the best reward for a sailor far from home, was a letter from each in a mailbag that arrived some weeks later.

In 1944, Thanksgiving services were held at Saint Paul's American Church in Rome, as they had been from the time the church was built in 1879 until the last prewar service in 1941. That service was held without the pastor, who was in a fascist prison. Now, an interfaith service was held for soldiers and civilians in the liberated church. American forces in France in 1944 held Thanksgiving services at the great cathedrals of Reims and Notre Dame, the Rothschild Synagogue and the American Episcopal Church in Paris.

Soldiers at the front, of course, could not attend these services, but, like the unit described in this report under the wartime censorship dateline "With the Third Army," somewhere in France, 1944, they were sent hot dinners.

Down here on Thirty-fifth Division's front lines our artillery was booming at a rate that must have been maddening to the enemy, whose shells were coming in with uncomfortable accuracy. Back from foxholes knee deep in water came a squad of the 155th Infantry that had been relieved for the occasion. The men arrived wet and disconsolate in the little shell-torn village just behind their outpost. The sight of the town itself was enough to break anyone's spirit. . . . Most of the houses were just masses of brick and mortar without contour. These boys headed straight for a burned-out barn where, they had been told, they could make a rendezvous with the meal truck. The barn had four walls and part of a roof. . . .

Promptly at 11:30 a truck pulled up in front of the barn with great steaming cases of food. While it was being unloaded, the GI's started a fire in the barn and brewed their own coffee. Then they lined up with their mess kits and one of great moments of the year was at hand. Their eyes literally popped when they saw the generous portions and unexpected variety.

There were large slabs of turkey, a mound of potatoes with savory gravy, carrots, peas, raisin bread, butter, cookies and candy. And each man got a cigar. To make the meal complete, and this can be attributed to GI ingenuity, one of them discovered a barrel of excellent wine in a near-by cellar. This was served with the meal.

. . . when the feast was over the principal topics of conversation were home and their wives or girl friends. The war was not discussed, even though the conversation was blacked out on several occasions when shells fell too close for comfort or our batteries opened up on all sides. The only reference to the war was a unanimous opinion that Christmas would see the last of it and that this Thanksgiving dinner, their first in France, would certainly be their last.

In fact, the war in Europe continued until May, and, in the Far East, until Japan surrendered in August 1945. Tyranny was defeated and the men and women in the armed services came home. On Thanksgiving Day 1945, Americans gave thanks for a world of peace and for victory over Japanese and German aggression.

Tradition
in an
Irreverent Age_____ 16

Thanksgiving has been a vital part of American life for three
and a half centuries, reliable in its advent every autumn, yet
changing to accommodate new patterns in American culture. The
pious days of prayer set aside by the Puritans became jolly days of
family reunion in the young republic and the occasion of great
football matches in turn-of-the-century America. Thanksgiving
in our own generation has gracefully accommodated still more
new attitudes and inventions and, at the same time, maintains its
venerable traditions.

The central traditions of Thanksgiving Day as they are
observed in the 1980s would have been familiar to our great-
grandparents and are too commonplace to need lengthy description here. Families still gather for the holiday. Churches open as
they always have, ministers deliver Thanksgiving sermons and
presidents still color their Thanksgiving proclamations with the
tincture of partisan politics. Football teams do battle on Thanksgiving afternoon. And, of course, the traditional turkey dinner is

eaten by families across the land. All of these customs continue as they have for generations, but recent decades have added new twists to time-honored traditions.

Where an open sleigh once pulled into the farmhouse dooryard, sedans and station wagaons pull into suburban driveways. The vehicles that bring families home for Thanksgiving may have changed, but not the love that draws them together. The doors still open to release impatient children who rush into the waiting arms of grandparents; the trunk, like the hamper of old, is lined with carefully packed pies and vegetable dishes ready to be carried into a kitchen filled with the welcoming aroma of roasting turkey.

To be home for Thanksgiving is still, today, a national tradition and a personal imperative. By early afternoon on Wednesday, offices begin to empty and campuses are deserted, as Americans rush to get home for the holiday. Thanksgiving eve is the busiest travel day in the year. On Thanksgiving morning, the travelers and their hosts awaken to the pleasurable awareness that this is Thanksgiving Day, and their only mandatory task is to enjoy the holiday.

For millions of families, Thanksgiving begins with church services where the familiar harvest hymns are sung and sermons on giving thanks delivered. Others may either go to a Thanksgiving parade or watch one on television.

Television is a ubiquitous presence in the modern American household, on Thanksgiving as on other days. It may serve as a background as the family sets the table, greets guests, eats dinner and relaxes together, or it may provide the focus of attention for a family that sits, watching silently. Television networks, aware of the large holiday audience, provide special Thanksgiving programming from early morning until late at night, beginning with the Thanksgiving parades and continuing with football.

On Thanksgiving Day, since 1934, the Detroit Lions have played a Thanksgiving Day football game, always broadcast on national radio and, since 1956, on television. College and professional games have become Thanksgiving traditions. In the evening, the networks broadcast popular family movies and other entertainments, but for many football is the highlight of Thanksgiving on television. Indeed, 100 years and millions of enthusiastic fans have established football as an American Thanksgiving tradition.

Phrasing the Thanksgiving proclamation to serve political ends, a custom that predates the introduction of football, is an equally lively tradition today. The political issues may have changed but not the proclivity of politicians to seize an opportunity to promote favorite programs. "Thanksgiving has become a day when Americans extend a helping hand to the less fortunate," President Ronald Reagan told Americans in his proclamation for 1981, at a time when his conservative administration was making massive reductions in social welfare programs and urging that the needy be cared for by private charity. "Long before there was a government welfare program," Reagan continued, "this spirit of voluntary giving was ingrained in the American character." Americans opposed to the reductions gritted their teeth, while the president's supporters applauded.

President Lyndon Johnson managed to anger both liberal and conservative constituents with his Thanksgiving proclamations. In 1966, filled with enthusiasm for sweeping economic and social reforms designed to create a "Great Society," Johnson proclaimed that Americans ought to be grateful because

> Never, in all the hundreds of Thanksgiving Days, has our nation possessed a greater abundance, not only of material things, but of the precious intangibles that make life worth living. Never have we been better fed, better housed, better clothed. Never have so many Americans been earning their own way, and been able to provide their families with the marvelous products of a momentous age. Nor has America ever been healthier, nor had more of her children in school and in college. Nor have we even had more time for recreation and refreshment of the spirit, nor more ways and places in which to study and to enrich our lives through the arts.

Time magazine labeled this "one of the most palpably political Thanksgiving messages" in a century, coming as it did just a week before congressional elections. But, then, the magazine's conservative editors openly opposed Johnson's social programs.

In 1967, at a time of growing opposition to American involvement in Vietnam, Johnson told the nation in his proclamation that "We are engaged in a painful conflict in Asia which was not of our choosing, and in which we are involved in a sacred promise to help a nation which has been the victim of aggression." The liberal Protestant magazine *Christian Century* called the statement a deliberate untruth and, for the first time in its history, the magazine refused to publish a presidential Thanksgiving proclamation.

President John Kennedy managed to use his 1961 Thanksgiving proclamation to promote a favorite project without displeasing any political faction. "In the midst of our Thanksgiving," Kennedy suggested, "let us not be unmindful of the plight of those in many parts of the world to whom hunger is no stranger. . . . " He went on to praise the Food for Peace and Freedom from Hunger programs. America, in the second half of the twentieth century, began to realize that the abundance of its natural resources entailed an obligation, or at the very least, provided an opportunity to help the people of world's impoverished nations. In 1973, the Fast for a World Harvest campaign of the international relief agency Oxfam offered Americans a vivid way to express their commitment to end hunger in the world.

Oxfam America, which sponsors self-help development projects in the world's poorest regions, conceived the idea of asking Americans to fast on the Thursday before Thanksgiving and send the money they would have spent on food to the organization's headquarters. The fast gained immediate popularity on high school and college campuses, where food service mangers agreed to donate the cost of meals not eaten by fasting students. The number of participants has grown every year since. Participants gain a new realization of the blessing of abundant food and a deeper appreciation of Thanksgiving Day. The following letter, from an Oxfam supporter, shows how the fast helped one family realize how very much they had to be thankful for.

"What's for dinner, Mom?"

It was 6 o'clock. My two children were milling around the kitchen. My husband was just driving up from the office.

I smiled. "It's a surprise," I told them.

Usually we're your basic "meat-and-potatoes" family. But tonight was going to be different. Tonight was November 17th, a week before Thanksgiving. And like hundreds of thousands of other Americans, for me and my family, tonight was going to be Fast for a World Harvest night.

I wanted to help my family understand a little more about the one billion people in the world who go to bed hungry every night. Instead of a roast and vegetables, we were having just one thing: a modest bowl of white rice. And the money we saved on the meal we would send to Oxfam America for its work overseas.

I checked the rice.

"Dinner's ready!" I put the bowl on the table.

"So what's for dinner?" asked my husband.

"Rice."

"Is that all?"

"That's all—tonight we're going to eat like millions of people in the world eat every night."

I began to explain why this meal was a special meal. They'd heard me talk about world hunger before. But as they stared at the lonely bowl of rice, they began to realize what it might feel like to be hungry and not have enough to eat.

Helping the needy at Thanksgiving has deep roots in the holiday, but while the charitable impulse is as old as the juxtaposition of poverty and wealth, charity's favored recipients change with the times. Victorian Americans preferred to help poor children—just the children, not their presumably shiftless parents. During the Great Depression, charitable efforts were concentrated on helping families. Heads of families were given preference as workers were hired, and in 1930 charity workers distributing food baskets from New York City police stations regretfully but firmly turned away adult supplicants with no young children living at home. With not enough food to go around, preference was given to families with children to feed.

In the 1970s, elderly Americans became fashionable objects of philanthropy. Newspapers highlighted Thanksgiving dinners given at senior citizen centers quoting the elderly beneficiaries, just as reporters had once described nineteenth-century newsboys and settlement house waifs being treated to a Thanksgiving feast.

The yellow school bus has Vinnie Clifton at the wheel and he steers it gently, as if back through time, watching all the gray heads seated two-by-two in the rearview mirror and braking slowly as he pulls up to the Polish-American Hall [in Port Washington, New York].

The old people carefully disembark and the smell of roast turkey is in the hall already, wafting from the kitchen where Marie Doscher has the hall's women's auxiliary working on all burners. The greetings range from hugs to simple nods. Friends get together in little groups, and after Vinnie's second trip up from Main Street, 147 people have gathered for a Thanksgiving meal, beating the double-isolation of long years and suburbs. . . .

Rose Colon, for example, has to pause next to her husband, Joseph, trying hard to figure back when she last cooked a real Thanksgiving dinner with a family and a 20-pound turkey and the clean-up and the leftovers and all that.

"Ten, no, 12 years ago, after Rosemarie married and moved out," she says. "She was the last to go." The girl was one of four children the Colons raised here after moving from the Bronx 30 years ago to get "lots of country space for them." No regrets, they say; the children grew up fine and moved out on their own, and the Colons will have a second Thanksgiving meal tomorrow with their son, James, a New York City fireman and his family, farther out on the Island. . . .

"She cooked turkey, but lots of pasta, too," Frank Nitto, who is 81 now, says, recalling his mother, Domenica, preparing an early immigrant family holiday meal in Greenwich Village long ago. He needs a walker to get around to his friends here, but Mr. Nitto hardly deals in regret or the past tense. . . .

"I'm from upstate—and I don't mean Rockland—I mean real country, near Utica," Ruth Nitto says. "It was over the river and through the woods to grandmother's house, really, when I was a girl. My father had a horse and buggy!"

A trip over the river and through the woods to share Thanksgiving dinner with family remains the ideal Thanksgiving Day. Whether relatives have flown in for the week or come just for the afternoon, Thanksgiving dinner is the holiday's confidently anticipated highlight. Abundance is the hallmark of Thanksgiving dinner. Numerous side dishes, generous servings, rich ingredients, second helpings and luxurious desserts are enjoyed openly, and thoughts of calories and cholesterol are banished. Part of the enjoyment comes of knowing precisely what foods to expect on the Thanksgiving table and of savoring the dishes not merely as they appear on our plates, but also as we remember them from Thanksgiving days long ago.

A marksman loads his rifle while another contestant takes aim at the annual turkey shoot held at Old Strubridge Village, Massachusetts on the Saturday before Thanksgiving. Tourists stand in the background near the crate holding the turkey that the best marksman will win.

Participants in the Virginia Thanksgiving Festival kneel in prayer during a reenactment of the service of Thanksgiving held when settlers landed at Berkeley Hundred on December 4, 1619. The festival is held every year on the first Sunday in November.

Dinner on Thanksgiving has been preceded by grace since the first Thanksgiving dinner was eaten, and grace precedes Thanksgiving dinner today in thousands of families in which a blessing is asked before no other meal in the year. Fathers and grandfathers unaccustomed to offering public prayers awkwardly clear their throats and ask the Lord for His blessing because, after all, saying grace is a Thanksgiving tradition.

Interest in early American history has flourished in the modern era while religion has faded from its central position in American life. If asked to list Thanksgiving traditions, many people would think of turkey, cranberries and Pilgrims but omit grateful prayers and worship services—an ironic situation for a holiday conceived by pious people as an opportunity for prayer, but a true reflection of modern attitudes. Americans know far more about the ship on which the Pilgrims sailed, the food they ate and the clothes they wore than about the way they worshiped.

Lively interest in the details of colonial life is apparent in the re-creation of pioneer villages as popular tourist attractions. Virtually all of them present special programs at Thanksgiving time. At Old Sturbridge Village in Massachusetts, for example, men dressed in early nineteenth-century clothing hold a turkey shoot, albeit deferring to modern sensibilities by shooting at targets in place of live turkeys. At the Mystic, Connecticut, Seaport Museum, cookery buffs can learn to prepare an old-fashioned Thanksgiving feast over an open-hearth fire. But the largest crowds are drawn to those towns that claim to have hosted the first Thanksgiving.

Members of the Virginia Thanksgiving Festival unabashedly welcome visitors "to the celebration of America's first Thanksgiving—in Virginia." Every year on the first Sunday in November, tourists watch 38 men in period costume reenact the arrival of colonists at Berkeley Hundred in Virginia on December 4, 1619. Upon disembarking, the settlers fell to their knees and offered prayers of thanksgiving for their safe arrival. The modern-day reenactment of this event includes tribal dances performed by the Chickahominy Redmen Dancers and a lively program calculated both to delight spectators and "gain appropriate recognition for Virginia's documented claim to the first official Thanksgiving in America."

Plymouth, Massachusetts, has long considered itself to be the home of the first Thanksgiving, and most townsfolk still do, despite the objections of historians at Plimouth Plantation. Plimouth Plantation, the "living history museum of 17th Century Plymouth," features a carefully authenticated replica of the Pilgrim village as it looked in 1627. Tourists can watch costumed employees prepare and enjoy a seventeenth-century harvest feast, but, they will be told, the feast is not a Thanksgiving dinner. Plantation historians explain that Puritan Thanksgivings were irregularly scheduled days of thankful prayer. What the tourists are invited to watch is an English Harvest Home being celebrated in colonial New England style.

The town of Plymouth, regardless of what historians say, considers itself the home of the first Thanksgiving. On Thanksgiving Day, 55 Plymouth citizens, garbed to represent the settlers who survived the first winter in the wilderness and lived to celebrate the Plymouth Thanksgiving of 1621, walk in procession through the town toward the First Parish Church, where tourists are welcome to join the worshipers in an interdenominational service. Most of the nation subscribes, along with the people of Plymouth, to the legend of the first Thanksgiving there in 1621, for it is a wonderful story and, while it may be historically inaccurate to describe it as the ancestor of the modern Thanksgiving Day, the harvest feast of Pilgrims and Indians has been recounted for so many years that it has itself become a Thanksgiving tradition.

Traditions define a holiday and make it special. In any generation, they form a link with the past and comprise a heritage for future generations, valued by the individual as a way to participate in something that endures beyond a single lifetime. In our era of rapid, continuous and often disruptive cultural change, it is comforting to know that although the details of some customs may change, Thanksgiving endures, a lodestar in a changing landscape.

The Harvest Feast, A Culinary History Appendix

Thanksgiving dinner is a national institution. Each dish must be prepared, each condiment served, the very seasonings selected according to immutable laws codified beside the kitchen fire of a Pilgrim mother and not subject to modification by whim or culinary fashion. Americans would no sooner change the menu for Thanksgiving dinner than paint the White House beige. There is no substitute for turkey with chestnut stuffing. Or should it be sausage stuffing? Or simple herbed bread crumbs?

Alas, the menu is immutable only in idealized memories of the Thanksgiving dinners of childhood. In reality, dishes appear on contemporary Thanksgiving tables that were unheard of a century ago, and dishes that were once fixed traditions have disappeared. This, in the changeable realm of culinary fashion, is hardly surprising. More remarkable than the reality of change, though, is the strength of tradition, for some of the dishes on modern Thanksgiving tables have been served on Thanksgiving day for three centuries and more.

The first New England Thanksgiving dinners were prepared three and a half centuries ago in settlements freshly carved out of a rocky, forested wilderness by men and women interested in worshiping God, not in pampering the flesh. Thanksgiving was a day of prayer with a holiday meal wedged in between morning and afternoon services. Resources were scarce. Wives made a harvest feast with what they had at hand, and what they had were pumpkins, game, corn, pumpkins, fruit and more pumpkins.

Pompions, as pumpkins were first called, were easy to grow and would keep all winter long in a root cellar. They served the early colonists as a basic dietary staple, eaten at nearly every meal and in every possible preparation. In the words of one of America's first folksongs:

> For pottage and puddings and custards and pies
> Our pumpkins and parsnips are common supplies;
> We have pumpkin at morning and pumpkin at noon,
> If it was not for pumpkin, we should be undone.

Long before turkey was associated with Thanksgiving, the holiday was known for the special attention lavished by New England cooks on fancy pumpkin dishes. Pious Puritans, in fact, derided folk who paid more attention to Thanksgiving dinner than to Thanksgiving devotions by labeling the holiday St. Pompion's Day. Placed on the table beside whatever game the men of the family could shoot or buy from an Indian hunter, pumpkin pies, baked in large, square pans, were the first culinary Thanksgiving tradition.

Early Thanksgiving dinners were simple but ample, featuring fresh game, which was as likely to be venison, duck or goose as turkey, and Indian corn boiled or steamed as Indian pudding. Maple syrup and cranberries, which Indians taught the settlers to use, were also served. Cranberries, a native American fruit that once grew wild in salt bogs along the Atlantic coast, are harvested in the fall. Early settlers learned from the Indians how to dry the fruit for winter use.

The berries were prepared in the way seventeenth-century English settlers prepared apples, pumpkins, beach plums and, in fact, most fruits and vegetables. These women, unaccustomed to eating raw foods, chopped and stewed fruits in boiling water, sometimes adding herbs, sweetening or vinegar for flavor. The resulting dish they called sauce—apple sauce, pumpkin sauce, cranberry sauce. A seventeenth-century pumpkin recipe reads this way:

> But the Huswives manner is to slice them when ripe, and cut them into dice, and to fill a pot with them of two or three Gallons, and stew them upon a gentle fire the whole day, and as they sink, they fill again with fresh Pompions, not putting any liquor to them; and when it is stew'd enough, it will look like bak'd Apples; this they Dish, putting Butter to it, and a little Vinegar, (with some Spice, as Ginger, &c.) which makes it tart like an Apple, and so serve it up to be eaten with Fish or Flesh: It provokes Urin extreamly and is very windy.

Some families along the coast may have eaten oysters, clams and lobsters, but these shellfish were so abundant and easily gathered that they were deemed poor people's food; few wives would have chosen them for a feast day. Oats, rye, barley and wheat ground into flour and baked as bread or served boiled in pudding completed the feast.

The financial and culinary resources of the colonists grew during the years when Thanksgiving gained prominence as a holiday. By the early 1700s, savory dishes crowded Thanksgiving tables, and Thanksgiving dinner crowded the afternoon church service out of existence. New England was now a land of prosperous farmers, producing ample food and wealthy enough to trade for imported molasses and tea. Domesticated turkeys cackled in barnyards along with geese and chickens, pigs rooted in their pens, cows grazed in pastures and game could be hunted in the nearby forests. Farm families in this land of plenty commonly enjoyed three or four kinds of meat on Thanksgiving Day. Turkey would not become the star attraction of Thanksgiving dinner until the early nineteenth century.

In the 1700s and early 1800s, a turkey, goose or other bird would be roasted by suspending it directly over the fire by means of an iron hook or by impaling it on the central rod of a more elaborate culinary device known as a tin oven. The tin oven was made from a sheet of metal bent into a half cylinder, with its concave side set toward the fire in the open hearth. A spit ran through the axis, with a handle so that the bird skewered on it could be rotated. Drippings that fell to the bottom of the oven were ladled over the bird as it roasted. A child was often delegated to sit near the scorching fire turning the spit and basting the fowl.

Other fowl or joints of meat could also be cooked in a roasting pan. The meat was laid in a pan with slices of bacon, onions, spices and herbs. Then the pan was covered with a tight-fitting lid and set into the fire. Embers were heaped atop the lid. In the words of the author of a set of instructions for preparing turkey or mutton in this fashion:

> For turkey braised,
> The Lord be praised.

Besides roasting and braising, meats were boiled in large kettles, the special feature of Thanksgiving dinner being not the particular type of meat served, but the abundance of mutton, venison, beef, pork and poultry on the table. The presence of three or four kinds of meat emphasized the status of this meal as a major feast, but a chicken pie signified that the feast was Thanksgiving dinner. An extinct tradition, chicken pies were a Thanksgiving institution from the seventeenth century well into the nineteenth. In the words of Sarah Josepha Hale, "This pie, which is wholly formed of the choicest parts of fowls, enriched and seasoned with a profusion of butter and pepper, and covered with an excellent puff paste, is, like the celebrated pumpkin pie, an indispensable part of a good and true Yankee Thanksgiving."

Chicken pie, joints of meat and roasted poultry were accompanied by dishes of winter vegetables. Mashed pumpkin, turnip and potatoes, cabbage, succotash (dried corn and beans boiled until soft) appeared along with creamed onions—that is, onions served in freshly skimmed cream. There are families today for whom creamed onions are still a hallowed Thanksgiving tradition. Along with the vegetables came pickles, preserves and cranberry sauce, all washed down with cider.

Apple cider was the beverage of the New Englander, as beer is the drink of Germans and wine the choice of the French. Pressed from a carefully selected blend of tart and sweet apples, the unfiltered juice was stored in great hogsheads in every farmhouse basement. It fermented to become a sparkling, mildly alcoholic beverage. Farmers were proud of their individual blends and compared the cider of different farms and types of apples, as wines from different vineyards are compared.

Indians had introduced the colonists to pumpkins and cranberries; in return, the colonists introduced the Indians to cider. A story is told of Reverend Whiting, a seventeenth-century minister of Lynn, Massachusetts, who, like all New England householders, always had a barrel of apple cider on tap for guests.

> Mr. Whiting had a score of apple trees from which he made cyder. And it hath been said yt an Indian once coming to hys house and Mistress Whiting giving him a drink of ye cyder, he did sett down ye pot and smaking his lips say yt Adam and Eve were rightlie damned for eating ye appills in ye garden of Eden, they should have made them into cyder.

Some apples were reserved from cider making to be made into pies. Pies, their flaky crusts filled with meat, vegetables, fruit or custard, are the crowning glory of New England cuisine. They were served in rich families and poor, and might appear at any meal. Daniel Webster, New England's great statesman, is said to have liked apple pie for breakfast. Such excessive pie eating earned the ridicule of outlanders:

> In Massachusetts, sad to say,
> From Boston down to Buzzard's Bay,
> They feed you till you want to die
> On rhubarb pie and pumpkin pie
> Until, at last, it makes you cry,
> "What else is there that I can try?"
> They look at you in some surprise
> And feed you other kinds of pies.

Others might mock, but New Englanders loved their pies, and when the time for the great annual feast came around, New England wives embarked on a veritable orgy of pie baking, described here by Harriet Beecher Stowe in her novel *Oldtown Folks*:

> The making of pies at this period assumed vast proportions that verged upon the sublime. Pies were made by forties and fifties and hundreds, and made of everything on the earth and under the earth.

The pie is an English institution, which, planted on American soil, forthwith ran rampant and burst forth into an untold variety of genera and species. Not merely the old traditional mince pie, but a thousand strictly American seedlings from that main stock, evinced the power of American housewives to adapt old institutions to new uses. Pumpkin pies, cranberry pies, huckleberry pies, cherry pies, green-currant pies, peach, pear, and plum pies, custard pies, apple pies, Marlborough-pudding pies,—pies with top crusts, and pies without,—pies adorned with all sorts of fanciful flutings and architectural strips laid across and around, and otherwise varied, attested the boundless fertility of the feminine mind, when once let loose in a given direction.

Fancy the heat and vigor of the great panformation, when Aunt Lois and Aunt Keziah, and my mother and grandmother, all in ecstasies of creative inspiration, ran, bustled, and hurried,—mixing, rolling, tasting, consulting,—alternately setting us children to work when anything could be made of us, and then chasing us all out of the kitchen when our misinformed childhood ventured to take too many liberties with sacred mysteries. Then out we would all fly at the kitchen door, like sparks from a blacksmith's window.

In the corner of the great kitchen, during all these days, the jolly old oven roared and crackled in great volcanic billows of flame, snapping and gurgling as if the old fellow entered with joyful sympathy into the frolic of the hour; and then, his great heart being once warmed up, he brooded over successive generations of pies and cakes, which went in raw and came out cooked, till butteries and dressers and shelves and pantries were literally crowded with a jostling abundance.

A great cold northern chamber, where the sun never shone, and where in winter the snow sifted in at the window-cracks, and ice and frost reigned with undisputed sway, was fitted up to be the storehouse of these surplus treasures. There, frozen solid, and thus well preserved in their icy fetters, they formed a great repository for all the winter months; and the pies baked at Thanksgiving often came out fresh and good with the violets of April.

Pies, like Thanksgiving itself, have ascended from simple origins in the New England countryside to glory as an American institution. Of the infinite variety of pies, two, the pumpkin and the mince, are intimately associated with Thanksgiving dinner. Ellen Chapman Rollins described the classic mince pie in *Child-*

life, (1881)Old-time, a memoir of her girlhood in Wakefield, New Hampshire.

> A true Thanksgiving mince pie should be an inch thick, with a thin, flaky crust, tinted by its imprisoned juices, which threaten to break through like blood from overfull veins. Around its edge must be a slight crinkle made by the tines of a fork or castor-bottle cover; and in its top a hole here and there from the stroke of a knife to let the steam out. This steam, once known, can never be forgotten—the intermingled exhalation of beef and pork or suet, and apples and raisins and citron and sugar and spices and boiled cider, and, in profane families, of a dash of good brandy. When you press upon its upper crust, there should gush up from the slashes a brown gravy, sparkling with tiny gobules of fat, and deliciously scenting the room. Fortunate they who have been permitted to relish, with a slice of cream cheese, and a mug of sweet cider, this healthful, bliss-giving pie!

There is no more quintessential Thanksgiving dish than mince meat pie, and yet, unlike the native pumpkin pie, mincemeat was a tradition borrowed from the Christmas feasts of merry old England. Puritans in both England and America banned Christmas; the "high-shoe lords of Cromwell's making" frowned on all of the ancient Yuletide customs: "Plum broth was Popish, and mince pie—/O, that was flat idolatry!"

But, by the early 1700s, mince pie was enshrined in the New England Thanksgiving menu. As part of her long campaign to instruct Americans in the proper observance of Thanksgiving Day, Sarah Josepha Hale included a recipe for mince pie in the November 1858 edition of *Godey's Lady's Book*.

Mince Pie

1 lb. lean beef, shredded
¾ lb. suet
1 lb. apples, pared, cored
1 lb. currants, chopped fine
1 lb. brown sugar
1 tsp. salt
½ ounce allspice & cloves
two nutmegs, grated
juice of two lemons
half a pound citron (preserved peel)

Mix thoroughly and add ¼ a pint brandy or light wine. Line tart tins with light pastry, fill with the mixture and cover with paste, bake ½ hour.

The housekeeper following this recipe would presumably have her own pastry recipe and have been experienced enough to realize that she ought to sauté the meat and stew the ingredients in a kettle before filling the pie shells. Temperance mincemeat, which came into fashion after the Civil War, substituted molasses for the time-honored brandy.

When New England Puritans borrowed mincemeat from Christmas, they also took the plum pudding. This rich suet pudding studded with raisins was the great finale of the Thanksgiving feast: "But what did their eyes behold! Roxy Jane, with beaming face, bearing aloft a huge platter, on which reposed a great, rich-brown, plummy-looking pudding!" Roxy Jane, the hired girl, entered the dining room at the climax of Sophie Sweet's Thanksgiving story "All the Plums," in the November 1882 issue of *St. Nicholas* magazine.

Plum pudding made a very rich ending to a very heavy meal. Meat with gravy, boiled winter vegetables and pies were not a diet for the delicate of palate, but there was one traditional dish on the old-time Thanksgiving table that would merit the approval of a modern health food devotee. Among the gravies and pickles stood a bunch of fresh celery stalks, the only item on the menu served raw.

How celery came to be part of the Thanksgiving dinner is not precisely clear, but its presence was a fixed institution. Perhaps celery was featured because it is among the few salad vegetables that can be kept in a root cellar until late November. Probably it first came to the Thanksgiving table as a novelty. There is a long tradition of buying luxurious and generally unavailable foods for the Thanksgiving feast; imported figs, dates, lemons and oranges appeared in many New England homes at Thanksgiving if at no other time of year, and celery, introduced in this country only at the time of the Revolution, was both luxury and novelty.

However it began, celery was established and remained a true Thanksgiving custom. When the charitable overseers of Saint Barnabas's House in New York distributed the fixings for

Thanksgiving dinner to 115 poor families in 1895, they packed each basket with the ingredients deemed essential to the Thanksgiving feast: "A turkey, potatoes, cranberries, celery, three and one-half pounds of sugar, and a quarter-pound of tea."

Pumpkin pie, mince pie, chicken pie, cranberry sauce, cider, plum pudding and celery complete the list of Thanksgiving traditions developed in seventeenth- and eighteenth-century New England. In the new century, Thanksgiving dinner grew into a national institution, and turkey assumed its proud place as keystone of the feast.

The turkey is an American native first domesticated by the Aztec in Mexico. Spanish conquistadors brought the birds to Spain, and it may be that the first English people who saw one thought that it came from Turkey. It also is possible that the name derives from the bird's call, which sounds something like "turk-turk." Whatever the derivation of the name, domestic turkeys came to New England from Europe, descendants of the Aztec stock.

Eastern woods were also once full of wild turkeys that could be hunted in the fall, beautiful game birds that caught the imagination of Benjamin Franklin—he wanted to make the wild turkey the symbol of our nation:

> For my part, I wish the bald eagle had not been chosen representative of our country; he is a bird of bad moral character. . . . For in truth, the turkey is in comparison a much more respectable bird withal, a true original native of America. Eagles have been found in all countries, but the turkey is peculiar to ours; . . . he is besides (though a little vain and silly, it is true), a bird of courage who would not hesitate to attack a grenadier of the British Guard who should presume to invade his farmyard with a red coat on.

Whether our forebears admired the turkey for its courage or for its flavor, whether it was chosen because it could be hunted in the November woods or because it was the largest fowl in the barnyard, we will never know. But early in the nineteenth century, turkey became the American Thanksgiving bird. An old bit of doggerel points out that we effectively have two national birds, the eagle and the turkey:

May one give us peace in all our states,
The other a piece for all our plates.

Once the question of the proper main course for Thanksgiving dinner had been definitively settled, the question of what to stuff the turkey with was raised. It is a question that will never be settled. Rice, fruit, oysters, sausage, day-old biscuit, fresh bread, soft bread, stale bread and corn bread are all cherished traditions in somebody's family. There is not even any absolute answer to the question "What was the traditional stuffing in old New England?" for even then, there were many ways to stuff a turkey.

In 1857, Sarah Hale, the lady who devoted more effort to making Thanksgiving a national holiday than anyone else, printed this recipe for "Roasting Turkey" in *Godey's Lady's Book*:

Roasting Turkey
Chestnut Stuffing, peel, chop and pound chestnuts in a mortar, quantity—one and a half pounds. Rasp that same weight of bacon fat and mix it with the chestnuts.
Stuff the turkey with it, placing stuffing in turkey two days previous to cooking. It is supposed to impart a flavor to the flesh of the fowl.
Cut thin slices of bacon fat and place over the breast of the turkey; secure it with half a sheet of clear white paper, and roast.
The paper will catch the fire and become scorched; but keep the heat well to the breast, in order that it may be as well done as the rest of the bird; baste well, froth it up; serve with gravy in the dish, and bread sauce in a tureen.

Modern home economists will cringe at the suggestion that rasped bacon fat be allowed to sit in the cavity of an uncooked turkey for two days—a perfect recipe for food poisoning. But it is wholly unnecessary to turn to an 1857 magazine to find a recipe for turkey stuffing. Mrs. Hale was the first editor to devote her November cooking pages to advice on preparing the holiday meal, but her example has been followed by editors every November since.

Turkey with cranberry sauce was already well established as the traditional and, indeed, the only desirable Thanksgiving dinner when Sarah Hale began her Thanksgiving campaign. And so it is to this day. A few malcontents grumble that eating the same meal every November is boring. But far from finding "turkey and fixings" boring, most Americans look forward to enjoying on Thanksgiving Day precisely the same array of dishes that they ate last year, and every year back to childhood. Americans, in fact, enjoy turkey with cranberry so much that many families have borrowed the Thanksgiving menu to serve on Christmas Day. Turkey and cranberries as a Yuletide tradition is a fitting denouement to the culinary history of a holiday that began with the Puritan rejection of Christmas and that borrowed its traditional mince pie and plum pudding from that banished holiday.

Thanksgiving dinner, as it was created in New England and known to the nation at mid-nineteenth century, was a simple, home-style feast. Roast turkey, cranberry sauce, mashed winter vegetables, homemade cider, pies and plum pudding were the hearty, filling fare of the farmhouse kitchen. The Victorian passion for elegance would attempt to change all that.

Godey's Lady's Book, which had once confined advice on its Thanksgiving cooking pages to instructing young cooks in the preparation of old-fashioned dishes, now included recipes for Piquant Potatoes á la Baviére, Cocoanut Cake, Meringue Custard Tartlets, Rice Croquettes and Turtle Soup. This last, a "recipe for a small turtle," begins with a straightforward instruction, "Boil the turtle until it is tender."

Coconut, meringue and turtles were stylish additions to the Thanksgiving menu, but none of them matched oysters in popularity. Every Victorian magazine article on "Recipes for Thanksgiving" included an oyster recipe, and every housekeeper with pretensions to stylishness served oysters at Thanksgiving. The November 1879 *Lady's Book* ran recipes for Scalloped Oysters, Fried Oysters, Broiled Oysters and Oyster Soup. Oysters were the symbol of culinary luxury, and it was natural for Victorian wives to add their favorite delicacy to the menu of the great feast. Oysters at Thanksgiving are still a tradition in some families.

A host of new foods was introduced to Thanksgiving dinner as modern technology brought unheard of delicacies to American tables. Railroads, for example, now brought oranges to cold northern cities. Oranges were, to be sure, far too expensive to be eaten every day, but a few might be purchased as a holiday treat.

By the 1880s, refrigerator cars brought California lettuce and pears east, although purchasers agreed that long transportation "affects the taste and flavor."

Some nostalgic Victorians complained that cooked food lost much of its savor when big cast-iron stoves replaced open-hearth cooking and baking in Dutch ovens at midcentury, but housewives found the new stove a blessed improvement over the old methods. Cooking and baking with a cast-iron stove was easier and less dangerous, and the greater evenness of the heat made more elaborate preparations possible for the home cook. Many more cakes, for example, were baked after the introduction of cast-iron stoves.

Most wonderful of all the Victorian culinary innovations, however, was ice cream; for although this heavenly treat was introduced to Europe by Marco Polo, only in the 1850s did it become available to the middle classes. Even then, it was a very extravagant treat—far too expensive for regular indulgence, but a fitting dessert for the harvest feast.

Even more radical than the addition of oysters and ice cream to the menu was the Victorian introduction of service by courses. Traditionally, the meal began when every hot savory dish was set on the table for the main course and ended when the plum pudding emerged from the oven. Victorian women, however, divided the meal into a rigid succession of courses from soup to nuts. In many families, this entailed interspersing the old-fashioned chicken pie and mashed turnips with more elegant dishes and serving them in the new, "correct" order, as suggested by this 1887 menu from the *Woman's Home Companion*:

DINNER
Raw Oysters   Turtle Soup
Boiled Fish, with Anchovy Sauce
Roast Turkey, Giblet Sauce
Smothered Guinea Fowl   Chicken Pie
Roast Haunch of Venison
Mashed Potatoes   Sweet Potatoes
Mashed Turnips
Cauliflower   Boiled Onions
Baked Salsify   Cabbage Salad
Cranberry Sauce   Celery

Sweet Peach Pickle
Pumpkin Pie   Mince Pie
Thanksgiving Pudding
Ice Cream   Thanksgiving Cake
Crackers   Cheese   Pickles
Fruit   Oranges
Grapes

Some well-to-do families, however, became so carried away by the urge to imitiate French haute cuisine that they abandoned American tradition completely. This menu, suggested by *Harper's Bazaar* in 1900, retains roast turkey alone of all the traditional dishes; even cranberry sauce is omitted.

MENU FOR TWELVE COVERS
Huîtres
Buzzard Bay.

Soup
Purée of game.

Hors-d'oeuvre
Olives farcies. Salted almonds.
Canapés of caviare.
Canapés with anchovy sauce.

Fish
Lobster in shells, garnished with oyster crabs.
Potato croquettes with cheese.

Entrées
Small timbales, Bretonne.
Filet of venison with artichokes.
Jellied pâté of goose livers with truffles.
Romaine salad.

Roast
Turkey decorated with glazed chestnuts.

Dessert
Thanksgiving monument of ice-cream.
Cakes.
Camembert cheese.
Coffee.

When the fashion for culinary elegance reached the point where a Thanksgiving dinner without cranberry sauce or pumpkin pie could be seriously proposed, Americans called a halt and brought old-fashioned Thanksgiving dishes back into style. Most families had continued to enjoy the time-honored menu, even at the height of the craze for the elaborate French meals, because on Thanksgiving pleasure is taken from doing things the traditional way. In the words of America's great cooking teacher, Fannie Farmer, "What hopes center on the golden-brown turkey, the flaky pastry, the spicy plum pudding! Surely no American will forego these traditional dishes on this traditional day. . . ."

The basic traditions of Thanksgiving dinner have not changed since Fannie Farmer offered her 1914 Thanksgiving menu, suggesting roast, stuffed turkey, giblet gravy, cranberry molds, curled celery, mashed potatoes, onions in cream, oyster and chicken pie, Thanksgiving plum pudding, hard sauce, mince pie, pumpkin pie and assorted nuts. Families add a side dish or argue over the relative merits of whole berry versus jellied cranberry sauce, but only an occasional restless food editor proposes major changes in the menu.

In Miss Farmer's day, food editors suggested such additions as Escalloped Sweet Potatoes with Mushrooms, Orange and Chestnut Salad, Roast Ducks with Orange Slices and Jelly, or Pumpkin Ice in Blossoms. Editors have continued to propose replacing turkey with individual Cornish game hens or omitting potatoes, onions and peas in favor of asparagus, wild rice and broccoli. But few cooks pay them heed: broccoli and game hens can grace a festive table any time of the year; sweet potatoes and turkey define Thanksgiving dinner.

It is often pointed out that turkey, cranberries, pumpkin, corn and potatoes are all native American foods and for this reason constitute a fitting repast on our national feast day. There is truth in this reasoning, and it may explain how these foods came to be eaten on Thanksgiving but it cannot explain why we eat them still.

Thanksgiving Day, the emotions we attach to the holiday, the people we share it with and the foods we eat on it are hopelessly bound together. Every slice of turkey is a serving of tradition, each ladle of cranberry sauce a pouring out of American history, each slice of pie an offering of love, of family, of tradition, of—Thanksgiving.

Annotated Bibliography

The best source on the early history of Thanksgiving is *The Fast and Thanksgiving Days of New England* by William DeLoss Love, Jr. (Cambridge, Mass.: Houghton Mifflin, 1895). This thorough study includes a list of all fast days and days of thanksgiving—congregational, town, colony, state and national—for which Love could find documentation through the end of the eighteenth century. The best short article on the origins of Thanksgiving is "Our New England Thanksgiving, Historically Considered," *The New Englander* 38, no. 149 (March 1879): 240–52.

Two works deal specifically with proclamations for Thanksgiving: Franklin Benjamin Hough, *Proclamations for Thanksgiving, Issued by the Continental Congress, President Washington, by the National and State Governments on the Peace of 1815, and by the Governors of New York Since the Introduction of the Custom; With Those of the Governors of the Several States in 1858. With An Historical Introduction and Notes* (Albany, N.Y.: Munsell and Rowland, 1858). Hough wrote near the culmination of the campaign to make Thanksgiving a national holiday, and his introduction illuminates the process whereby Thanksgiving became a holiday in New York State. *Thanksgiving; Its Source, Philosophy and*

History with all National Proclamations and an Analytical Study Thereof, by H. S. J. Sickel "of the Philadelphia Bar" (Philadelphia: International Printing Co., 1940), was written in response to President Franklin Roosevelt's decision to change the date of Thanksgiving. It helpfully collects the proclamations issued by the Continental Congress and all presidential proclamations of fast and thanksgiving days in one volume. However, it mislabels the two John Adams's proclamations and James Madison's 1814 proclamation as proclamations of thanksgiving when they were, in fact, for solemn days of humiliation and prayer. The historical introduction is not accurate.

The place of Thanksgiving in the church-state relationship is well explicated in Anson Phelps Stokes, *Church and State in the United States* (New York: Harper and Brothers, 1950).

Edwin T. Greninger, "Thanksgiving: An American Holiday," *Social Science* 54, no. 1 (Winter 1979): 3–15, is a brief summary of the history of Thanksgiving. Generally accurate, it does contain some potentially misleading errors, such as the statement that Virginia was the second southern state to observe Thanksgiving.

Innumerable magazine articles have been published on the history of Thanksgiving, and these often repeat myths and inaccurate accounts of the holiday's history. The historical introduction to *Thanksgiving,* by Robert Haven Schauffler, in the series Our American Holidays (New York: Dodd, Mead, 1929), is in this casual, historical tradition. The book comprises an interesting collection of poems and short stories about Thanksgiving.

That Elusive First Thanksgiving

Mourt's Relation, or Journal of the Plantation at Plymouth contains the contemporary account of the 1620 Plymouth thanksgiving. Printed in 1662, it has been reprinted by Corinth Books (New York, 1963), Dwight B. Heath, editor.

Many accounts of the "first Thanksgiving" as presented by partisans of the various sites exist; more are printed every November. For examples of the genre, see Camille Benson Bird, "The First Thanksgiving" [Popham, Maine], *Daughters of the American Revolution Magazine* 45, no. 5 (November 1914): 225–27; Mary F. Miller, "Thanksgiving" [Plymouth, 1623], *Our Young Folks* (November 1866): 671–73; J. H. A. Bone, "The First New England Thanksgiving" [Plymouth, 1621], *Our Young Folks* (November 1869): 722–29; Virginius Dabney, "A Setting for the First Thanksgiving" [Jamestown and Berkeley Hundred], *Saturday Evening Post,* November 1981, pp. 12, 14, 88, 114; John Gould, "Who Says They Were First?" [Maine], *Saturday Evening Post* November 29, 1958, pp. 38, 112; "First Christmas, First Thanksgiving" [Florida], in *The Florida Handbook*, comp. Allen Morris (Tallahassee, Fla.: Peninsular Publishing Co., 1983), p. 316; and Mrs. Clyde W. Warwick, "The Feast of the First Thanksgiving" [Texas], in *The Randall County Story* (Randall County Historical Survey Commission), pp. 3, 4.

A Holiday is Born

The most accurate accounts of the creation of Thanksgiving are found in William DeLoss Love, *The Fast and Thanksgiving Days of New England* (Boston: Houghton Mifflin, 1895), and "Our New England Thanksgivings, Historically Considered," *The New Englander,* No. CXLIX, Vol. 38, March 1879. Early proclamations from Connecticut are maintained by the Archivist of the Connecticut State Library in Hartford. *The Records of the Colony of New Plymouth in New England* were edited by Nathaniel Shurtleff and published in Boston in 1855 by order of the Legislature of the Commonwealth of Massachusetts, and reprinted by AMS Press, New York, 1968. See *Pilgrim Colony; A History of New Plymouth 1620–1691*, by George D. Langdon, Jr. (New Haven: Yale University Press, 1966), for an account of the Scituate Thanksgiving of 1636. See *Redeem the Time: The Puritan Sabbath in Early America*, by Winton V. Solberg, Harvard University Press, Cambridge, Mass., 1977, for an understanding of the Puritan attitude toward holy days.

Thanksgiving Comes of Age in New England

Love, *The Fast and Thanksgiving Days of New England,* is the best source on the period. Information on the development of Thanksgiving in Massachusetts is found in Halsey M. Thomas, ed., *The Diaries of Samuel Sewall, 1674–1729* (New York: Farrar, Straus & Giroux, 1973); and in James Kendall Hosmer, ed., *Winthrop's Journal; History of New England, 1630–1639* (New York: Charles Scribner's Sons, 1908). "Our New England Thanksgiving, Historically Considered" is an excellent summary of the growth and origins of the holiday. Shurtleff's *Records of the Colony of New Plymouth in New England* contains the Thanksgiving orders for that colony.

Revolutionary Holiday

An overview of the revolutionary period is given in Love, *The Fast and Thanksgiving Days of New England*. Proclamations by the Continental Congress and early federal proclamations are reproduced in Hough, *Proclamations for Thanksgiving*. Marilyn Gombosi, *A Day of Solemn Thanksgiving; Moravian Music for the Fourth of July, 1783 in Salem, North Carolina (Chapel Hill: University of North Carolina Press,*

1977), presents an interesting musical picture of a Moravian celebration of a special Thanksgiving.

Information on the Hutchinson proclamation in Massachusetts can be found in Love, p. 333; and in Thomas Hutchinson, The History of the Colony and Province of Massachusetts-Bay, edited by Lawrence Mayo and reprinted by Harvard University Press (Cambridge, Mass., 1936), pp. 249 and 250; see also John Gorham Palfrey, *History of New England from the Revolution of the Seventeenth Century to the Revolution of the Eighteenth*, reprinted by AMS Press (New York, 1966), Vol. 2, pp. 448 and 449.

Proclamations of individual governors are maintained in state archives.

Information on President Washington's proclamations can be found in Rose S. Klein, "Washington's Thanksgiving Proclamations," *American Jewish Archives*, November 1968, pp. 156–62; in Paul F. Boller, Jr., *George Washington and Religion* (Dallas: Southern Methodist University Press, 1963), pp. 52–65; and in Donald Jackson and Dorothy Twohig, eds., *The Diaries of George Washington* (Charlottesville: University of Virginia Press, 1979), Vol. 5, pp. 501 and 502.

The early federal period is covered in Stokes, *Church and State in the United States*, Vol. 3, pp. 194 and 195, and Vol. 1, pp. 486–91.

Colonel Henry Dearborn's diary is reproduced in *Proceedings of the Massachusetts Historical Society*, Vol. 2, Second Series, 1886–1887 (Boston: Massachusetts Historical Society, 1888). Juliana Smith's diary is excerpted in Helen Evertson Smith, *Colonial Days and Ways* (New York: Century, 1900).

The sermon delivered at the Spanish and Portuguese Synagogue in New York is reprinted as *A Religious Discourse: Thanksgiving Day Sermon, November 26, 1789*, by Reverend Gershom Mendes Seixas, with an introduction by Isidore S. Meyer (Jewish Historical Society of New York, 1977).

Political Feast in a Young Republic

All federal fast and thanksgiving day proclamations are reprinted in *Thanksgiving* by Sickel. Some fast day proclamations are, however, inappropriately listed as thanksgiving proclamations in this book.

Love's *The Fast and Thanksgiving Days of New England* continues to be an excellent source on this period.

Information on the Episcopal liturgy for Thanksgiving can be found in William Stevens Perry, *History of the American Episcopal Church*, Vol. 2 (Boston: James R. Osgood & Co., 1885), pp. 113 and 114.

Governor John Jay's Thanksgiving proclamation is detailed in *The Life of John Jay with Selections from His Correspondence and Miscella-*

neous Papers by his son William Jay (New York: J. & J. Harper, 1833), pp. 385–88. The incident is also treated in George Pellew, *John Jay* (Cambridge, Mass.; Houghton Mifflin, 1890), p. 321; and Jabez D. Hammond, *The History of Political Parties in the State of New York* (Syracuse, N.Y.: Hall, Mills, 1852), Vol. 1, p. 446.

Reverend Joseph Lymen's discourse, *A Thanksgiving Sermon Delivered November 29, 1804* (printed by William Butler, Northampton, Mass., 1804), is in the collection of the Presbyterian Historical Society in Philadelphia.

An account of Governor Gerry's 1811 proclamation can be found in George Billias, *Elbridge Gerry: Founding Father and Republican Statesman* (New York: McGraw-Hill, 1976).

The early federal period is covered in Stokes, *Church and State in the United States*; Vol. 1, pp. 486–92, covers Madison and Jefferson, and Vol. 3, pp. 179–84, covers Tyler, Jackson and Taylor. The letter from Zachary Taylor to Reverend Nicholas Murray, written on November 5, 1849, in which Taylor declines to issue a Thanksgiving proclamation, is reprinted in the *New York Times*, November 26, 1931, p. 3. At that time the letter was for sale by an autograph dealer.

The quotation from President Adams' diary is taken from the *Memoirs of John Quincy Adams; comprising portions of His Diary from 1795 to 1848,* ed. by Charles Francis Adams, Vol. II, pages 53, 54, entries for November 15, 16, 1825 (Philadelphia: J. B. Lippincott and Co., 1875.)

It Never Rained on Thanksgiving

Reminiscent descriptions of Thanksgiving can be found in Edward Everett Hale, *A New England Boyhood* (New York: Cassell, 1893; reprint ed., New York: Garrett Press, 1970), pp. 136–47; C. H. Rockwell, "A New England Thanksgiving Day Forty Years Ago," *Harper's Weekly*, December 1, 1984, p. 1139; Ruth Tirrell, "I Remember, I Remember," *Good Housekeeping*, November 1974, pp. 44–52; E. P. Powell, "Thanksgiving Fifty Years Ago," *The Independent*, November 1900, pp. 2842–44; and Martha J. Lamb, "One New England Thanksgiving," *Magazine of American History* 16, no. 6 (December 1886): 505–15.

Fictional accounts of the holiday include Caroline Orne, "The Walbridge Family, A Thanksgiving Story," *Gleason's Pictorial Drawing Room Companion*, November 27, 1852, pp. 346 and 347; Harriet Beecher Stowe, "How We Kept Thanksgiving at Oldtown," in *Oldtown Folks* (Boston: Fields, Osgood, 1869; reprint ed., New York: Library of America, 1982); and Sarah Josepha Hale, "Thanksgiving Dinner," in *Northwood; Or, Life North and South* (Boston: Bowles & Dearborn, 1827; reprint ed., Freeport, N.Y.: Books for Libraries, 1972).

Old Holiday in a New Home

Information on the westward expansion of New England culture can be found in Lois Kimball Matthews, *The Expansion of New England Settlement and Institutions to the Mississippi River, 1620–1865* (Boston: Houghton Mifflin, 1909); Frederick Jackson Turner, *The United States, 1830–1860*, Chap. 3, "New England" (New York: Henry Holt, 1935); and William Warren Sweet, *Religion on the American Frontier*, Vol. 3, *The Congregationalists* (Chicago: University of Chicago Press, 1939).

Material on Thanksgiving in New York is taken from Hough, *Proclamations for Thanksgiving;* I. N. Phelps Stokes, *Iconography of Manhattan Island, 1498–1909* (New York: Robert H. Dodd, 1915); and *The New York Times,* November 23, 1890, p. 17, col. 1.

Wisconsin is covered by Edward Noyes, "Thanksgiving Day in Early Milwaukee," *Historical Messenger of the Milwaukee County Historical Society*, December 1964, pp. 54–59. The Wisconsin State Archives contain the Journal of the House of Representatives of the Second Legislative Assembly of Wisconsin, Second Session. Thanksgiving was debated on March 4, 5 and 7, 1839. The reminiscences of Mrs. Mary Spielman Roller were quoted in an unidentified newspaper clipping, courtesy of the Milwaukee County Historical Society.

Thanksgiving proclamations for Michigan were provided by the state archives. In fact, Thanksgiving proclamations for every state are available from the state archivist, except where they have been lost, as some have been, or been rendered illegible by tearing, folding and careless treatment.

Thanksgiving in the Western Reserve is touched on briefly in William Ganson Rose, *Cleveland: The Making of a City* (Cleveland: World, 1950), p. 166. It is covered more fully in the yearly listing under "holidays" in the *Annals of Cleveland, 1818–1876,* an index and a collection of reprints of articles from Cleveland newspapers compiled by the Work Projects Administration in 1938.

Isabel Jamison describes "The First Official Thanksgiving in Illinois," *Journal of the Illinois State Historical Society* 2, no. 3 (October 1918): 370–78. Chicago material comes from the Chicago Historical Society archives.

Information on Kansas was provided by the Kansas Historical Society in Topeka. Marie MacDonald's article, "Out of Adversity—Thanksgiving," appeared in the November 27, 1969, Witchita *Eagle and Beacon*. Ray Morgan's article, "Johnson County Site of First Recorded Holiday Observance in Kansas," which describes Thanksgiving at the Shawnee Methodist Indian Mission, appeared in the Kansas City, Missouri, *Times*, November 28, 1969.

Sources on Thanksgiving in Hawaii were provided by the Hawaii

State Library in Honolulu. The missionary-sponsored newspaper *The Friend* contained Thanksgiving articles on November 15, 1856 (p. 85), January 1, 1857 (p. 1), December 5, 1864 (p. 92), December 1897 (p. 91), November 1931 (p. 246) and December 1939 (p. 228). Books that refer to early Thanksgiving days include M. C. A. (Mrs. Theodore) Richards, *The Chief's Children's School* (1937), pp. 90–91 and 345; Laura Fish Judd, *Sketches of Life in the Hawaiian Islands* (New York: Randolph, 1880; reprint ed., Honolulu: Honolulu Star Bulletin, Ltd., 1928), p. 80; *Thrum's Hawaiian Annual* (Honolulu: Thomas G. Thrum, 1911), p. 115; and Mary Emma Dillingham Frear, *Lowell and Abigail* (New Haven: Yale University Press, 1934), p. 135.

William J. Petersen's two articles—"The First Iowa Thanksgiving," *The Palimpsest* 25, no. 11 (November 1944), and "Thanksgiving in Iowa," *The Palimpsest* 49 no. 12 (December 1968)—offer a complete history of Thanksgiving in that state.

Robert O'Brian's article on "San Francisco's First Thanksgiving," quoting from the *California Star* of November 20, 1847, and a letter from Edward Kimbel in the San Francisco *Bulletin* of December 1888 are in the collection of the California Historical Society in San Francisco.

Proclaiming Thanksgiving Throughout the Land

John C. Calhoun is quoted from Horace Bushnell, *Work and Play: Literary Varieties* (London:, Alexander Strahan, 1864; reprint New York: Charles Scribner's Sons, 1903), Vol. 1, p. 220.

Information on Thanksgiving in Pennsylvania was communicated to me by the Pennsylvania Historical and Museum Commission in Harrisburg. Reverend Samuel Lowrie's memoir is in the collection of the Historical Society of Western Pennsylvania in Pittsburgh.

Missouri Thanksgiving proclamations are reprinted in *Messages and Proclamations of the Governors of Missouri*. I quote from Vol. 1, pp. 520–21. This, along with the Hammond letter, information on dates of early Thanksgivings, and the quote from the Liberty *Weekly Tribune*, were obtained from the State Historical Society of Missouri in Columbia.

Dates of early Thanksgiving days in Maryland were obtained from the Hall of Records, Department of General Services, in Annapolis.

Richard Collins, *History of Kentucky*, Vol. 1, first published in Covington, Kentucky, 1874, discusses Thanksgiving on pp. 49 and 52 (Frankfurt, Kentucky: Kentucky Historical Society, 1966).

Early Thanksgivings in Florida are mentioned in Sidney Walter Martin, *Florida During Territorial Days* (Athens: University of Georgia

Press, 1944), p. 104; and Bertram Groene, *Ante-Bellum Tallahassee* (Tallahassee: Florida Heritage Foundation, 1971), p. 149.

The best source on the activities of Sarah Josepha Hale is her monthly column, "The Editor's Table," in *Godey's Lady's Book*. Ruth Albright Finley's biography *The Lady of Godey's*, was published by Lippincott, Philadelphia, 1938.

The letter describing the first Thanksgiving in Louisiana is from the "Samuel Merrill Collection," of the Indiana Historical Society in Indianapolis. Dated December 23, 1845, it was written by Julia Merrill to Catharine Merrill. There is an article on "The First Thanksgiving in New Orleans," by T. E. Tedd, that appeared in *Inn Dixie* in November 1946 on pages 15 and 16. Two dates in the article are incorrect. January 15, 1845 should read January 15, 1846, and December 21, 1841 should read December 21, 1848.

The passage on Mississippi is quoted from the *Journal of John Mudd*, Volume 17, pp. 148–50, manuscript collection of the Chicago Historical Society.

Information on Minnesota Thanksgivings is quoted from *The Frontier Holiday*, editor, Glenn Hanson, North Central Publishing Co., St. Paul, Minn., 1948 and from an address by Solon J. Buck, "The Minnesota Historical Society and Some Early Thanksgiving History," delivered on November 29, 1928, in the collection of the Archives & Manuscripts Division, Minnesota Historical Society, Ms. #FF602 B92. Further information was gleamed from Ruth Thompson, "First Thanksgiving Day in Minnesota Territory," Minneapolis *Tribune*, November 22, 1948, and from a newspaper clipping "Mary Knopik Uncovers an Early Thanksgiving Here," dated November 23, 1977, in the collection of the Hennepin County Historical Society, Minneapolis.

Texas Thanksgivings are described in Clifford Snowden, "Early Texas Had Days of Thanksgiving," from the November 12, 1939, Dallas *Morning News*, which reprints Governor Wood's 1849 proclamation; and in J. Oliver Wade, "Texas' First Thanksgiving," *The Texas Magazine* 7, no. 1 (November 1912): 67–69.

Arkansas information was drawn from Diane Sherwood, "When Arkansas Had Its First Thanksgiving Day—1847," *Arkansas Historical Quarterly* 4 (Autumn 1945): 250–56.

California material is drawn from several sources: "Life in Early California in 1849—Journal of I. Kent," *California Historical Society Quarterly* 20 (1941): 40; and Jay Ellison, "The Struggle For Civil Government in California," *California Historical Society Quarterly* 10 (1931), which contains a copy of Governor Riley's proclamation. The R. P. Putnam diary, which mentions Thanksgiving on p. 236, is manuscript no. 1734 in the collection of the California Historical Society in San Francisco. In the library of the same society is an article by W. W.

Ferrier on Thanksgiving Day from a November 1924 edition of the Berkeley *Daily Gazette.*

Gubernatorial proclamations for Oregon were obtained from the collection of the Oregon Historical Society in Portland. Further information is found in Charles Oluf Olsen, "Thanks to the Gracious Author of All Our Mercies," Portland *Sunday Journal*, Sec. 5, *Pacific Parade Magazine*, November 18, 1945, pp. 1 and 2; and Dorris Holmes Bailey, "Thanksgiving in Pioneer Days," Portland *Sunday Journal, Northwest Living Magazine*, November 1, 1954, p. 17.

Governor Young's 1852 proclamation for Utah was reproduced in the *Deseret News* of November 25, 1939, on p. 1 of the Church section. A very useful article is by E. Cecil McGavin of the Church Historian's Office, "The First Thanksgiving in Utah," *Improvement Era* 49 (November 1946): 696–97.

Information on Nebraska comes from the Western Heritage Society in Omaha.

Yankee Abolitionist Holiday

Sermons quoted in this chapter include the following: "A Discourse delivered at the Plymouth Church, Brooklyn, New York, Upon Thanksgiving Day, November 25, 1847 by Henry Ward Beecher" (New York: Cady and Burgess, 1848), Collection of the Presbyterian Historical Society, Philadelphia; "Fugitive Slave Law; The Religious Duty of Obedience to Law. A Sermon Preached in the Second Presbyterian Church in Brooklyn, November 24, 1850, by Ichabod S. Spencer, D.D." (New York: M. W. Dodd, 1850), Collection of the Pittsburgh Theological Seminary; "Israel and the United States Compared. A Discourse, delivered to the Associated Presbyterian Church, New Lisbon, Ohio, on Thanksgiving Day, November 20, 1856, by Samuel T. Herron" (Wilson & McCaskey, Buckeye State Office, 1857), Collection of the Pittsburgh Theological Seminary; "Our Blessings and Responsibilities: A Discourse preached at the Annual Thanksgiving, observed in Franklin, Tennessee, November 26, 1857 by Rev. A. Hartpence" (Franklin: Haynes & Balch, Printers, 1857), Collection of Eugene C. Barker, Texas History Center, University of Texas at Austin.

Governor Bell's proclamation is reprinted in Wade, "Texas' First Thanksgiving."

The *Daily True Democrat* is quoted from the *Annals of Cleveland.*

A Review of the Thanksgiving Day controversy in Virginia is found in M. E. R., "The Thanksgiving Day Contention," *Virginia Cavalcade* 1, no. 2 (Autumn 1951): 9–11.

Sarah Josepha Hale's views on Thanksgiving are set forth in the "Editor's Table" sections found toward the back of the September, October, and November editions of *Godey's Lady's Book* from 1846 onward.

Information on Thanksgiving in Kansas and Missouri can be found in MacDonald, "Out of Adversity;" in "The First Official Thanksgiving Day in Missouri Was Celebrated 110 Years Ago," Kansas City, Missouri, *Times*, November 25, 1954; and in the *Missouri Register of Civil Proceedings 1852-1860*, p. 404, courtesy of the State Historical Society of Missouri in Columbia.

Years of Sorrow, Day of Thanks

Sermons quoted are "A Thanksgiving Sermon preached before the Thirty Ninth Ohio Volunteers, U.S. Army at Camp Todd, Macon, Missouri, November 28, 1861, and a Sketch of the Regiment by Rev. B. W. Chidlaw, Chaplain" (Cincinnati: George Crosby, 1861), Property of the Ohio Historical Society Library, Columbus; and "The Right of the Sword. A Thanksgiving Discourse at the Union Church, Worcester, Massachusetts, November 21, 1861, by Ebenezer Cutler, Pastor" (Worcester, Mass.: Henry J. Howland), Collection of Eugene C. Barker, Texas History Center, University of Texas at Austin.

The Cleveland *Leader* is quoted from the *Annals of Cleveland.*

Gubernatorial Thanksgiving proclamations for 1861 were excerpted in the *New York Times* of November 10, 1861, p. 4, col. 3. The Massachusetts proclamation appears in full in *The Living Age*, December 14, 1861, pp. 520–21.

An account of the southern Thanksgiving proclamation of 1861 is in the *Journal of the Congress of the Confederate States of America, 1861–1865*, 58th Congress, 2nd Session, Document no. 234, p. 275, Monday, July 22, 1861 (Washington, D.C.: U.S. Government Printing Office, 1904), Vol. 1. The proclamation for and a sermon preached on the second Confederate Thanksgiving is reprinted in "A Thanksgiving Discourse Delivered at Washington, Georgia, on Thursday, September 18, 1862, by H. A. Turner" (Macon, Ga.: Burke, Boykin & Co., 1862), Collection of the Museum of the Confederacy, Richmond.

The Visalia, California, *Expositor* is quoted in Benjamin Franklin Gilbert, "The Confederate Minority in California," *California Historical Society Quarterly* 20 (1941): 161.

Reports of Thanksgiving day in camp in 1862 are drawn from the Cleveland *Leader* of December 1, 1862, p. 2, col. 1; and from three manuscripts in the collection of the Indiana Historical Society in Indianapolis: Civil War Diary of Michael Frosh, November 24, 1862; Civil War Diary, George Washington Tambert Collection, April 13, 1862; and Civil War Diary of James P. Burke, November 27, 1862, p. 21. See also Allan Nevins, ed., *A Diary of Battle: The Personal Journals of Col.*

Charles S. Wainwright, 1861–1865 (New York: Harcourt, Brace and World, 1962).

Descriptions of Thanksgiving Day 1863 are drawn from the *New York Times* of August 6, 1863, "The National Thanksgiving," p. 7, col. 4, and August 7, 1863, "Thanksgiving and Its Fruits," p. 1, col. 4; see also "God in the War: A Discourse preached in behalf of the U.S. Sanitary Commission on the day of The National Thanksgiving, August 6, 1863, by Rev. Henry Smith, D.D., Pastor of the North Presbyterian Church, Buffalo, New York" (Buffalo: Wheeler, Matthews & Warren, 1863), Collection of the Pittsburgh Theological Seminary.

The November 1863 Thanksgiving Day is described in "Letter of Custus Morse of December 9, 1863," Collection of the Indiana Historical Society, Indianapolis; "Letter to Robert Conley from Lissie S. Pollack of December 7, 1863," Robert Conley Collection, Indiana Historical Society; and H. Clay Trumbull, *War Memories of an Army Chaplain* (New York: Charles Scribner's Sons, 1898), pp. 68–69.

Lincoln's Thanksgiving proclamations can be found in Roy P. Basler, ed., *The Collected Works of Abraham Lincoln* (New Brunswick, N.J.: Rutgers University Press, 1953), Vol. 3. pp. 32, 185–86; Vol. 4, pp. 55–56, 322–23, 496–97. An account of the decisions to issue the proclamations is given in Carl Sandburg, *Abraham Lincoln: The War Years* (New York: Harcourt, Brace, 1939), pp. 46, 229–30, 359, 446.

Thanksgiving Day 1864 is described in the *New York Times*, September 10, 1864, "Gratitude for Victory; The Thanksgiving To-Morrow," p. 4, col. 2; November 24, 1864, "The Thanksgiving Feast," p. 4, col. 5; and November 25, 1864, "Thanksgiving," p. 1, col. 5. See also "The Grand Thanksgiving Dinner: To Our Sailors and Soldiers," *Frank Leslie's Illustrated Newspaper*, December 3, 1864, pp. 1, 168, 169.

Victorian Holiday

Information on Thanksgiving during Reconstruction was drawn from several sources. *New York Times* articles treating the topic include "The National Thanksgiving," October 29, 1867; "Thanksgiving Ignored by the Governor of Louisiana, He Refused to Appoint a Day," November 29, 1872; "Thanksgiving in Georgia, November 18, 1874; and "Special Thanksgiving in Alabama," December 9, 1875, p. 2, col 3. An undated article, "Thanksgiving in Helena in 1865," is in the collection of the Historical Society of Montana Library. Texas material is drawn from Snowden, "Early Texas Had Days of Thanksgiving." Louisiana's Reconstruction Thanskgivings are described in T. E. Tedd, "The First Thanksgiving in New Orleans," *Inn Dixie*, November 1946, pp. 15 and 17. A contemporary account of the Georgia Thanksgiving is found in the Cleveland *Leader* of November 23, 1874, quoted from the *Annals of Cleveland.*

Information on Thanksgiving Day in late Victorian New Orleans is drawn from the New Orleans *Daily Picayune* of November 24, 1897, p. 3, col. 5; and November 25, 1897, p. 3, cols. 4 and 5; p. 4, col. 2; p. 8, cols. 1–7.

The quotation describing an old-fashioned Thanksgiving in upstate New York is taken from Powell, "Thanksgiving Fifty Years Ago."

The Whittier quotation is found in John B. Pickard, ed., *The Letters of John Greenleaf Whittier* (Cambridge, Mass.: Harvard University Press, Belknap Press, 1975), Vol. 2, p. 480.

Accounts of Thanksgiving traffic are given in the *New York Times* of November 29, 1888, "The Thanksgiving Dinner; Annual Exodus of New Englanders Who Want to Eat It at Home"; and November 24, 1881, "Exodus to New England," p. 10, col. 2.

The Kingston, Rhode Island, Thanksgiving of the 1890s is described in Tirrell, "I Remember, I Remember." The turn-of-the-century Arizona Thanksgiving is described in Freddie Hanson, "Thanksgiving: Memory Unrationed," *Christian Science Monitor*, November 1947, p. 5.

The tale of the gluttonous boardinghouse lodger from Iowa is recounted in Petersen, "Thanksgiving in Iowa."

Articles recounting Catholic participation in Thanksgiving ran in the *New York Times* on November 28, 1884, p. 6, col. 4, "A Catholic Recognition, The Puritan Feast Observed by the Plenary Council"; November 22, 1888, p. 5, col. 3 and p. 4, col. 4, "A Catholic Innovation," and "Thanksgiving Among Catholics"; and on November 24, 1890, p. 1, col. 6, "Cardinal Gibbons' Address to Roman Catholic Churches."

Descriptions of American Thanksgiving banquets in Berlin, Rome and other foreign cities appeared annually, usually a day or two after the holiday, in *The New York Times.* Thanksgiving celebrations at American embassies and in American colonies abroad were often described or listed in the "Editor's Table" section of *Godey's Lady's Book*; the November 1861 edition is especially useful. The program of the *Thanksgiving Day Banquet of the American Society in London*, "Henry S. Wellcome In The Chair, R. Newton Crane In The Vice Chair," held at the Hotel Cecil in London on November 26, 1896, was published as a small book. A copy is in the collection of the Carnegie Library in Pittsburgh.

Accounts of theatrical performances were given annually in the newspapers, see the *New York Times* of November 27, 1891, "Great Day for the Theaters p. 3, col. 2."

The custom of pardoning prisoners in Massachusetts is described in the *New York Times* of November 26, 1875, p. 1, col. 2. Charitable activities in Cleveland are quoted from the Cleveland *Leader* of November 28, 1874, found in the *Annals of Cleveland.*

Charitable activities and other customs were chronicled in the contemporary press. I have read and drawn upon the yearly Thanksgiving coverage of the *New York Times*, the Cleveland papers as excerpted in the *Annals of Cleveland*, *Harper's Weekly*, *Frank Leslie's Illustrated Weekly*, *Ballou's Pictorial Drawing Room Companion*, the New York *Tribune*, the New York *Sentinel*, the Pittsburgh *Post*, the Pittsburgh *Gazette* and the Pittsburgh *Telegraph*. Both the New York and Pittsburgh papers published useful round-up columns detailing the day's activities around the nation, usually called "The Day Elsewhere," or simply "Thanksgiving."

General descriptions of Victorian Thanksgiving customs can be found in Mary Ellis, "How to Spend an Old-Fashioned Thanskgiving Day," *Ladies' Home Journal*, November 1905; Edward Everett Hale, "Thanksgiving in 1901 as We Do It in Boston," *The Independent*, November 1901, pp. 2814–16; and Petersen, "Thanksgiving in Iowa."

Thanksgiving Kicks Up its Heels

The fantastical parades were covered every year in the *New York Times*. Especially descriptive articles include November 25, 1881, p. 8, col. 1, "Young America in the Streets—The Squareback Rangers and Other Organizations Parade"; November 28, 1884, p. 6, col. 3, "Parades of the Fantastics: The Noisy Way in Which Some Persons Enjoyed Themselves"; November 30, 1900, p. 5, col. 1, "Original Hounds Parade: Ancient Organization Celebrated in Characteristic Way: Thanksgiving Day Spent at Staten Island Drinking Beer, Eating Turkey and Dancing"; and November 27, 1885, p. 8, col. 3, "Fun of a Lively Sort—The Hamilton Rangers Disport Themselves at Riverview Park."

Information on Thanksgiving activities in various cities was drawn from the same newspapers cited in Chapter 11.

The Norwich, Connecticut, bonfires are described in the *New York Times*, November 15, 1891, p. 3, col. 5, "Thanksgiving Bonfires, Norwich People Celebrate the Day in a Peculiar Way."

The quotation from Clara Louise Root Burnham's story "A Thanksgiving Revival," in which Maynard Senior and Junior differ over the propriety of holiday football, is taken from *A West Point Wooing and Other Stories*, 1899 (reprint ed., Freeport, N.Y.: Books for Libraries Press, 1969). The role of football is detailed in "Thanksgiving Day in New York Up to Date," *Harper's Weekly*, November 28, 1891, p. 950. Giuseppe Giacosa is quoted from Oscar Handlin, *This Was America* (Cambridge, Mass.: Harvard University Press, 1949), pp. 369 and 397.

Thanksgiving Day in California is described in " 'California's Bantam Cock,' The Journals of Charles E. DeLong 1854–1863," *California*

Historical Society Quarterly 10 (1931): 258; and Dorothy Huggins, comp., "Annals of San Francisco," *California Historical Society Quarterly* 15 (1936): 184.

Thanksgiving Day in Honolulu is described in the *Diary of Mary Atkins,* pp. 7 and 8, entry for November 28, 1863, Collection of the Hawaii State Library, Honolulu.

Outlaws and Turkey in the Wild West

Kansas material is from the collection of the Kansas Historical Society in Topeka.

Washington material comes from the collections of the Washington State Historical Society and the Eastern Washington State Historical Society and from *Told by the Pioneers* (Olympia: Washington State Historical Society, 1938), Vol. 2, p. 189.

The Fort Apache turkey hunt is described in Will C. Barnes, "Our Thanksgiving Turkey," *The Cattleman,* November 1936, pp. 19–23.

Arizona information was provided by Joan Metzger of the Arizona Historical Society in Tucson.

Montana material comes from newspaper clippings in the collection of the Historical Society of Montana Library: "Plummer Was a Gracious Turkey Day Host," Montana Newspaper Association Inserts, November 24, 1941; and "First Montana Thanksgiving Came in Bloody 1865," Bozeman *Daily Chronicle,* November 23, 1967.

The Elko, Nevada, *Daily Independent* of November 24 and 26, 1888, was consulted for advertisements of balls, dinners and turkey shoots.

The Thanksgiving party given by Butch Cassidy and the Sundance Kid is delightfully described in Dick Dunham, "When the Outlaws Gathered for Thanksgiving," *Denver Post,* Empire Section, November 20, 1977.

Thanksgiving at Fort Browning, Montana, was described in "1868 Thanksgiving Dinner Set Scene for Search for Gold in Little Rockies Area," *Phillips County News* (Malta, Mont.), November 24, 1955, Historical Society of Montana Library.

Material on Wyoming is drawn from "Buffalo Bones" by Phil Roberts, Research Historian, Wyoming State Archives and Historical Department, printed in the *Glenrock Independent,* November 23, 1978.

Texas material is taken from Catherine Ikard Carrow, "Amusements for Men and Women in the 1880's," *Western Texas Historical Association Yearbook,* 23 (October 1947): 94 and 95.

The Cherokee proclamation is taken from "Indian Thanksgiving," *New York Times,* November 19, 1889. Other Cherokee proclamations are in the collection of the Oklahoma Historical Society, Oklahoma City.

All-American Thanksgiving

The position of the patriotic societies is described in "Object to Parade on Thanksgiving," *New York Times*, November 4, 1926, p. 27, col. 1. Thanksgiving dinners at Ellis Island and Castle Garden were usually mentioned in the *New York Times* summary of holiday observances published on the Friday after Thanksgiving. See particularly November 27, 1883, p. 8; November 30, 1894, p. 10; and November 29, 1895, p. 2.

Pearl Kazin's words are taken from her delightful story "We Gather Together," *The New Yorker*, November 25, 1955, pp. 51–56.

Reaction to President Cleveland's proclamation can be found in the *New York Times*, "No Mediator Says the Rabbi," November 19, 1896, p. 8; and "Topics of the Times," November 27, 1896, p. 4.

Danny Thomas's childhood Thanksgiving is described in Arlene and Howard Eisenberg, "Thanksgiving with a Lebanese Flavor," *Good Housekeeping*, November 1971, pp. 84, 86, 88, 93.

The quotation from *The Delineator* is taken from Julia Sedgwick King, "The Evolution of Thanksgiving Dinner," November 1910.

Claims by partisans of various purported sites of the first Thanksgiving appeared in "Thanksgiving Day and Christmas," *William and Mary College Quarterly Historical Magazine*, January 1915, p. 1; Bird, "The First Thanksgiving"; and L. I. Gracey, "Beginnings of the American Thanksgiving Day," *The Chautauquan* no. 2, 16 (November 1892): 174–76.

James F. Vivian, "The Pan-American Mass, 1909–1914: A Rejected Contribution to Thanksgiving Day," *Church History*, September 1982, pp. 321–33, covers the topic, which also made a splash in the newspapers of the day. Contemporary articles can be found in the *New York Times Index*.

Thanksgiving during World War I is described in "Thanksgiving a la Hoover," *St. Nicholas*, November 1917, pp. 26–29; and in the *New York Times*: "Six Hoover Menus Issued;" November 27, 1918, p. 11; "Big Dinners at the Front;" November 30, 1917, p. 7; "Baker Asks Nation to Sing," November 17, 1918, p. 19; and "Dinners for Servicemen," November 23, 1917, p. 11.

The Fourth Thursday in November

News of the Retail Dry Goods Association's desire to move the date of Thanksgiving first appeared in the *New York Times* on August 5, 1939, p. 25, col. 3. Earlier efforts by the Seafood Advisory Committee were reported on May 25, 1935, p. 17, col. 6; and efforts to merge the holiday with Armistice Day were reported on November 17, 1929, Sec. 3, p. 5, November 12, 1927, p. 16, December 22, 1932, p. 22, and November 15, 1932, p. 4.

The previous, unsuccessful, effort by the Dry Goods Association was reported in the *New York Times* of September 24, 1933, Sec. 2, 15:6, and October 14, 1933, p. 7, col. 5.

"Roosevelt to Move Thanksgiving: Retailers for It; Plymouth Is Not," was a page one headline in the *New York Times* of August 15, 1939. The ensuing flap generated extensive coverage in the press. *New York Times* articles on the topic, on which I have relied heavily, can be found under the heading "Thanksgiving Day" in the *New York Times Index* for 1939.

Governor Pennoyer's proclamation for Oregon can be found in the November 3, 1893, *Oregonian*, p. 8, col. 3.

Articles consulted on the 1939 furor, aside from the *Times*, include "Two Thanksgivings Breed Grief," *Business Week*, November 18, 1939; "Turkey Days," *Newsweek*, November 20, 1939, p. 17; "O'Daniel Finds Solution for Thanksgiving Change," *Austin* (Texas) *Statesman*, August 16, 1939, p. 1; and "Turkey Tempest," *Newsweek*, August 28, 1939, p. 15.

Thanksgiving Day 1940 is covered in the *New York Times*, "Plymouth in U.S. Hails Bombed City," November 29, 1940, p. 1, col. 3; and "Cooks of the 27th Daunted by Turkey," November 21, 1940, p. 32, col. 1.

Thanksgiving Day 1941 is described in the *New York Times*: "Eden Confident of U.S. on Orient," November 21, 1941, p. 5; and "U.S. Gives Thanks for Its Strength in World at War," November 21, 1941, p. 1, col. 1; November 18, 1941, p. 52, and November 20, 1941, p. 36, were whole pages devoted to Thanksgiving coverage.

The effect of an earlier Thanksgiving on trade was chronicled in *Business Week* on January 13, 1940, "Did Nov. 23 Pay?" and on October 26, 1940, "Thanksgiving Score"; and in the *New York Times*, "Thanksgiving Plan No Spur to Trade," March 15, 1941, p. 27, col. 1.

The legislative move to create a permanent date is detailed in the *New York Times*: "Asks Standardized Thanksgiving," October 31, 1939, p. 23, col. 1; "Thanksgiving Goes Back to Old Date in '42," May 21, 1941, p. 25, col. 5; "Thanksgiving Day Restored" (which included the Ogden Nash poem) May 22, 1941, p. 20; "House Votes to Legalize Old Thanksgiving Day," October 7, 1941, p. 5; and "Thanksgiving Day Fixed by Law," December 27, 1941, p. 14. *Time* covered the story in "President Admits Mistake," June 2, 1941, p. 12; and *Newsweek* in "Thanksgiving Line-Up," October 20, 1941, p. 5.

Wartime Thanksgiving days were thoroughly covered in the *New*

York Times, my primary source for the period. Although the index for these years lists only a few relevant articles, many pages of articles actually appeared in the paper and these can be found by reading through the late November editions. The long quotation from Gene Currivan, "Hot Turkey Cheers Third Army Squad," appeared in the *Times* of November 24, 1944, p. 16, col. 7. "Thanksgiving in London," a letter from Vera Brittain, describes the 1942 Thanksgiving services in Westminster Abbey; it appeared in the *Saturday Review*, January 9, 1943. Alex Haley is quoted from his article "Thank You," *Parade*, November 21, 1982, pp. 4–6.

Tradition in an Irreverent Age

Reference is made to two articles on Thanksgiving traffic: "Pennsylvania Turnpike in a Jam," *New York Times*, November 20, 1959, p. 11, col. 4; and "Neighbors Warm Extra Turkey for Snowbound in the Middle West," *New York Times*, November 23, 1979, p. 24, col. 3.

Lyndon Johnson's Thanksgiving message is recounted in "Now, the Grateful Society," *Time*, October 28, 1966, p. 27. His controversial Vietnam era message is written up in "Falsehoods Discerned in Johnson's Message," *New York Times*, November 29, 1967, p. 4, col. 1.

The Oxfam letter is taken from a September 1983 fund appeal letter, "The Tenth Fast for a World Harvest," signed by Joe Short, Executive Director, Oxfam America, Boston.

Quotations from the article about Thanksgiving at a senior citizen center are taken from Francis X. Clines, "About Port Washington; Thanksgiving at Twilight," *New York Times*, November 23, 1978, Sec. B, p. 10.

Information on television programming was taken from the *New York Times* television page and from the Thanksgiving week edition of *TV Guide*.

Information on the reenactment at Berkeley Hundred is taken from "An Early Thanksgiving," *New York Times*, September 23, 1979, Sec. 10, p. 5, col. 4; and from press releases and brochures provided by the Virginia Thanksgiving Festival, Richmond, Va.

Information on Plymouth is taken from the *New York Times*, "A Sampling of Events at Thanksgiving," November 9, 1980, Sec. 10, p. 9, col. 1; and Diane McWhorter, " 'Plimouth' Harvest Feast in Original Style," *New York Times*, October 13, 1982, p. 20, col. 1; and from press kits provided by Plimouth Plantation, Plymouth, Mass., and the Pilgrim Society, Plymouth Mass.

The Harvest Feast, A Culinary History

The pompion recipe is found in J. Joselyn, *New England Rarities* (1672), and quoted from "Recreating the First Thanksgiving Dinner," by

James W. Baker, Research Librarian, Plimouth Plantation. Further material on food at Plymouth can be found in James Deetz and Jay Anderson, "The Ethnogastronomy of Thanksgiving," *Saturday Review of Science*, November 25, 1972, pp. 29–38. The recipe for "Turkey Braised," comes from *The Living Age*, December 13, 1862, p. 505.

Harriet Beecher Stowe is quoted from her novel *Oldtown Folks*, which describes late eighteenth-century life in her husband's hometown of Natick, Massachusetts (see pp. 1211–12). Mince pie is described in a paean taken from *Old Time Child Life* by E. H. Arr. Old-fashioned recipes are also described in Anna Barrows, "Old Fashioned Thanksgiving Dishes," *Ladies Home Journal*, November 1911.

The quotation describing the entry of the plum pudding is taken from Sophie Sweet, "All the Plums," *St. Nicholas*, November 1882, pp. 34–39. Fanny Farmer's plum pudding recipe is taken from "Good Things for Thanksgiving," *Woman's Home Companion*, November 1912, p. 52

Thanksgiving dinners distributed by St. Barnabas's House are described in "The Day at St. Barnabas's House," *New York Times*, November 29, 1895, p. 2.

* Produce arriving by the new refrigerator cars is described in "Ready for Thanksgiving," *New York Times*, November 20, 1892, p. 7.

Fannie Merritt Farmer is quoted from "An Old Fashioned Thanksgiving Dinner," *Woman's Home Companion*, November 1914.

The November issues of numerous women's magazines were consulted, starting in the post–Civil War era; they all published Thanksgiving menus and stories. The two quoted menus are taken from *The Ladies Home Companion* of November 1887 and *Harper's Bazaar* of November 24, 1900.

Index

Credits

Grateful acknowledgement is made to the following for permission to reprint illustrations:

"The First Thanksgiving," by N. C. Wyeth, Courtesy of Metropolitan Life

"Thanksgiving Week—1621," by C. S. Reinhart, *Harper's Weekly,* December 1 1894

Berkeley Hundred "First Thanksgiving" Reenactment, Courtesy of the Virginia Thanksgiving Festival

"Praise God from Whom All Blessings Flow," artist unknown, *Godey's Lady's Book,* December 1854

"Open Hearth Cooking," Courtesy of Plimouth Plantation

"Thanksgiving Dinner Among the Puritans," artist unknown, *Harper's Weekly,* November 30, 1867

President George Washington's Thanksgiving Proclamation of 1789, Courtesy of the Library of Congress

"Thanksgiving Day—Ways and Means," by Winslow Homer, *Harper's Weekly,* November 27, 1858

"Preparing for Thanksgiving," artist unknown, *Ballou's Pictorial Drawing Room Companion,* November 24, 1855

"Thanksgiving Day—Arrival at the Old Home," by Winslow Homer, *Harper's Weekly,* November 27, 1858

"Thanksgiving Sketches—Frolic with the Children," by C. G. Bush, *Harper's Weekly,* December 8, 1866

"Coasting Out of Doors," by Winslow Homer, *Ballou's Pictorial Drawing Room Companion,* November 28, 1857

"Thanksgiving Day—The Dinner," by Winslow Homer, *Harper's Weekly,* November 27, 1858

"Thanksgiving Sketches—After Dinner," by C. G. Bush, *Harper's Weekly,* December 8, 1866

"Thanksgiving Day—The Dance," by Winslow Homer, *Harper's Weekly,* November 27, 1858

"A Thanksgiving Dinner Among the Descendants of the Puritans," by J. W. Ehringer, *Harper's Weekly,* November 30, 1867

"Trapping Wild Turkies," by A. R. Waud, *Harper's Weekly,* November 28, 1868

"Preparing for Thanksgiving ," by Joseph Becker, *Frank Leslie's Illustrated Weekly,* November 30, 1878

"Thanksgiving Sketches—Preparation," by C. G. Bush, *Harper's Weekly,* December 8, 1866

"In Luck," by A. B. Frost, *Harper's Weekly,* December 20, 1884

"Home to Thanksgiving," by George H. Durrie, Currier and Ives, 1867, reproduced with permission of the Beatrice Companies, Inc. Collection of Currier & Ives

"Thanksgiving in Camp," by Winslow Homer, *Harper's Weekly,* November 29, 1862

"Press Thanksgiving Dinner," by Mr. Crane, *Frank Leslie's Illustrated Weekly,* December 19, 1863

"Holiday in Camp—Soldiers Playing Football," by Winslow Homer, *Harper's Weekly,* July 15, 1865

"Receiving Contributions for Soldiers' Thanksgiving Dinner," artist unknown, *Frank Leslie's Illustrated Weekly,* December 3, 1864

"Preparing Poultry to be Cooked for Soldiers' Thanksgiving Dinner," artist unknown, *Frank Leslie's Illustrated Weekly,* December 3, 1864

"Thanksgiving Day in the Army—After Dinner: The Wish Bone," by Winslow Homer, *Harper's Weekly,* December 3, 1864

"United We Stand," by Thomas Nast, *Harper's Weekly,* December 3, 1864

"Preparing for Thanksgiving," by J. W. Ehringer, *Harper's Weekly,* November 24, 1868
"On the Tip Toe of Expectation," artist unknown, *Harper's Weekly,* December 8, 1866
"Family Party Playing at Fox and Geese," by Winslow Homer, *Ballou's Pictorial Drawing Room Companion,* November 28, 1857
"Thanksgiving Dinner of the American Colony in Berlin at the Kaiserhof," *Collier's,* January 5, 1901
"Thanksgiving Dinner at the Colored Orphans Asylum," artist unknown, *Frank Leslie's Illustrated Weekly,* December 12, 1874
"Thanksgiving Dinner at Five Points Mission," artist unknown, *Harper's Weekly,* November 27, 1858
"The First Thanksgiving Dinner," by W. S. L. Jewett, *Harper's Weekly,* November 24, 1868
"Target Excursion in Broadway," artist unknown, *Harper's Weekly,* October 23, 1858
"Ragamuffins in New York," artist unknown, *Once a Week (Collier's),* November 29, 1894
"Parade of the Metropolitan Police Department," artist unknown, *Harper's Weekly,* December 8, 1866
"Raffling for Turkies," artist unknown, *Frank Leslie's Illustrated Weekly,* December 7, 1872
"A Run from Behind Interference," by Frederick Remington, *Harper's Weekly,* December 2, 1893
"Thanksgiving in New York—As it Was," by W. T. Smedley, *Harper's Weekly,* November 28, 1891
"Thanksgiving in New York— As It Is," by W. T. Smedley, *Harper's Weekly,* November 28, 1891
"Thanksgiving Dinner for the Ranch," by Frederick Remington, *Harper's Weekly,* November 24, 1888
"Cause for Thanksgiving," by Gilbert Gaul, *Harper's Weekly,* November 26, 1887
"Castle Garden—Their First Thanksgiving," by St. John Harper, *Harper's Weekly,* November 29, 1884
"Pilgrim's Progress" in Plymouth, Massachusetts, Courtesy of Plymouth Public Library
Franklin Delano Roosevelt at Thanksgiving Dinner on November 24, 1938, in Warm Springs, Georgia, Courtesy of the Roosevelt Library in Hyde Park, New York
Thanksgiving Services in Westminster Abbey, Courtesy of the Navy Historical Center
Thanksgiving at the Front—World War II, Courtesy of National Air Survey Center
Turkey Shoot at Old Sturbridge Village, Courtesy of Old Sturbridge Village
Berkely Hundred "First Thanksgiving" reenactment, Courtesy of Virginia Thanksgiving Festival